MEDICAL MALPRACTICE

MEDICAL MALPRACTICE

Theory, Evidence, and Public Policy

PATRICIA M. DANZON

HARVARD UNIVERSITY PRESS
Cambridge, Massachusetts, and London, England

LIBRARY OF CONGRESS CATALOGING IN PUBLICATION DATA

Danzon, Patricia Munch, 1946–
  Medical malpractice.

  Bibliography: p.
  Includes index.
    1. Medical personnel — Malpractice — Economic aspects —
United States.   2.   Physicians — Malpractice — Economic
aspects — United States.   3.   Insurance, Malpractice —
United States.   I. Title.   [DNLM: 1. Malpractice.
2. Public Policy.   W   44   D199m]
RA1056.5.D36   1985   368.5   84-29764
ISBN 0-674-56115-5 (alk. paper)

Preface

AS THIS BOOK goes to press, medical malpractice is once again in the headlines, after almost a decade of quiet. Malpractice rate increases of more than 50 percent have been granted in some states, resulting in premiums of $80,000 for specialists in high-risk areas. Malpractice claim frequency is now rising by roughly 12 percent a year, after remaining stable for several years after the surge in the early seventies that precipitated the 1975 crisis. Claim severity (average amount per paid claim) has outpaced the rate of inflation throughout the last decade. Change in the malpractice system, either through incremental tort reform or more radical no-fault alternatives, is under consideration at the federal level and in several states. Concern is particularly acute in states such as New York and Florida, where the solvency of the insurance mechanisms established after the last crisis is in doubt.

Research cannot fully keep pace with these rapidly changing events. Much of the analysis in this book draws on data from the 1975 crisis and the years immediately following, through 1978. But the results of that analysis remain immediately relevant today. Current developments in malpractice insurance markets resemble in mild form the much more severe crisis of the mid-seventies. More fundamentally, the fact that claim frequency and severity have continued to rise tends to confirm that the reforms enacted in response to the last crisis did not radically change the malpractice system. Thus the results of the empirical analysis and the evaluation of reforms remain valid, even if the mid-1970s dollar values of premiums and awards seem low by today's standards.

Since this book synthesizes research done over a long period, I would like to acknowledge support and help from a correspondingly long list of sources and individuals. My work on malpractice began at the Rand Corporation at the time of the malpractice crisis of 1974, with support from the U.S. Department of Health, Education, and Welfare and the California Citizens' Commission on Tort Reform, with continued support from the Institute for Civil Justice. The book was largely written while I was a National Fellow and then a Senior Research Fellow at the Hoover Institution, with support from the Weingart Foundation and the J. M. Foundation. Duke University has provided the resources necessary to complete it. Funds from all these sources are gratefully acknowledged.

The list of individuals who have contributed in some way is too long to enumerate. In particular, I would like to acknowledge the contributions of Dennis Smallwood and Lee Lillard, who (separately) coauthored work I have drawn on here and have been invaluable colleagues. For their helpful comments and advice (not always followed) on various parts of the research, I would like to thank Robert Bell, William Butz, Robert Ellickson, David Hartman, Joseph Newhouse, Charles Phelps, A. Mitchell Polinsky, and Gary Schwartz. Special thanks are due to Christina Peck and Christine Peterson for very able research assistance. Preparation of the final manuscript has benefited greatly from the editorial advice of Michael Aronson and Mary Ellen Geer. Finally, I would like to thank the Alliance of American Insurers, the American Insurance Association, the American Medical Association, and the Insurance Services Office for providing data.

Contents

Introduction

A PHYSICIAN who fails to meet the profession's customary standard of adequate care and thereby injures a patient can be sued for negligence. The injured patient is entitled to compensation under the law of medical malpractice, which is a particular application of tort law — that amorphous web of rules that governs injuries to person or property where crime or contract is not at issue.

Within tort law, physicians and other learned professionals — including architects, attorneys, and accountants — have been singled out from other callings and occupations in their professional liability to clients. The grounds for the great majority of professional liability suits is negligence. To establish a cause of action under a negligence rule of liability, the plaintiff must show that a duty of care existed; that the defendant failed to conform to the required standard of care, either by his acts or by failure to act; that the plaintiff sustained damages; and that the breach of duty was the proximate cause of the damages. The plaintiff need not prove these allegations beyond all reasonable doubt, as in criminal cases, but must only show that the preponderance of the evidence supports them. If negligence is proved, the tort plaintiff has traditionally been entitled to full compensation for all pecuniary and nonpecuniary damages. Thus, in principle, the law of medical malpractice holds physicians and other health care providers liable only for that subset of iatrogenic injury (adverse outcome of medical care) that results from professional negligence. Adverse outcomes consistent with normal risk are in principle the burden of the patient. Nevertheless, most professionals consider liability insurance against malpractice suits to be a prerequisite of professional practice.

Although physicians, hospitals, and other practitioners have been liable for malpractice for centuries, such actions have been relatively rare until recently. But in the late 1960s and early 1970s the frequency of claims alleging medical malpractice began to expand at unprecedented rates, as did the dollar amounts awarded to successful plaintiffs. Rough estimates indicate that claim costs were increasing by up to 40 percent a year in some states during this period. At first malpractice insurance premiums did not keep pace with rising claim costs. Then in 1974–75 the malpractice insurance crisis broke. Insurance carriers sought premium increases of up to 500 percent in some states; surgeons in southern California saw their rates jump from $12,000 to $36,000 a year; in other states the crisis of price became a crisis of availability, as traditional insurers restricted coverage or withdrew from the market entirely, leaving health practitioners to choose between forming their own insurance companies or going without coverage altogether. Although somewhat similar developments occurred for other professionals and in other liability areas, notably product and municipal liability, the rate of change in the medical field was more extreme. So was the drama created by the reaction of the health care professions, who threatened to retaliate with strikes or withdrawal of services. Fear became widespread that failure of the liability system and liability insurance mechanisms might result in at least a temporary collapse of some elements of the health care delivery system.

During 1974 and 1975 most state legislatures were under intense pressure to take steps to resolve the crisis. Opinions differed as to both causes and appropriate cures, but consensus grew that something had to be done. By the end of 1976 most states had enacted new laws designed to dampen or eliminate the apparent causes of the eruption in insurance premiums and to ensure the availability of malpractice insurance. Individual states adopted quite different combinations of corrective measures, but all were founded in some set of perceptions about the purpose of the malpractice system, how it works in practice, and the likely effects of changes in the laws that underlie and govern the workings of the system. Participants in the debate over tort reform did not have available to them then, nor do they now, much empirical evidence to resolve the conflicting views of what caused the crisis of the mid-1970s and, more generally, of how the liability and insurance mechanisms operate in practice.

Nevertheless, the crisis was apparently resolved in most states, although it has continued to simmer in one or two, notably Florida and New York. Overall, the rate of growth of claim frequency slowed and even fell in many states in 1976, and premium increases were modest throughout the late 1970s. There are some ominous clouds on the horizon, however: awards have continued to outpace the rate of inflation, and claim frequency has resumed its upward trend since the late 1970s. Insurance is widely available, but recent premium increases have averaged 20 or 30 percent, with even sharper increases for some specialties in some states. In general, though, medical malpractice only makes news in the relatively rare instances of a multimillion-dollar jury award.

Although our institutions for handling medical malpractice appear to be functioning relatively smoothly, two basic questions remain unanswered. First, did the changes adopted in the wake of the last crisis resolve its underlying causes sufficiently to prevent a recurrence, or is the subsequent lull unrelated to those changes? This question acquires urgency as the evidence mounts that the frequency and severity of claims are rising at substantial rates. Although supreme courts in several states have rejected major remedial changes adopted in response to that crisis, legislatures in other states are attempting to enact new restrictive measures. Second—and a more fundamental question—even if current institutions are robust against shocks, do they perform the function for which they are intended in an efficient manner? Much of the current concern over the medical malpractice system involves its contribution to the cost of health care in general.

The tort system of liability for negligence has two main purposes. First, it provides compensation to those injured as a result of the negligence of others, thereby acting as a source of insurance. Second, by imposing sanctions on persons found negligent, it acts as a deterrent to future negligent behavior. However, if the tort system is to be evaluated on grounds of economic efficiency, then it can be justified, if at all, only by its performance in deterring negligent behavior. Compensation and risk spreading could be accomplished at lower cost, and arguably more equitably, through either public or private first-party health and disability insurance. Such programs are already in place, and we rely on them for the great majority of injuries that are not eligible for compensation through the tort system, including all iatrogenic injuries not attributed to negligence. Thus if the concern is compensation, doing it through the tort system, which is more costly to operate and serves at most a tiny fraction of accidents, makes little sense.

The costs of operating the current medical malpractice system add up to several billion dollars. Most obvious are the tangible items, such as litigation costs and overhead, which absorb two-thirds of every malpractice insurance premium dollar, and the costs of defensive medical practices. Less tangible but no less real are the time and anxiety costs to physicians and plaintiffs involved in litigation. Are these costs out of all proportion to the problem they are intended to correct, or are they offset by at least equivalent benefits, in terms of deterrence of potential injuries, because physicians are more careful as a result of the threat of suit? Unfortunately, both the underlying incidence of malpractice and the deterrent benefits of the malpractice system are hard to quantify. But that does not justify ignoring them and focusing concern solely on the more visible costs of malpractice claims, which is the tendency underlying many reform proposals. From a public policy perspective, the problem is one of designing liability rules and insurance mechanisms that minimize the total cost of injuries, including the utility costs of injuries, the resource costs of prevention, and the overhead costs of effecting compensation. Reforms designed to reduce claim costs — and any other reform — must be evaluated in this broader context.

Much has already been written on the malpractice problem and its potential solutions, mostly by physicians, attorneys, and insurance experts. But even though these practitioners draw on valuable, firsthand knowledge, personal experience often does not provide a basis for sound generalizations about the system as a whole. For example, it is widely believed that there is an excessive number of suits, brought by disgruntled patients urged on by ambulance-chasing lawyers, who sue whenever medical care fails to deliver a perfect cure. No doubt such cases exist, but they are far from the whole story. According to a California study (CMA, 1977), roughly 1 in 126 patients admitted to California hospitals in 1974 suffered an injury resulting from malpractice. I estimate that at most 1 in 10 of these injured patients filed a claim, and less than half of those who filed a claim received any compensation. Thus it appears that the incidence of malpractice is much higher than the frequency of malpractice claims. Another common allegation is that the disposition of claims is arbitrary and bears little relation to the legal standards of negligence and compensable damages, because the great majority of claims are settled out of court. But statistical analysis of more than 5,000 insurance claim files tends to refute this view, showing that the settlement process follows predictable patterns and reflects to a fair degree what the outcome would have been had a case gone to verdict. Whether this process results in optimal compensation to victims and appropriate incentives to physicians, and whether the whole system is worth its costs, remain open questions.

The problem of deterring medical malpractice is thus real, as is the problem of efficient compensation of victims. This book brings economic analysis and empirical evidence to bear on the public policy issues raised by the malpractice liability system and associated insurance mechanisms. It is intended to fill some of the gaps in our understanding of how the malpractice system operates in practice and how it might be improved.

In Part I of the book I develop a theoretical framework by which to evaluate the existing system and proposed reforms. The theory demonstrates how an appropriately defined rule of liability can in principle operate as a highly efficient substitute for more cumbersome regulation of the quality of medical care. Specifically, liability for negligence is a means of providing health care practitioners with efficient incentives for injury prevention when patients lack the information to choose and monitor the quality of care themselves. I then present empirical evidence on the incidence of malpractice injuries and claims, the disposition of claims through the courts, and determinants of the frequency and severity of claims. These data provide some evidence on the extent to which the actual operation of the system conforms to the theoretical ideal.

Part II examines issues in malpractice insurance. Liability insurance is a key component of the tort system. Most obviously, the smooth functioning of the insurance market is essential for stability in the health care delivery system, as the events of 1974–75 showed. But more fundamentally, since insurance tends to insulate the physician from the penalties meted out by the legal process, insurance can undermine the deterrent function of the malpractice system. The chapters in this section analyze the causes and solutions of the 1974–75 malpractice insurance crisis, the efficiency of current malpractice insurance institutions, and the case for government intervention in this market.

Part III discusses various proposals for changing the current system, including the restructuring of tort awards, shorter statutes of limitations, and various proposals to reduce litigation costs. I then evaluate more radical alternatives, ranging from allowing patients and providers to contract out of the tort system to extending compensation on a no-fault basis to all victims of iatrogenic injury. The final chapter summarizes the evidence and the conclusions.

I

FRAMEWORK AND EVIDENCE

CHAPTER 1 lays out a framework for evaluating the malpractice system from the standpoint of economic efficiency. It shows how in principle liability for negligence operates as an efficient system of quality control. The following chapters then present evidence on the operation of the system in practice. Chapter 2 reports on the incidence of injuries resulting from malpractice and compares this to the number of claims filed and paid. Chapter 3 analyzes the disposition of claims through the courts and the settlement process, showing what determines which claims get paid and how much is paid, and evaluating how far the outcome conforms to the legal standards of negligence and damages. Chapter 4 examines the trends over time and the huge differences among states in the frequency and severity (dollar amount paid) of malpractice claims. It presents estimates of the contribution of medical, demographic, and legal factors to these trends, and of the impact of the tort reforms enacted after the 1975 crisis.

1

Tort Liability as a System of Quality Control

CONCERN over medical malpractice tends to focus on the cost of claims and of insurance premiums. Reforms are generally designed with a view to reducing these costs, without a clear perspective on the role of claims or the role of the tort system as a whole. I argue in this chapter that the primary economic rationale for tort liability is deterrence. In principle, the law of negligence can create an incentive structure designed to induce physicians to invest optimally in injury prevention (Posner, 1977). Since injuries are costly but prevention is also not free, optimal prevention requires balancing the costs and benefits of reducing injury risk.

Why are physicians and other professionals subject to liability for their professional acts, whereas in other economic activities we rely on market mechanisms to allocate resources efficiently? The reason is that the efficient functioning of markets requires that consumers be informed about the risks and benefits of alternative services and be able to monitor the quality of care actually delivered. These assumptions are obviously violated to some degree in the case of medical and other professional services, where the professional is trained to have superior knowledge and expertise. Tort liability can be viewed as a device to correct the inefficiencies that could result from market signals when consumers misperceive risk.

The Optimal Prevention of Injury

Injuries are costly. Most obvious are the costs of medical treatment, rehabilitation, and wages lost as a result of temporary or permanent disability. Harder to measure but no less real are the pain and suffering and the diminution in the quality of life that result from physical impairment. These are irreplaceable losses that cannot be recompensed by monetary compensation. In addition, there are administrative and overhead costs of effecting compensation. In the case of medical malpractice, these overhead costs add up to roughly twice as much as the compensation actually received by the victim.

On the other hand, injury prevention is also costly. Averting medical injuries requires time of physicians and other personnel, perhaps additional tests and other procedures. But injury prevention, like most activities, is subject to the law of diminishing returns. The initial dollars spent on basic safety measures — sterilizing medical instruments, checking labels — have a large payoff. But as more is spent, the reduction in risk per dollar spent diminishes. Thus the marginal or incremental costs of injury prevention rise as we attempt to reduce injury rates to lower and lower levels. Since resources devoted to prevention must be diverted from other socially valuable uses, the elimination of all injuries is not feasible. Although we may say we would pay any price to avoid an injury, our behavior in innumerable contexts — driving speed, dangerous sports — reveals that we do make trade-offs between risk reduction and other valuable uses of time and money.

Definition of the optimum. Since preventing all injuries is prohibitively costly, we cannot avoid the question of how much to spend on prevention. In addressing this question, the economist takes as the objective of social policy the maximization of the value of total societal resources. An allocation of resources between competing uses is efficient or "optimal" if the total value of the goods and services produced cannot be increased by switching resources to produce more of one good and less of another. Thus, an efficient allocation of resources to prevention exists if, at the margin, a dollar spent on prevention saves a dollar of injury costs; this is true for each prevention activity — tests, monitoring of personnel, physician care, and so on. Another way to say this is that the efficient or optimal prevention policy is that which minimizes the total cost associated with injuries, including the resource and utility costs of injuries themselves, the costs of prevention, and the administrative costs of effecting compensation (Calabresi, 1970). "Optimal" is used throughout the book in this technical sense of economic efficiency. It has normative connotations only to the extent that economic efficiency is a major goal of social policy. Whether economic efficiency is or should be the only criterion for evaluating social policy toward injuries is not debated here.

Policy options. Several policy tools are available for achieving the prevention and compensation of injuries. The government may attempt to regulate safety directly, by setting standards. For example, the Highway Safety Commission sets safety standards for automobiles; the Food and Drug Administration regulates pharmaceutical products; licensure requirements define minimum training and skill levels for practicing medicine. Similarly, the government may mandate levels of insurance coverage, either through private insurance mechanisms, such as the compulsory automobile insurance required in some states, or public insurance mechanisms, such as Social Security Disability Insurance.

In contrast to direct regulation of safety standards and insurance coverage, liability rules are an indirect method of regulation. A liability rule determines in the first instance who should pay for an injury and, if someone other than the victim is assigned liability, how much should be paid. But the assignment of liability, in addition to compensating victims retrospectively, also has prospective impact. The anticipation of liability affects the incentives of persons involved in hazardous activities to take preventive measures and to buy liability insurance. Thus liability rules are an indirect way of influencing private choices with respect to safety precautions and insurance, through incentives rather than regulatory fiat.

Different societies choose different assignments of liability for injuries. In the United States, liability rules differ depending on the source of the injury. Under a rule of first-party liability or caveat emptor (let the buyer beware), the person who suffers the loss also pays for it, in the first instance. He may, of course, buy first-party insurance, which provides indemnification in the event of a loss. Losses due to illness are typically borne on a first-party basis, and private and public health insurance programs provide a means of spreading this risk.

At the other extreme is a rule of strict third-party liability, in which case the loss is paid for, in the first instance, by the party who is in some sense causally responsible for the injury. Again, the third party to whom the loss is transferred may buy insurance — in this case, liability insurance. The workers' compensation system, which requires employers to compensate employees for all work-related injuries, exemplifies a rule of strict third-party liability.

Injuries arising out of medical treatment — iatrogenic injuries — are currently governed by a negligence rule of liability which is a hybrid of first-party and third-party liability. Under this rule a medical provider is liable for injury to a patient if the injury was the result of failure to meet the "due" standard of care. But if the injury is judged an adverse outcome consistent with the normal risk of non-negligent care, then the medical provider is not liable and the patient bears the cost. Whether the victim or the injurer is liable depends on whether or not the injurer's level of care met or fell short of the due-care standard.[1] Again, the initial assignment of liability does not necessarily determine who ultimately bears the loss, because of the intermediation of insurance. The person at risk typically has first-party health and disability insurance that covers injuries which are part of the normal risk of the activity — those which occur even when the due-care standard is met. Defendants typically carry liability insurance to cover costs in the event of suit.

Thus a liability rule performs two functions: first, a distributive function, to determine who should pay for the injury; and second, in the long run, an allocative function, to determine the total societal cost of injuries. This societal cost of injuries depends on the incentives of people to invest in injury prevention and to buy insurance, which in turn depend on their expectations about the assignment of liability for future injuries.

A liability rule may therefore be evaluated in terms of its distributive effects and its allocative effects. In this book I shall be concerned primarily with evaluating the medical malpractice system from the standpoint of its allocative effects. Specifically, I shall address the following two questions: Does the law that holds medical providers liable for injuries arising out of professional negligence provide benefits at least equal to costs? Could the law be modified to reduce the costs without loss of benefits, or to increase the benefits for a given cost? Distributive questions will be addressed to the extent of trying to show who bears costs and risks under this and possible alternative liability rules. The ethical issue of who *should* pay for iatrogenic injuries will not be discussed in any detail, partly because it is a question on which economists have no particular expertise, partly because the analysis will show that it may be an elusive goal to pursue: the person made liable for an injury in the first instance may not end up ultimately bearing the cost, because of the operation of markets and insurance mechanisms.

Why Hold Physicians Liable?

Although at first sight the rules of caveat emptor, strict liability, and negligence appear to assign injury costs very differently and hence create very different incentives for injury prevention, in fact under certain conditions the liability assignment does not matter. In his seminal article on liability rules, Ronald Coase (1963) showed that if both parties are fully informed about risks and if the costs of contracting are negligible, then the allocation of resources to loss prevention and hence the frequency of losses will be unaffected by who is held liable. In competitive markets, the distribution of income — who ultimately bears the costs of prevention and costs of accidents — may also be unaffected by the liability rule.

To see how outcomes can be invariant to the liability rule, consider the case of a patient deciding whether or not to have a particular medical test. When the rule is first-party liability, the patient bears the cost of injuries. Assume that the test costs $100 and that there is one chance in a hundred of a harmful side effect, which would entail monetary expenses of $5,000. The full expected cost of the procedure, including the expected cost of injury, is thus $150 ($100 + 0.01 × $5,000). If the patient is fully informed, indifferent to risk (risk-neutral), and cares only about the expected cost, then he would have the test if it has an expected therapeutic value of at least $150. However, the maximum he would be willing to pay for the test would be $100.[2] If he were averse to risk but disability insurance were available on actuarially fair terms (premium equal to the expected loss, or $50 = 0.01 × $5,000), then he would fully insure the potential loss, for a premium of $50, and still be willing to pay $100 for the procedure. If the chance of injury were greater or the damages larger, then he would not choose to have the test if it offered a therapeutic value of only $150 because the expected benefits would be less than the expected costs, including the risk of injury.

Now consider the same situation under a rule of third-party liability, that is, the physician is liable for any injuries that occur. The cost to the physician of performing the test now includes the $100 resource cost for the procedure itself plus $50 for the expected cost of injuries for which he will be liable. If he is risk-averse and can buy liability insurance on actuarially fair terms, he will buy a liability insurance policy for $50. Since the patient will be fully compensated in the event of an injury, he would choose to have the procedure provided its expected therapeutic value is at least $150, which is the fee the physician would charge under a rule of third-party liability.

Thus under either first- or third-party liability, the procedure will be performed provided it yields at least $150 in expected benefits. Furthermore, under either liability rule the patient bears the expected cost of injuries. With first-party liability he bears them directly, either by bearing the risk of a 1 in 100 chance of a $5,000 loss, for an expected value of $50, or by buying first-party insurance coverage, thereby substituting a sure $50 premium. With third-party liability, although the physician is liable for injury costs in the first instance, the expected cost of injuries is reflected in the fee he charges for his services. Under third-party liability the competitive fee for this procedure is $150, compared to $100 under first-party liability. Under both liability rules the patient is fully insured; the difference is that under a first-party rule he buys the insurance himself, whereas under third-party liability the insurance is tied in with the purchase of the procedure. The $50 higher fee reflects the cost of this compulsory insurance. Since outcomes are identical under the two liability rules, there are no grounds for choosing between them. Both result in an efficient allocation of resources to prevention and insurance.

This conclusion, that the allocation of resources and the distribution of income are invariant to the liability rule, holds only under the extreme assumption that patients and physicians are equally well informed about the risks and benefits of alternative procedures, and that patients can easily monitor the quality of care actually delivered.[3] But in general, if the consumer has imperfect information about the quality of a product or service, either because he lacks the technical expertise to evaluate its risks and benefits or because he cannot monitor whether the product actually delivered is the one he thought he had contracted for, then the rule assigning liability for injuries will affect the quality and quantity of services that are produced, the allocation of resources to injury prevention, and the frequency of injury.

To see the effect of consumer misperceptions in the medical context, consider the extreme case in which the patient is totally oblivious to the risk. With first-party liability, the fee for the test would simply be the $100 resource cost. The patient would not insure and would be willing to have the test if it yielded only $100 in expected benefits. Thus if patients tend to systematically underestimate risk, they will underinsure and will incur more risk and more injuries than they would wish to if they comprehended the risks they were incurring. Conversely, if patients systematically overestimate risk, they will overinsure and will incur higher costs of prevention and fewer injuries than they would choose to if fully informed.

Transferring liability from a poorly informed patient to a better informed physician provides a means of correcting these distortions. If the physician correctly estimates the risk of injury, when he is liable he will charge a fee of $150, composed of $100 for the resource cost and $50 for the expected liability cost. The patient confronted with a $150 fee will now only have the procedure if he values it at

$150. Despite his ignorance of the risks, he is induced to make the optimal decision about risk taking and to purchase the optimal amount of insurance, which is implicit in the fee. Thus placing liability on producers provides a means of correcting the inefficiencies that would result from consumer misperception of risks. This correction of defective market signals is the economic justification for holding manufacturers liable for product-related injuries and for the professional liability of physicians, attorneys, architects, and engineers.[4]

Obviously the example just given is a gross oversimplification of medical decision making. Nevertheless, because of their information advantage, physicians have considerable discretion in guiding the choice of quantity and quality of services. Most providers may well try to act as a perfect agent for the patient, making those choices the patient would have made if he were fully informed. Medical training, codes of ethics, and norms of decent human conduct are conducive to this end. But financial gain and preference for leisure create incentives that conflict with the patient's interests. The physician who orders unnecessary treatments, fails to refer a difficult case to a specialist, skimps on taking a history, or hurries through a procedure can increase his income, but thereby exposes the patient to more risk. If patients accurately perceived these risks, they would adjust their demand for the physician's services, thereby transferring or "internalizing" to the physician the risk consequences of his level of care. But if patients do not accurately perceive the risks, then the costs of injuries or, equivalently, the benefits of reduction in risk of injury are not internalized to the physician, and his financial incentives to engage in risk reduction are suboptimal.

Liability for Negligence

Although the example in the previous section was developed for the case of strict liability, a rule of liability for negligence can also, in principle, correct the defective market signals for prevention that flow from consumer misperception of risk, provided courts define negligence in an optimal manner. A precise definition of the legal standard of negligence was formulated by Judge Learned Hand in U.S. v. Carroll Towing.[5] Negligence is said to occur if the loss caused by the accident, multiplied by the probability of the accident's occurring, exceeds the burden of the precautions the defendant might have taken to avert it. In other words, negligence consists of failure to take precautions if their cost is less than the expected damages averted. But this is precisely the economic definition of efficient investment in prevention. To achieve full efficiency, however, the legal definition of negligence must encompass liability for "unnecessary" treatments, that is, treatments in which the expected benefits are less than the expected costs.[6] A negligence rule thus defined creates incentives for the physician to act precisely as the patient would have chosen if fully informed.

In fact, in applying the negligence standard to the practice of medicine and other professions, the courts do not attempt to apply the Hand cost-benefit calculation on a case-by-case basis. Rather, they typically defer to the customary practice of the profession, determined on the basis of expert testimony. Professional negligence is defined as a departure from customary standards of good practice. Provided that customary practice is in fact optimal, holding physicians liable for departure from such practice provides the optimal incentives that would flow from the Hand definition of negligence.

The argument so far, favoring physician liability, has considered only deterrence — incentives for prevention. It has ignored administrative costs and the burden of risk, both of which tend to be higher under a rule of third-party liability than under caveat emptor. Any transfer of liability to third parties adds costs of litigation, since defendants naturally oppose such liability. Both strict liability and negligence require determination of the causal relationship between the defendant's actions and the plaintiff's injuries. Fewer claims will be filed under a negligence rule than under strict liability, but for those claims that are filed there is the additional issue of whether the defendant's actions fell short of the due standard of care, that is, of distinguishing those injuries consistent with the normal risk of acceptable care and those injuries deemed preventable under standard care and therefore attributable to negligence. The added administrative costs incurred under a third-party liability rule are reflected in the lower fraction of the insurance premium dollar available to compensate patients. Roughly 80 cents of the first-party health insurance premium dollar is returned to policyholders as compensation, compared to 60 cents for workers' compensation, where the liability rule is third-party liability without regard to fault, and roughly 40 cents for medical malpractice and automobile liability, where the rule is third-party liability for negligence only.[7] Because both strict liability and negligence entail higher administrative costs than first-party liability, they can be deemed efficient overall only if these added overhead costs are at least offset by lower costs of injuries, as a result of more efficient deterrence.

If the malpractice system is to provide optimal compensation to patients and optimal deterrence incentives to physicians, certain conditions must be met.

1. The legal standard of due care must be optimally defined.
2. Damage awards must be structured to provide optimal compensation to victims and optimal incentives to defendants.
3. Patients must detect and file claims for all injuries due to negligence and unnecessary treatment.
4. The courts must make accurate findings of liability and damages.

As we shall see, in practice all of these conditions appear to be violated to some degree. The legal standard of due care — the customary standard of the profession — is only a rough approximation to the optimal standard of care, and is at best only approximately applied by the courts. The legal standard of compensable damages — full compensation for all monetary and nonmonetary loss — is not optimal from the standpoint of either deterrence or compensation. Many valid claims are not filed, and some invalid claims are filed. Most claims that are filed are settled out of court. Thus even if the legal standards of negligence and damages were appropriately defined and applied by the courts, there remains the question of how far the settlement process mirrors the potential outcome in court and hence reflects the legal standards. And even if the legal process did generate correct signals, most physicians carry liability insurance which insulates them to a large extent from the penalties meted out through the liability system.

The extent and causes of the discrepancies between theory and practice in the negligence system are analyzed in the following chapters. I defer to Part III an evaluation of current legal rules with regard to standard of care and compensable damages.

2

Malpractice: A Problem of Injuries or Claims?

IN 1984 malpractice insurance premiums cost roughly $3 billion, and the total cost of the malpractice system, including other public and private costs, was much higher. Is this cumbersome and costly system disproportionate to the problem it is designed to control? There is widespread belief that most malpractice claims simply reflect the unrealistic expectations of litigious patients, who sue whenever the results of health care intervention are less than perfect. How accurate is this perception? Answering these questions is crucial to determining whether public policy should focus on controlling the cost of malpractice claims or controlling the incidence of malpractice. As I argued in Chapter 1, the tort system can be justified, if at all, only as a system of deterrence. But is deterrence unnecessary, and are we in fact simply operating an expensive and inequitable system of compensation?

To determine the extent of malpractice, as opposed to malpractice claims, I examine in this chapter the limited evidence available on the frequency of incidents of malpractice — the "injury universe" — and compare this to the frequency of claims — the "claim universe." Data on the frequency of incidents of malpractice are very sparse. The only broad-based study is a pioneering but nevertheless limited study of injuries occurring in a sample of 23 California hospitals in 1974. Unfortunately, this study did not determine how many of the patients involved filed claims. However, reasonably complete aggregate claim data are available from the National Association of Insurance Commissioners (NAIC) survey of claims closed by private insurers between July 1975 and December 1978. By comparing these data on claims closed in California with the California injury data, we can get a crude measure of the number of claims relative to the number of injuries by age of the plaintiff, severity of the injury, and type of medical error.

The results are striking. Roughly 1 in 126 patients admitted to hospitals in California in 1974 suffered an injury due to negligent medical care. Of these, at most 1 in 10 filed a claim, and only 40 percent of these claims resulted in payment to the plaintiff. Just why 9 out of 10 potential claims are not filed is explored in this and later chapters. A second issue is how the probability of a claim being filed, given an injury, differs by type of injury, age of plaintiff, or medical procedure. To the extent that systematic differences exist, the sanctions of the medical malpractice system fall unevenly on different medical activities and hence may induce distortions in the delivery of care.

The Data Sources

Medical injuries. In 1974 the California Medical Association and the California Hospital Association jointly sponsored a study to evaluate the feasibility of a no-fault system of compensation for medical injuries (hereafter referred to as the CMA study). A team of four experts in legal medicine examined the hospital records of 23 nonfederal short-stay hospitals in California to identify "incidents of disability caused by health care management."[1] The hospitals were chosen to be representative in terms of size, ownership, teaching status, and region. The records were chosen to be representative of hospital discharges in California in terms of age, race, sex, and payment source.

Three classes of injury were identified: (1) adverse effects of treatment; (2) effects of incomplete diagnosis or treatment; and (3) effects of incomplete prevention or protection. Injuries were rated on an eight-point severity scale: categories 1–3 represent temporary injuries of increasing severity; categories 4–7 represent permanent injuries of increasing severity; category 8 represents death.

For each injury, the investigators evaluated the likelihood of a jury finding of liability under current negligence law. They noted that their determination of liability was based not only on professional negligence but also on other factors they considered relevant from their experience in handling malpractice claims, such as the type and severity of the injury, whether it was preventable under ordinary standards, why certain things were done and others not, and the state of the records. Thus what I shall refer to as a "malpractice incident," a "liability injury," or a "negligent injury" was admittedly a subjective evaluation but was made by medical-legal experts experienced in handling malpractice claims.[2]

Malpractice claims. The NAIC survey of medical malpractice claims closed by insurers between July 1975 and December 1978 provides a comprehensive nationwide data base on malpractice claims. For purposes of this comparison with the CMA data on injuries, I estimated the number of claims closed in California, arising from treatment in hospitals, by age of patient and severity of injury. Claims involving only emotional damage or legal issues were omitted, since such incidents are excluded from the injury universe by design. Multiple claims arising from the same incident were consolidated, and claims related to incidents that occurred outside hospitals were omitted.[3]

Frequency of Injuries and Claims

Injuries. The CMA investigators identified 970 incidents of disability caused by health care management in the 20,864 records they studied. This implies an average injury rate of 4.65 injuries per 100 hospital admissions, or roughly 1 in 20. Extrapolating from the hospitals in the sample yields an estimate of 140,000 iatrogenic injuries in California hospitals in 1974. If California hospital admissions were representative of hospital admissions nationwide (which may not be a valid assumption), this would imply 1,535,211 injuries nationwide. This figure certainly understates the total universe of iatrogenic injuries, for several reasons. First, injuries occurring outside hospitals were omitted, unless they resulted in hospitalization.[4] Second, some injuries occurring in hospitals may not have been recorded in hospital records. Third, certain types of medical injury were specifically excluded from the CMA study, such as nonindicated treatments that did not result in adverse outcome; unauthorized treatments, and injuries resulting in emotional damage only, or disability that did not prolong hospitalization and probably would not cause continuing disability following discharge.[5]

Of this total number of iatrogenic injuries—roughly 1 per 20 admissions—the investigators estimated that 17 percent would probably result in a jury finding of liability under current negligence law. Hereafter I refer to these injuries as "negligent injuries." The remaining 83 percent were categorized as adverse outcomes consistent with the normal risk of medical treatment. This implies that the average risk of injury due to negligence (that is, injury compensable under the current tort system) was four-fifths of 1 percent, of 1 per 126 hospital admissions in 1974. If applied nationwide, this figure implies 260,000 negligent injuries.

Table 2.1 Injury rates per 1,000 hospital admissions, by age and severity

Severity[a]	Age				
	19	20–44	45–64	65	All ages
1	8.05	16.94	19.32	24.68	16.63
2	7.49	13.17	14.70	12.49	11.94
3	2.99	8.83	11.55	12.49	8.62
4	0.56	2.46	5.88	3.90	3.02
5	0.38	0.72	1.89	1.56	1.06
6	0.75	0.80	0.21	0.26	0.38
7	0.19	0.14	0.42	0.78	0.34
8	1.68	1.30	6.30	11.95	4.51
Total	22.09	44.36	60.27	68.11	46.50

Source: CMA (1977).

a. Severity index: 1 = Minor Temporary Disability: not exceeding 30 days and not requiring surgery; 2 = Minor Temporary Disability: not exceeding 30 days but requiring surgery; 3 = Major Temporary Disability: lasting more than 30 days but no longer than 2 years; 4 = Minor Permanent Partial Disability: most functionally nondisabling disabilities; 5 = Major Permanent Partial Disability: substantial damage, but not sufficient to cause complete loss of ability to perform most ordinary functions; 6 = Major Permanent Total Disability: substantial damage, usually sufficient to alter patient's life-style into a dependent position; 7 = Grave Permanent Total Disability: complete dependence or short-term fatal prognosis; 8 = Death.

Table 2.1 shows how this average risk of injury per admission is distributed by age and severity level. In reviewing this and later breakdowns from the CMA study, it is important to keep in mind that the small sample size (the total number of injuries is 970) makes some inferences tentative. The great majority of injuries were minor: 80 percent of all injuries were categorized as temporary, 6.5 percent were minor permanent injuries, 3.8 percent involved major permanent disability, and 9.7 percent were fatal.[6] The risk of injury increased with age, from 2.2 percent for patients under age 20 to 6.8 percent for patients over 65. A pattern of gradually increasing risk with age occurred at most severity levels, but the risk of fatal injury was significantly higher for the elderly.

The percentage of injuries attributed to negligence rather than normal risk increased dramatically with the severity of the injury (see Table 2.2), from 8 percent for minor temporary disabilities to 83 percent for grave permanent total disability. Thus for nonfatal injuries, the more severe the injury, the higher is the probability that it was due to negligence rather than normal risk. For fatal injuries, only

Table 2.2 Distribution of injuries and claims, by severity (percentages)

	Injuries				Claims[c]		
Severity	All injuries	Negligent injuries[a]	Non-negligent injuries	Injuries with liability[b]	All claims	Paid claims	Unpaid claims
1	35.8	17.6	39.5	8.4	11.2	8.6	13.1
2	25.7	18.2	27.2	12.0	34.0	30.4	36.8
3	18.6	20.0	18.3	18.3	14.7	17.1	12.9
4	6.5	9.1	6.0	23.8	13.5	15.9	11.8
5	2.3	4.9	1.7	36.4	5.3	6.4	4.5
6	0.9	3.0	0.5	55.6	2.4	2.7	2.3
7	0.6	3.0	0.1	83.3	1.9	2.3	1.5
8	9.7	24.2	6.7	42.6	16.9	16.7	17.1
Total	100.0	100.0	100.0	17.0	100.0	100.0	100.0

Sources: CMA (1977), NAIC (1980), based on countrywide totals.
a. Distribution of negligent injuries, by severity.
b. Percentage of injuries in each severity class deemed negligent.
c. Related claims have been consolidated. Excludes claims reporting no injury, or emotional or legal issue only (8.3% of total).

43 percent were categorized as negligent. Consequently, whereas only 20 percent of all injuries were permanent, 44 percent of negligent injuries involved permanent disability.[7] Normal risk was a slightly more important cause of injury for the elderly: the ratio of negligent to nonnegligent injuries decreased with age from 19.5 percent for those under 20 to 16.1 percent for those over 65 (Table 2.3).

Claims.   We do not have data on the number of claims filed by the

Table 2.3 Percentage of injuries with liability, by age

Age	Injuries with liability (%)
19	19.5
20–44	17.6
45–64	16.2
65	16.1
All ages	17.0

Source: CMA, 1977, p. 99.

patients whose injuries were recorded in the CMA study. We do, however, have estimates of the number of claims closed with and without payment in California from July 1975 through December 1978. Since the great majority (more than 90 percent) of these claims were settled prior to verdict, we do not have a legal evaluation of liability. As will be shown in Chapter 3, whether or not a claim received payment in out-of-court settlement is a rough but imperfect indicator of the probability of a finding of liability at verdict, because litigation costs and other factors influence the settlement outcome. Where possible, therefore, I report data on total claims and claims closed with payment.

Table 2.2 shows the distribution of total claims and paid claims by severity of the injury. Sixty percent of all claims and 56 percent of paid claims were categorized as temporary disabilities (categories 1–3). This is similar to the 56 percent of negligent injuries categorized as temporary, and significantly less than the 80 percent of total injuries. Death accounted for a lower fraction of total and paid claims (17 percent) than of negligent injuries (24 percent).

Putting together these data on injuries and claims, Table 2.4 presents rough estimates of the proportion of negligent injuries for which a claim was filed and the proportion that received compensa-

Table 2.4 Ratio of malpractice claims to negligent injuries, by severity

Severity	Total claims	Paid claims
1	0.057	0.023
2	0.076	0.081
3	0.082	0.028
4	0.15	0.052
5	0.17	0.065
6	0.13	0.050
7	0.11	0.037
8	0.058	0.020
Total	0.10	0.039

Sources: CMA (1977), NAIC (1980).
Note: Related claims have been consolidated. Excludes claims reporting no injury, or emotional or legal issue only, and claims occurring outside hospitals. Claims for classes 1 and 2 taken from 1976; classes 3, 4, and 8 from 1977; and classes 5–7 from 1978. See note 3.

Table 2.5 Ratio of paid claims to injuries, by age of plaintiff

Age	Ratio of paid claims to injuries
19	0.048
20–44	0.056
45–64	0.026
65	0.018
Total	0.039

Sources: CMA (1977), NAIC (1980).

tion. Overall, at most 1 in 10 negligent injuries resulted in a claim, and of these only 40 percent received payment. In other words, at most 1 in 25 negligent injuries resulted in compensation through the malpractice system. The likelihood of filing a claim appears to be slightly higher for permanent than for temporary injuries, and lowest for death. There is greater variation by age: the likelihood that a negligent injury will receive payment ranges from 1 in 55 for persons over 65, to 1 in 18 for persons aged 20 to 44 (Table 2.5). These patterns — decreasing probability of payment with age and higher probability of filing for permanent injuries — strongly suggest that the expected award is an important factor in determining whether a claim is filed.

This rough estimate that at most 1 in 10 negligent injuries results in a claim is probably an upper bound for several reasons. First, it is likely that the hospital records do not reveal all negligent injuries. Second, it seems plausible that injuries occurring from office-based practice, which are excluded from this comparison, are less severe and thus are discovered and pursued less frequently than injuries arising in hospitals. Third, California has one of the highest frequencies of claims per physician and claims per capita nationwide, so if the frequency of injury is no higher in California than the national average, the frequency of claim per negligent injury must be even lower in other states.[8] Fourth, if some of the claims that were filed were related to injuries that the CMA panel would have excluded as nonnegligent, this would imply that even fewer than 1 in 10 negligent injuries were reported. On the other hand, the estimate that 1 in 25 malpractice victims receives compensation is downward-biased to the extent that hospitals or physicians provide corrective medical care free of charge to forestall a potential claim, in the event of a mishap.

Two main conclusions emerge from this comparison of injuries and claims. First, if the California experience is typical, the risk of injury due to negligent medical care is not trivially low: 1 per 126 hospital admissions in 1974. If this risk were uniform nationwide, it would imply a total of more than 260,000 negligent injuries per annum. Second, at most 1 in 10 incidents of malpractice resulted in a claim at the height of the malpractice crisis, and at most 1 in 25 received compensation. Even for major permanent disabilities, at most 1 in 7 patients filed a claim. Unfortunately we do not have more current data on injuries and claims. But let us assume (1) that claim frequency has increased at 12 percent a year since 1978, which implies a doubling of claims by 1984, and (2) no change in the incidence of negligent injury, with the increased frequency of treatment and hence exposure offset by higher quality of care. Under these assumptions, a rough current estimate is that only 1 in 5 incidents of malpractice gives rise to a malpractice claim. Thus the cost of malpractice — the cost of injuries due to negligence — is probably still several times greater than the cost of malpractice claims.

Medical Characteristics of Injuries and Claims

To determine whether the tort system can provide efficient incentives for avoiding injuries, we need a better understanding of the nature of the medical errors, and of whether the tort system is equally effective at detecting and deterring different types of error. If certain mistakes are easier to discover than others, then the malpractice system may impose an uneven penalty on different types of error or on different procedures or treatments and hence may distort the delivery of care.

Although the CMA study provides some interesting information on the characteristics of iatrogenic injuries, it has two important limitations. First, the data base includes only injuries detectable from hospital records. Second, although some information is reported on the medical procedure and body part involved in each injury, inference about the *frequency* or *rate* of injury is not possible in the absence of information on the universe of treatments or procedures. If, for the sake of illustration, procedures on the heart and procedures on the stomach each account for the same percentage of injuries, this would imply that these procedures are of roughly equal risk only if they are performed with roughly equal frequency. If procedures on the stomach are twice as numerous as those on the heart, the frequency of injury would be twice as high for heart procedures. The necessary data on the universe of treatments were not collected as part of the CMA study.[9]

Nevertheless, the CMA study does report on the frequency of different types of medical error, and these data have important implications for prevention. Table 2.6 shows that roughly 82 percent of all injuries were categorized as adverse effects of treatment; 15 percent were classified as effects of incomplete diagnosis or treatment; and 3 percent were classified as effects of incomplete prevention or protection. Thus of the iatrogenic injuries detectable in hospital records, the great majority (82 percent) result from medical intervention (commission) rather than omission, and an even larger percentage (85 percent) involve a new abnormal condition rather than an imperfect resolution of the original condition for which health care was sought. Table 2.6 also shows the distribution of injuries by primary causal event. Specific procedures accounted for 66 percent of all injuries, and of those in which the causative factor was known, 73 percent involved manner of performance. Diagnosis-related injuries (misdiagnosis and nondiagnosis) accounted for only 4.9 percent of all injuries.

These findings may be biased by the nature of the sample: it may be that iatrogenic injuries due to omissions in health care management are as common but harder to detect from hospital charts than injuries due to commission. For the same reason, diagnostic error may be underrepresented relative to procedural error. This is suggested by the fact that diagnostic injuries occurred disproportionately outside the sample hospitals, suggesting that they were detectable only when their adverse results were sufficiently severe to result in hospitalization. Similarly, of the 19 percent of incidents involving drugs or biologics, 76 percent occurred outside the sample hospitals, again suggesting that such incidents were underdetected in the charts of these hospitals.[10]

Errors of commission also appear to be the most common basis for claims, although a precise comparison of the likelihood of a claim for different types of injury is not possible because the injury categories used in the injury and claim studies are not strictly comparable. The NAIC distinguishes three main categories of medical causation — misadventures in diagnosis, misadventures in planning treatment, and improper performance — and a fourth category which includes legal issues and emotional injuries only. Table 2.7 shows the propor-

Table 2.6 Distribution of injuries by primary causal event and class of injury

Class of injury	Mis-diagnosis	Non-diagnosis	Specific procedure	General medical management	Nursing management	Anesthesia management	Drugs and biologics	Nondefective devices	Defective devices	Total
1	0.36	—	70.5	0.72	0.24	2.0	21.6	1.1	3.5	82.3[a]
2	12.8	18.2	51.4	11.4	—	1.4	3.4	—	1.4	14.6
3	—	—	19.4	9.4	45.2	3.2	16.1	6.5	—	3.1
Total	2.2	2.7	66.1	2.6	1.6	2.0	18.8	1.1	3.1	100

Percentages of each class of injury

Source: CMA (1977, pp. 10–13, 58).
Note: The injury classes are defined as follows. Class 1: Adverse effects of treatment. The occurrence of a new abnormal condition caused by a treatment or procedure, either diagnostic or therapeutic. Includes the adverse effects of commission in health care management regardless of the degree of care rendered. Class 2: Effects of incomplete diagnosis or treatment. The occurrence of a discrepancy between expected and demonstrated outcomes of an original abnormal condition for which health care management was sought. Involves the failure to realize an expected outcome, based on optimal capacity, through acts of omission and commission in health care management. Class 3: Effects of incomplete prevention or protection. The occurrence of an abnormal condition caused by incomplete preventive or protective health care management. Involves de novo abnormal conditions, foreseeable and preventable under optimal capacity, caused by omissions in health care management.
a. Percentage of total injuries in each class.

Table 2.7 Distribution of claims and average indemnity, by
medical cause, 1975–1978

Cause	Claims (%)[a]	Indemnity ($)[b]
Diagnosis only	6	17,333
Planning treatment only	12	32,313
Improper performance only	31	31,006
Diagnosis and planning	19	38,071
Diagnosis and improper performance	4	32,250
Planning and improper performance	5	56,008
Diagnosis, planning, and improper performance	3	65,759
Not applicable	15	15,117
Total	100	34,091

Source: NAIC (1980, p. 455).
a. Claims closed with and without payment.
b. Excluding claims closed without payment.

tion of claims in each category and the average indemnity on paid
claims. Forty-three percent of claims allege improper performance,
41 percent allege planning errors, and 34 percent allege diagnostic
errors, while 15 percent of claims involve legal issues or emotional
injuries only. Whereas 31 percent of claims allege procedural error
alone, in only 6 percent is diagnostic error the sole allegation. Thus it
appears that misdiagnosis alone is rarely a sufficient basis for a claim,
and when successful the average indemnity on these claims is
roughly half the average indemnity on all claims.

Taken at face value, these data suggest that the prevention of injuries and claims requires taking more care, not simply performing
more tests or x-rays. A mere 2.7 percent of all injuries (or 54 percent of
the injuries resulting from misdiagnosis) were attributed to the absence of diagnostic tests or x-rays, and diagnostic error is the sole
allegation in only 6 percent of claims. The CMA study concludes,
"Problems of performance, rather than purely judgmental issues,
were the overwhelmingly responsible mechanisms" (CMA, 1977,
p. 62).

Feasibility of a No-Fault System

The CMA study was undertaken to evaluate the feasibility of a system of no-fault compensation for iatrogenic injury. One of the potential problems in operating such a system is the uncertainty surround-

ing causation, that is, the difficulty of distinguishing an adverse outcome resulting from medical care from an imperfect cure of the underlying condition. In this regard, the finding that 85 percent of iatrogenic injuries result in the occurrence of a "new abnormal condition" may seem to suggest that the problem of identifying iatrogenesis is not insuperable. However, such a conclusion would be overly optimistic because it is based on a sample of potentially compensable injuries as identified by medical-legal experts, who intentionally eliminated imperfect results consistent with "optimal capacity," defined as "the ultimate capability of a well-trained specialist, under optimal conditions, to accomplish an intended medical or surgical goal in the majority of instances" (CMA, 1977, p. 12). The distinction may well be much less clear for many of the claims patients might choose to bring. The feasibility of a no-fault system is discussed more fully in Chapter 12.

Conclusion

California data for 1974 indicate that roughly 1 in 126 hospital admissions resulted in an injury due to medical negligence. Only 1 in 10 of these led to a claim. Even assuming a doubling of claims since the mid-1970s, it is almost certainly still true that the cost of injuries due to malpractice far exceeds the cost of claims. Errors of performance rather than errors of judgment or diagnosis were the primary cause of injuries and the primary allegation in claims. These data suggest that the deterrence concerns of the malpractice system are well-founded; the problem is not simply one of litigious patients.

3

The Disposition of Malpractice Claims

IF THE MALPRACTICE SYSTEM is to perform its deterrent function efficiently, the legal process must send appropriate signals to physicians. This requires that the actual disposition of claims conform to the legal standards of due care and damages, assuming that these standards are appropriately defined. I defer until Part III an evaluation of the current legal standards. In this chapter I report on the disposition of a nationally representative sample of claims closed in 1974 and 1976. The purpose is threefold: first, to provide evidence on the accuracy of the actual disposition process relative to the legal standard, and to present hard facts to challenge or corroborate specific widely-held beliefs about the operation of the tort system; second, to test how far a model of rational bargaining behavior can explain the outcome of the settlement process; and third, to present estimates of the impact of tort reforms enacted in the mid-1970s. The Appendix at the end of the chapter compares this evidence on the disposition of malpractice claims with findings from other studies on the disposition of automobile and other tort claims.

According to current law, a health care practitioner is liable for an adverse outcome only if he departs from customary professional standards of adequate care. If found negligent, he is liable for the damages suffered by the plaintiff. Many believe that there is little resemblance between this standard and the actual disposition of malpractice claims. Lay juries allegedly lack the expertise to weigh the conflicting testimony presented by medical and economic experts, in order to evaluate liability and determine damages. Moreover, juries are widely believed to ignore such evidence, preferring to award compensation without regard to fault on the grounds that physicians and their insurance companies can better afford to bear the loss than can the innocent victim.

Even if lay courts have the competence and inclination to decide liability and damages with accuracy, the fact is that the great majority of cases — more than 90 percent — are not tried to verdict but are settled out of court. Cursory evidence seems to suggest that the outcome of the settlement process bears little relation to the potential outcome if the case were tried to verdict. Of cases tried to verdict, the plaintiff wins roughly one in four, whereas about half of the claims settled out of court result in some payment to the plaintiff. But when the plaintiff wins, the average award is much higher at verdict than in an out-of-court settlement. In the sample of claims closed in 1974 and 1976, the average award at verdict was $102,000, compared to an average settlement of $26,000.

Another important issue is how far the costs of litigation distort the process. In medical malpractice, as in product liability and automobile liability, only about 40 cents of the insurance-premium dollar reaches the plaintiff as compensation. An equivalent amount is spent on litigation.[1] Does the threat of litigation expense induce insurance companies to pay something to get rid of claims, no matter how specious their allegations? Conversely, do litigation costs bar claimants with valid but small claims from receiving compensation?

In this chapter I shall summarize the findings of a study of the disposition of 6,000 malpractice claims closed in 1974 and 1976 (Danzon and Lillard, 1983), focusing on the following questions.

1. Do the courts adhere to the standard of finding liability only where negligence is present, or do they tend to relax the negligence standard and compensate without regard to fault, particularly in cases of severe injury? How do awards relate to the legal standards of compensation and to the plaintiff's actual damages? The conventional wisdom, based on other studies of medical malpractice and automobile claims, is that the tort system systematically tends to overcompensate claims with small economic loss and undercompensate claims with large economic loss.[2] But the National Association of Insurance Commissioners concluded from their analysis of malpractice claims (NAIC, 1980) that there is no statistically significant relation between the amount paid to plaintiffs and their tangible or "economic" loss (wage loss; medical and other expenses).

2. Do out-of-court settlements bear any relation to the potential outcome in court? Since the great majority of claims are settled out of court, this is a key question in evaluating the entire tort system.

3. Is compensation unfairly distributed? Half of the dollars paid to plaintiffs in the claims studied were concentrated on only 3 percent of all claims (or 5 percent of the claims in which some payment was made). Would a more even distribution of compensation be more equitable?

4. Do costs distort the process, leading defendants to pay even nonmeritorious claims or plaintiffs to abandon valid claims?

5. Have the tort reforms adopted in response to the 1975 crisis affected the system in the intended direction?

6. From the perspective of an insurance company that must establish reserves to pay for claims, what lessons can be learned from statistical analysis of closed-claim files?

The data available to answer these questions are far from ideal, and it is important to understand these data limitations in order to assess the findings of this and previous studies. The data and methods of analysis are described briefly in the next section. The methodology of this study is significant because the findings are to some extent conditioned by the assumptions made about the bargaining behavior underlying the settlement process.

Data and Methodology

The data analyzed in this chapter come from two broadly representative surveys of medical malpractice claims closed by insurance companies during 1974 and 1976 (Danzon and Lillard, 1983). The disposition of these claims against physicians and hospitals follows a pattern typical in medical malpractice and product liability. About 43 percent of the claims were dropped without payment, while 50 percent were settled out of court with an average payment to the plaintiff of $26,000. Of the remaining 7 percent that were litigated to verdict, the plaintiff won roughly one in four, with an average award of $102,000.

For each claim, the files include information about the plaintiff, the defendant, the severity of the injury, the insurer's estimate of economic loss, the date of the injury, the dates of the filing and closing of the claim, and the outcome — amount of payment and stage of disposition. Only the 1974 survey reports specific allegations made by the plaintiff, and only the 1976 survey reports whether the plaintiff had attorney representation. The insurance company claim files give no information about the bargaining process that led up to the outcome, nor do they indicate what the outcome of a settled case might have been if it had been taken to verdict.

To these claim files we added a measure of delay in urban courts in the host state, as well as data on tort reforms enacted between the

1974 and 1976 surveys. These changes include measures to cap awards, particularly those for nonpecuniary loss; to reduce tort awards when the plaintiff is eligible for compensation from other sources (the collateral source rule); to revoke the plaintiff's right to name a specific dollar amount in his complaint (the *ad damnum*); to make compensation for future losses payable in periodic install-ments; and to limit the contingent fees that may be charged by plain-tiffs' attorneys.[3] No state enacted all of these changes, but most states enacted at least some.

Our task is to see how far these characteristics of the claims and the legal environment "explain" the observed pattern of outcomes. Pre-vious studies of closed-claim data have been largely descriptive, giv-ing averages and cross-tabulations for a range of characteristics of the plaintiff, the injury, the compensation paid, and the stage of disposi-tion.[4] But data limitations have severely restricted analysis, as op-posed to description of the disposition of tort claims, and limited the types of inference that could legitimately be drawn. For example, the two questions of primary policy interest are how well do the courts adhere to the legal standard, and how accurately does the settlement process reflect the potential outcome in court and hence the legal standard? But the sample of cases actually closed at verdict is too small to provide statistically reliable analysis of court behavior. Since more than 90 percent of claims are settled out of court, and the claim files do not indicate what they would have received if they had gone to court, there is no observable benchmark against which to compare the settlement outcome. Moreover, because the cases litigated to verdict are not representative of cases settled out of court, simple extrapolation from cases actually litigated to verdict would give biased estimates of the potential verdict for cases actually settled.

The statistical methodology used in the Danzon-Lillard study was designed to overcome these data limitations. It yields unbiased esti-mates of potential verdicts for cases that did not go to verdict, en-abling us to compare their actual outcome at settlement with the potential outcome at verdict. It thus permits analysis of the behavior of the courts based on potential verdicts for the full sample of claims, including claims dropped or settled as well as claims actually liti-gated to verdict. We also obtain estimates of the range of bargaining — the maximum the defendant would have been willing to offer and the minimum the plaintiff would have settled for — and can compare this maximum offer and minimum ask (demand) to the actual settle-ment.

In order to tease out these inferences from the limited data actually reported, we have to make certain assumptions about the bargaining behavior underlying the settlement process. These assumptions give rise to a set of predictions about when a case will be dropped, settled, or litigated to verdict, and the relation between the size of settlement and the potential verdict. Together, these relations constitute a theory or model of claim disposition, described briefly in the following section.[5] The model is then applied to the data on 6,000 closed claims and used to infer the unobserved quantities — potential verdict, maximum offer, minimum ask — from the observed data on the stage of disposition and settlement amount, if any. To the extent that the resulting estimates are plausible and meet certain statistical tests, it may be said that the underlying model — oversimplified though it may be — captures the fundamental or average behavior patterns governing claim resolution.

THE MODEL OF CLAIM DISPOSITION

The courts. Each claim has a potential verdict and a probability of the plaintiff winning if it were resolved in court, which depend on the facts of the case and the relevant body of law. According to the law of negligence, a plaintiff verdict requires a showing that the plaintiff was injured, that the defendant departed from the customary standard of care, and that the injury was causally related to that departure. If courts apply this law, the probability of a plaintiff verdict will depend on the facts of the case and the quality of the evidence, in addition to the applicable law.[6]

Once the liability of the defendant is established, the question shifts to the size of the award for damages. Damages may occur in two forms: compensable and punitive. Compensable damages are designed to compensate for the plaintiff's actual losses, including "economic" loss or special damages (wage loss; medical and other tangible expenses) and "noneconomic" loss or general damages (such as pain, suffering, shock, loss of consortium). If the injury is fatal, compensable damages are less than if the victim is badly injured but survives, because the survivors are not owed compensation for the decedent's noneconomic loss, consumption expense, and medical expense had he lived. In addition to compensatory damages, punitive damages may be awarded in cases of gross negligence and malicious or otherwise outrageous conduct by the defendant. Punitive damages are rare in medical malpractice suits.

Prior to 1975, basic tort damage rules governed how damages were calculated in malpractice cases and what facts could be disclosed to the jury. Under these rules, damages are paid in a single lump sum that covers both expenses incurred to date and expected future losses; the latter amount is usually discounted, at least in theory, to reflect the fact that it can earn interest prior to the time at which the expected loss materializes. Somewhat inconsistently, the plaintiff is traditionally not compensated for interest income lost in the interim between the occurrence of the injury and the payment of compensation. An increasing number of jurisdictions, however, are awarding prejudgment interest. Under the collateral source rule, evidence of compensation available from other sources, such as the plaintiff's health insurance, is not admissible in court.

Since 1975 many states have changed these basic tort damage rules expressly for cases of medical malpractice. As of 1978, fourteen states had enacted limits on either the total award or some component of it, usually noneconomic loss. Eighteen states modified the collateral source rule to admit evidence of collateral compensation; of these, eight mandated a reduction in the tort award for at least some collateral sources. Sixteen states made periodic rather than lump-sum payment of awards for future damages either mandatory or at the discretion of the court. Thirty-two states revoked the plaintiff's right to name a specific dollar amount in his complaint (the *ad damnum*; Danzon, 1984a). Few legislative changes have been made since then, although state supreme courts have since rejected some of these statutes, and there is renewed interest in tort reform. In cases where these changes were enacted early enough to affect the claims in the data base, the 1974 and 1976 outcomes are compared to see what effect the changes seem to have made.

Settlement out of court. The model adopts the simplifying assumption that each party acts (whether directly or through an attorney or insurer) to serve his own financial interest—the plaintiff to maximize his gain and the defendant to minimize his loss. This is not to deny that other nonrational or emotional factors play a role. In reality, outcomes are no doubt influenced by stubbornness, stupidity, risk aversion, and concerns that behavior on one case may affect credibility and bargaining power on others. But although the simplistic assumption of rational behavior does not capture every nuance of human motivation, the question is, are these departures from rationality sufficiently infrequent or mutually canceling to permit the overall patterns to be explained by the assumption of rationality? This is an empirical question. To the degree that the simple model yields plausible estimates when applied to actual data, the implication is that nonrational behavior can be ignored when the policy interest is in the overall structure of the current system or proposed changes in it.

The assumption of rational behavior implies that both parties have an incentive to settle because litigation is costly. The rational plaintiff would be willing to settle for his expected payoff in court — the probability that he will win times the award he expects to receive if he wins, minus his costs of going to court. For example, if he thinks there is a 50 percent chance that the jury would award him $10,000, but it would cost him $2,500 in attorneys fees and other outlays to get the verdict, then he is assumed to be willing to settle for $2,500 ($10,000 × 0.5 − $2,500). This amount is referred to as his "minimum ask" — the smallest amount for which he will settle.

The defendant is presumed to make a similar calculation to arrive at his "maximum offer." He multiplies what he believes is the plaintiff's probability of winning times the damages likely to be awarded, and adds his costs of going to court. Since he would be better off if he can settle for any lesser sum, this is the maximum he would offer to settle. In the above example, if his estimates were the same as the plaintiff's, he would be willing to offer at most $7,500 ($10,000 × 0.5 + $2,500).[7]

Note that the minimum ask and maximum offer are not the actual sums named in preverdict bargaining (which are not known), but are hypothetical amounts that define the range within which a settlement is possible, if the rational premise is correct. If both parties have identical expectations about the outcome in court, then the bargaining range is simply the sum of their costs of going to court.

These assumptions about rational settlement behavior imply a simple set of rules that determine the disposition of a claim. If the plaintiff's minimum ask turns negative (that is, his expected payoff from proceeding is less than the costs), the case is dropped without payment. If the plaintiff's ask is positive but less than the defendant's maximum offer, as in the example above, the difference between the ask and the offer defines the range within which settlement can occur. We assume that the parties settle for some weighted average of the ask and the offer. If the ask exceeds the offer, no mutually acceptable settlement exists. Each party expects to do better by going to verdict than by meeting the settlement demands of the other, and therefore the case is litigated to verdict.

IMPLICATIONS OF THE MODEL

To test how well this stylized model explains actual settlement behavior involves determining the patterns that the model would lead one to expect and then comparing these predictions to actual experience. In general the model predicts that the outcome at settlement will reflect to some extent the legal standards applied by the courts, but will also diverge in systematic ways on account of litigation costs. More specifically, the following patterns are predicted:

1. The probability of a plaintiff verdict and the size of the award, if any, will reflect the legal standards of negligence and compensable damages and the relevant facts of the case.

2. The size of out-of-court settlements will be influenced by the law of compensable damages through the litigants' expectations of the award at verdict. Settlements will be lower than potential verdicts, however, because of uncertainty about whether the plaintiff would win.

3. Settlements will tend to be lower, the higher are plaintiff costs and the lower are defense costs, because the plaintiff would be willing to settle for less, the higher are his costs of going to court, and the defendant would offer more, the higher are his court costs.

4. The likelihood that the plaintiff will receive some dollar amount in settlement will be related to the probability that the court would find the defendant liable. But because it is not rational for a plaintiff to pursue a case if the costs of going on exceed the expected recovery, the likelihood that a case will be dropped without payment depends not only on the evidence of liability but also on the size of the potential award and the plaintiff's costs of going to court.

5. The likelihood that a claim will be litigated to verdict will be greater, the greater is the gap between the plaintiff's and defendant's expectations of the likely award—or the more optimistic they both are about their own chances. The likelihood of litigation will be lower, the higher are the costs of going to verdict, since these costs represent the potential saving to be divided between them if they can agree to settle.

6. The sample of claims closed at each stage of disposition (dropped without payment, settled, or litigated to verdict) will not be a random sample of all claims; instead, it will be a subset "self-selected" on the basis of those case characteristics that affect the outcome at verdict and the costs of going to verdict.

7. In particular, claims that are tried to verdict are predicted to involve atypically large dollar amounts and more uncertainty about liability. Consequently, this small subset of claims will be an unreliable basis for predicting potential verdicts for cases actually settled or for evaluating how well the system functions for the great majority of claims that are settled out of court.

Evidence from the Analysis

This section reports on empirical testing of the model of claim disposition. It shows how characteristics of the case—the plaintiff, the defendant, the injury, and so on—affect the outcome at verdict and at settlement in ways predicted by the assumptions of rational, maximizing behavior, subject to the constraints of the law. The following section summarizes the findings on the impact of the post-1975 tort reforms.

In our sample, plaintiffs won in only 28 percent of the cases tried to verdict. Unfortunately, the information reported in the claim files about the facts of the case and the quality of the evidence is sparse and does not provide a solid basis for determining how well the courts adhere to the legal standard of finding the defendant liable only in cases of negligence. Nevertheless, some interesting and relevant patterns do emerge.

Severity of the injury. The plaintiff's probability of receiving an award was higher if the injury was permanent than if it was temporary, and highest if the injury was fatal. Although this evidence may seem to support the common allegation that courts relax the negligence standard and award compensation without regard to fault in cases of severe injury, this is a possible but not a necessary inference. As we have seen, the California Medical Association study found that the more severe the injury, the more likely it was to be due to negligence rather than a normal risk of adequate care — indeed, the proportion of iatrogenic injuries attributed to negligence rather than normal risk increased from 12 percent for minor, temporary injuries to 83 percent for permanent total disabilities. If one assumes that these patterns are typical nationwide, and that claims are drawn randomly from the universe of injuries, then the courts applying a negligence standard would correctly find for the plaintiff much more frequently in cases of permanent disability than in cases of minor or temporary injury. Without knowing what proportion of negligent and nonnegligent injuries in fact lead to a claim, we cannot use these data to evaluate the behavior of the courts precisely. But we can make the more limited inference that finding for the plaintiff more frequently in cases of severe disability is not sure proof of departure from the negligence standard.

Type of injury and allegations. In our study the plaintiff had a higher chance of winning if the injury involved an obvious error (treatment of the wrong patient or the wrong limb) or if he invoked the rule of res ipsa loquitur, literally, "the thing speaks for itself." This rule provides that when an event occurs that would not normally happen in the absence of negligence, the burden of proof shifts to the defendant to show that he was not negligent. The rule is very often invoked in cases of obvious treatment error (such as amputation of the wrong limb) or in cases where the patient could not have intervened or been expected to identify which person or process injured him (because he was anesthetized, for example).[8] Although we could not estimate directly how the probability of winning at verdict is affected, because so few of these claims reach verdict, we did find that plaintiffs in res ipsa cases were 50 percent more likely to receive a positive settlement. This suggests a high likelihood that the plaintiff would win if the issue were pressed to verdict, and shows that the evidence of negligence does indeed matter, both in court and in out-of-court settlement.

By contrast, plaintiffs alleging misdiagnosis or lack of informed consent were less likely to win in settlement or at verdict. A plaintiff verdict was 21 percent less likely if the charge was misdiagnosis, and 34 percent less likely if the charge was lack of informed consent.[9] This suggests that, at least in the mid-1970s when these were relatively new grounds for suit, plaintiffs tended systematically to overestimate their chances in such actions.

Multiple defendants. The plaintiff was almost twice as likely to win against multiple defendants as against a single defendant. Contrary to the popular belief that plaintiffs routinely add nonliable defendants to a claim solely in the expectation that one or more will offer to settle in order to "buy out" of litigation costs, in fact the defendants that are added do raise the probability of a plaintiff victory. The extent to which this occurs because multiple defendants try to shift liability among themselves, thereby producing evidence that aids the plaintiff, cannot be determined from the data.

SIZE OF THE AWARD

This analysis of the determinants of size of awards is based on the full sample of claims, not just the 2 percent that actually litigated to verdict and won. For the other claims, we can infer the "potential" or "shadow" verdict, given the assumption that settlements are a weighted average of the ask and the offer, which in turn are based on the parties' expectations of what would happen if the case went to verdict.

The available data permit much more to be said about the influence of the law and facts of the case on the size of the award than on the issue of liability. Contrary to the conclusion reached in NAIC (1980), that economic loss accounts for very little of the overall variation in payment size, we found that three crude measures of compensable damages (the insurer's estimate of economic loss, an index of severity, and the age of the plaintiff), together with indicators for whether or not the state adopted four specific legal rules between 1974 and 1976, account for more than 40 percent of the observed variation in shadow verdicts.[10]

Compensable damages. In principle the award should compensate for economic and noneconomic loss, but our data only report the insurance company's estimate of economic loss. The higher the economic loss, the higher is the award, but awards rise less than in proportion to economic loss. This finding has led others to conclude that the tort system tends to overcompensate small losses and undercompensate large ones. However, statistical analysis shows that errors in the data rule out such a judgment.[11] For the same reason, it is impossible to determine whether the courts tend to award proportionately greater noneconomic damages in cases where economic losses are greater.

The median (most typical) shadow verdict for claims involving permanent total disability is roughly twice that for claims involving death, which receive awards comparable to those for permanent partial disability. The awarding of lesser amounts for death than for total disability accords with the law which deducts from compensation to surviving dependents expenses that would have been incurred by the injured person had he lived but been totally disabled. Mean awards and settlements for different types of injury are shown in Table 3.1.

Shadow verdicts for permanent total disability average roughly 2 percent more for each remaining year of life expectancy, while for permanent partial disability the increment is 1 percent for each remaining year. Thus again this is evidence that awards are related to damages — in this case future damages. For minor injuries, awards first rise and then diminish with the age of the claimant, peaking in the late thirties, which is consistent with the pattern of earnings over the life cycle. It suggests that awards for minor injuries are influenced primarily by current wage loss.

We found no strong statistical evidence, however, that awards are related to the actual earnings of the plaintiff prior to the injury, and no systematic difference by sex of the plaintiff. This finding is tentative because the data on earnings were particularly poor. But taken at face value, it suggests that juries tend to disregard the intent of the law to place a higher value on lives with higher earning power. Such jury behavior would be consistent with survey evidence (Acton, 1973) that people do not believe that more should be spent to save the lives of those with higher earning power. It is also consistent with Wittman's finding (1983) that juries in automobile injury cases award

Table 3.1 Mean award, by stage of disposition and severity of injury: 1970, 1974, 1976

Year and stage of disposition	Temporary or permanent minor disability		Permanent partial disability		Permanent total disability		Death	
	Award (dollars)[a]	Sample size	Award (dollars)[a]	Sample size	Award (dollars)[a]	Sample size	Award (dollars)[a]	Sample size
1970								
Pre-suit	713	405	11,048	14	24,343	9	9,045	37
Suit	3,134	332	12,332	77	40,946	33	10,509	111
Verdict	10,097	26	21,163	7	32,860	2	18,770	3
1974								
Pre-suit	1,236	281	5,378	68	8,267	11	11,048	15
Suit	4,403	421	15,522	333	33,860	59	25,591	166
Verdict	5,710	25	34,201	19	438,011	6	52,575	17
1976								
Pre-suit	1,339	384	4,866	68	9,045	10	9,414	24
Suit	4,316	673	13,905	297	58,688	68	13,360	103
Verdict	9,414	7	22,026	16	331,042	4	141,492	16

Source: Danzon (1980).
a. Geometric means.

more, relative to reported damages, if the victim is female or Hispanic (categories with relatively low reported damages because of relatively low earnings.)

Most of these findings may seem obvious, and simply serve to put figures on relationships whose directions and rough dimensions appear to be determined by law. This may seem prosaic unless one remembers the frequent charge that actual decisions by juries and judges typically do not follow the precepts of the law. On the contrary, the conclusion of this analysis, based on almost 6,000 claims resolved nationwide in two different time periods, is that the courts are far from arbitrary and the law makes a substantial difference.

THE SETTLEMENT PROCESS

More than 90 percent of claims are settled out of court. Of these, about half are dropped without payment. In our study, the other half were settled for an average of $26,000, far less than the $102,000 average award in the small minority of tried cases that the plaintiffs won. This section examines why some claims are dropped, what influences the amount of settlement in those that are settled, and why some are litigated to verdict. Again, the findings are reasonably consistent with the model of claim disposition.

Reasons for dropping claims. The sheer fact that about half of the claims in the data base were dropped with no payment to the plaintiff—two-thirds of them without the filing of a lawsuit—contradicts the widespread belief that insurers stand ready to pay out money freely on small claims, including unfounded "nuisance" claims, in order to avoid more costly litigation.

The simple rational model suggests that a claim will be dropped if the claimant's ask becomes negative — that is, if the expected costs of pursuing it become greater than the prospective gains. The evidence confirms that low stakes or high costs increase the likelihood that a case will be dropped. In our study, the smaller the shadow verdict, the more likely a claim was to be dropped. This supports the belief that small malpractice claims are often barred from recovery because of the high fixed costs of participating in the legal process. A claim was also more likely to be dropped the greater the court congestion,[12] presumably because delay tends to reduce the present value of an award to the plaintiff. Thus, court congestion was an effective bar to recovery for some plaintiffs, although this pattern may be changing with the movement toward awarding prejudgment interest.

Claims were significantly more likely to be dropped in cases where there were statutory limits on the contingent fees that plaintiffs' attorneys could charge. States that enacted fee ceilings between 1974 and 1976 experienced a 13 percent increase in the percentage of dropped claims, from 34 percent in 1974 to 47 percent in 1976. We estimate that the ceilings contributed 5 of these 13 percentage points, presumably as a result of attorneys' increased reluctance to take on or pursue small or marginal cases if they were unable to charge a fee to cover the cost of their time.

The settlement process is a crude reflection of likely court rulings on liability. We estimate that between 39 and 53 percent of the claims dropped without payment—about one-quarter of all claims in the data base—would have produced an award for the plaintiff if taken to verdict. This indicates that the uncertainties and costs of litigation deny compensation to substantial numbers of claimants with small but legally valid claims. On the other hand, we estimate that 57 to 77 percent of the settled claims would have won if taken to verdict, a significantly higher percentage than the 39 to 53 percent estimated for dropped claims.[13] Contrary to some allegations, then, the settlement process is not random with respect to which plaintiffs receive compensation: those with a better chance in court have a better chance in settlement. Still, approximately 30 percent of plaintiffs who were paid something in settlement would have lost had they proceeded to verdict.

Size of settlement. The size of the settlement is closely related to the size of the shadow verdict. On average, paid claims settled for 74 percent of their shadow verdicts. The larger the claim, the wider is the dollar gap between the settlement and the shadow verdict. A $10,000 increase in shadow verdict results in only a $7,700 increase in settlement.

This widening gap between actual settlement and potential verdict is consistent with the conventional wisdom that the tort system tends to overcompensate small claims and undercompensate large ones. A plausible explanation for such a systematic bias in settlements is that the plaintiff's costs of going to court rise faster with larger claims (because of expert witness fees, for example) than do those of the defense. It would follow that plaintiffs would be willing to settle larger claims for a smaller percentage of what they could get in court. In other words, systematic bias between settlement amount and economic loss could occur even if verdicts were unbiased (which we cannot tell) if cases involving large economic loss entail relatively higher costs of going to trial for the plaintiff than for the defense. In fact, the limited evidence (NAIC, 1980) shows that the higher the stakes, the higher is the ratio of plaintiff costs relative to defense costs:

defense-allocated adjustment expense falls from over 100 percent of indemnity paid to claimants on claims under $3,000, to 10 percent of indemnity on claims paid over $140,000. By contrast, the plaintiff attorney's contingent fee percentage is not systematically related to the size of the award, although it is typically higher for more advanced stages of disposition (see Chapter 11). One factor contributing to this difference is that the plaintiff typically calls experts to testify on the size of damages, whereas the defense does not.

In our study, the defendant's maximum offer exerted much more influence on the settlement amount that the plaintiff's minimum ask. On a scale of 100, the imbalance is 87 to 13. Put another way, the amount of settlement was much closer to the maximum offer than to the minimum ask, suggesting that the plaintiff typically got the better of the bargain.

Although we cannot measure directly the magnitudes of the costs of going to trial for defense and plaintiff and the impact of these costs on settlement, nevertheless certain variables that are likely to affect these costs do have the predicted effects. Claims involving multiple defendants resulted in higher settlements, even after we controlled for the fact that such claims have higher potential verdicts. Multiple-defendant claims have higher defense costs because of the complexity of allocating liability, duplicative effort by defendants, and blame shifting that aids the plaintiff. Similarly, claims involving a physician defendant are expected to have higher costs of going to verdict than claims with only institutional defendants, because of the lost time and embarrassment to the physician of court appearance. Consistent with this, claims involving at least one physician yielded higher settlement offers, higher settlement rates, and higher settlement amounts than claims with only institutional defendants. This runs counter to the common notion that physicians are unwilling to settle because doing so is an implicit admission of liability; such concerns are apparently dominated by the desire to avoid the embarrassment and lost time that court appearances entail.

Our only proxy for plaintiff costs was court congestion. The logic is that delay reduces the present value of expected awards, in the absence of prejudgment interest, and raises the cost of evidentiary "decay" more to the plaintiff, who bears the burden of proof. Consistent with this, court congestion was found to reduce settlement size.

What difference do attorneys make? Virtually all plaintiffs who proceed to the point of filing a legal suit are represented by an attorney, suggesting that it is not feasible to file suit without one. Among claimants who settled prior to suit, those who were represented by attorneys received about 150 percent more than unrepresented claimants who settled at that stage. This clearly overstates the value of an attorney because of selectivity bias: many unrepresented claimants presumably had claims that had been rejected by attorneys. Still, the sheer size of the differential strongly suggests that an attorney who charged a typical fee of one-third of the settlement value was clearly worth his fee from the plaintiff's standpoint.

Limits on contingent fees to plaintiffs' attorneys appeared to reduce average settlement size by 9 percent. This suggests that fee ceilings do more than simply cut down on "windfall" returns — they also reduce the attorney's effort, and hence affect the probability of plaintiff victory and the likely gross recovery as well as the net amount realized by the plaintiff.[14]

Claims closed before the filing of suit were settled at much lower amounts than those settled after filing. It is doubtful, however, that the event of filing was as important as the fact that cases settled without formal litigation are likely to be precisely those in which the stakes are too small to warrant the expense of litigation.

Litigation to verdict. If the assumptions of the simple rational model are correct, litigation occurs when the plaintiff's minimum ask exceeds the defendant's maximum offer throughout pretrial bargaining. This is approximately the same as saying that the plaintiff's expected award in court exceeds the defendant's expectation by more than the sum of their anticipated litigation costs (see, for example, Landes, 1971; Posner, 1973; Gould, 1974). Thus any factor that increases the range of expectations or reduces litigation costs heightens the propensity to go to verdict. The evidence is consistent with these predictions.

In our study, by far the strongest predictors of how far a claim would be pursued were the size of the shadow verdict and the severity of the injury: the higher the shadow verdict, the less likely the case was to close prior to suit or to be dropped without payment, and the more likely it was to be tried to judgment. This suggests that the larger the shadow verdict, the greater are the litigants' errors in predicting it relative to their litigation costs. This conclusion is plausible for two reasons: first, major injuries entail large future losses, the estimation of which involves subjective judgment; second, because some of the costs of going to court do not vary with the stakes of the case, costs represent a larger proportion of the shadow verdict in smaller cases.[15] It follows that dollar caps on awards — or any other measure that reduces uncertainty — tend to encourage settlement out of court.

Claims involving multiple defendants were slightly less likely to go to verdict than were claims with only one defendant, even though the multidefendant claims have higher shadow verdicts. Thus the normal tendency for larger claims to go to verdict was apparently offset by the higher costs of defending them. Such costs would raise the defendants' maximum offer relative to the plaintiffs' ask, thereby making settlement more likely.

Litigation was also less likely—and settlement more likely—when there were limits on the contingent fees that could be charged by plaintiffs' attorneys, presumably because such fee ceilings reduce the attorney's return for a marginal hour of effort.

DISTRIBUTION OF INDEMNITY DOLLARS

The mean court award in the data base was $102,000, compared with a mean settlement of $26,000. It was also found that the top 5 percent of claims in terms of dollar payment (claims paid more than $140,000 each) received 49 percent of all dollars paid, while the bottom 50 percent of all claims (averaging less than $6,500 per claim) received only 4 percent of the dollars paid. Do these findings—the discrepancy between court awards and settlement amounts and the pronounced concentration of payments—imply severe inequities in the distribution of compensation?

Not necessarily. To a large extent, this discrepancy reflects the self-selection of cases by stage of disposition. Cases going to verdict usually involve more serious injuries and losses. In fact, there was a 103 percent disparity between the average shadow verdict of cases that settled and that of cases that went to verdict. By contrast, the settlement process—the tendency to settle for less than the shadow verdict—accounted for only a 30 percent differential between shadow verdicts and settlements. In other words, on average, plaintiffs who settle have suffered economic losses smaller than those of plaintiffs who go to verdict and win. The former therefore have smaller shadow verdicts, and are willing to settle for less than the average award won by plaintiffs in court.

Nor is the concentration of dollars on so few claims necessarily inequitable. The estimates of shadow verdicts (which have been shown to be heavily influenced by compensable damages) imply that 43.5 percent of all plaintiffs would have received less than $6,500 if their cases were pressed to judgment—a figure quite close to the 50 percent that actually did receive less than that amount. Thus the uneven distribution of dollars largely parallels the uneven distribution of injury severity and of compensable damages. Some further disparity is introduced by the disposition process and, in particular, by the costs of litigation, which influence whether a case is abandoned, settled, or litigated to verdict. But the most extreme charges, that the system is arbitrary and inequitable, are clearly unfounded.

Effects of the 1975 Tort Reforms

Assessing the effects of the 1975 tort reforms poses a threefold challenge. First, the precise form of a given measure varied from state to state. For example, in relaxing the collateral source rule, some states simply made evidence of collateral compensation admissible in court, whereas others authorized or mandated deductions from the court award. Second, identifying whether particular statutes could have affected claims in the data base is unavoidably imprecise. Our analysis (Danzon and Lillard, 1983) considered only those statutes that were enacted prior to the closing date of claims in the 1976 sample. Some statutes, however, did not become effective until several months after they were enacted, and several were subject to constitutional challenge. Claims in or near trial may have been exempt from recent changes in law, and there may have been further delays before changes in court decisions fed back into changes in out-of-court settlements. All these factors would lead our analysis to underestimate the full, long-run effect of tort reforms. Third, it was not possible for us to control for all of the statutory changes or for any changes in judge-made law, judicial instructions, or jury attitudes that may have occurred in response to the malpractice crisis. As a result, we may have overestimated the effect of those statutes we did measure.

For all these reasons, the effects realized in the period immediately following the enactment of reforms—the period captured by the 1976 claims—may not be reliable guides to the long-term effects of each measure. Consequently, these estimates should not be viewed as definitive but only as preliminary indicators. They were derived by comparing the change in awards between 1974 and 1976 in states that enacted a particular reform during that period and in states that did not.[16] Since the small sample size made it impossible to estimate separate effects of all the changes, we grouped some laws together and arbitrarily assumed that they had equal impact. The resulting estimates are particularly tentative. The effect of limits on contingent fees (which strictly is a change in rules rather than in law) has already been mentioned, but is repeated here for completeness.

In states that passed statutes to cap verdicts, or to eliminate specific dollar requests by plaintiffs (to bar the *ad damnum* clause), or to permit payment of awards for future losses in periodic installments, the apparent effect of these changes was as follows: reducing the average shadow verdict by 30 percent; cutting the average settlement by 25 percent; raising the share of cases dropped from 43 to 48 percent; and reducing the share of cases going to verdict from 5.1 to 4.6 percent. Relaxation of the ban on evidence of collateral sources of compensation for the injury appeared to reduce shadow verdicts by 18 percent, but the statistical significance of this finding was quite low.[17] Imposition of limits on contingent fees charged by plaintiffs' attorneys appeared to have the following effects: cutting the average settlement by 9 percent; raising the share of cases dropped from 43 to 48 percent; and reducing the share of cases going to verdict from 6.1 to 4.6 percent.

These results suggest that the tort reforms enacted in response to the crisis had substantial effects. How much they contributed to the resolution of the crisis is discussed further in Chapter 4.

Litigation costs. Among the most widely adopted changes was the introduction of pretrial screening panels or arbitration, which are intended to reduce expenditure on litigation by dispensing with the formal court rules of procedure and evidence. We were unable to estimate the effects of these changes directly because too few of the claims in our sample had been adjudicated in these new forums.

We did, however, use the model to simulate the effect of hypothetical changes. Our specific question was, what would be the effect of changes that reduce by 30 percent the costs of going to verdict of either party separately or both simultaneously? Such reductions are not unrealistic. In addition to the recent changes in statutory law, many of the common law changes adopted since the 1960s would have the effect of reducing litigation costs for the plaintiff—for example, the expansion of the locality rule to permit testimony by nonresident physicians on a local case, admitting textbooks as evidence, the more liberal interpretation of *res ipsa.* Although the simulations do not measure the effect of any specific change, they do reveal important effects of any change in rules or procedure that reduces costs and hence affects incentives to settle. In particular, cutting the plaintiff's costs of litigating to verdict will raise his minimum ask at the settlement stage because the ask is his expected payoff at verdict, net of his costs of going to verdict. Consequently, a reduction in the plaintiff's litigation costs tends to raise settlement amounts, lower the drop rate, and push more cases to verdict. Cutting defense litigation costs lowers the maximum the defense will offer in settlement, and consequently tends to lower settlement amounts and also push more cases to verdict.

To illustrate, we estimated that if the litigation costs of both parties were cut by 30 percent, the average settlement size would fall by 17 percent, the share of cases dropped without payment would fall from 42 to 40 percent, and the share of cases going to verdict would increase from 5.6 to 6.9 percent. Although this may seem a trivial absolute increase, it represents a 23 percent increase in the number of cases going to verdict.

These illustrative estimates make an important point: procedural reform that reduces the "per unit" cost of litigating may not reduce total expenditure on litigation. The reason is that when the cost of litigating falls, cases that previously would have been dropped or settled, because the expected costs of proceeding outweighed the benefits, will now be pushed to settlement or verdict. Thus total expenditure on litigation will fall by less than the reduction in cost per case, and may even rise. To return to the numerical example, assume first that the costs of settling are zero and the costs of going to verdict are 30 percent of the expected award initially, and 20 percent after the 30 percent cost reduction. With these assumptions and the estimates derived from the simulations, total expenditure on litigation falls by only 18 percent, although cost per case falls by 30 percent. If we now allow for the positive costs of settling, equal to 10 percent of the expected award, and assume that this amount is unaffected by the change that reduced the costs of going to verdict, then total expenditure on litigation falls by only 3 percent because we must add the additional costs of settling those cases that previously would have been dropped without payment.

Obviously, this analysis does not suffice to evaluate the efficiency of procedural reform because it ignores the effect of litigation on the accuracy of the outcome in court, on incentives to file claims, and ultimately on the deterrent effect of the tort system. It simply illustrates that procedural reform designed to reduce expenditure on litigation may have complex and unintended consequences, and is highly likely to increase court congestion and the public costs of operating the courts.

Conclusions

At the broadest level of generality, the major implication of these findings is that despite its apparent perversities, the tort system in practice is far from random. The plausibility of the estimates lends credence to the plausibility of the model and its underlying assumption, that simple, self-serving rationalism largely explains average behavior and outcomes in the disposition of medical malpractice claims. Consequently, there are reasonably stable and predictable relations between the rules that would be applied in formal court-room proceedings and the actual outcome in the great majority of cases that are settled informally out of court. Post-crisis tort reforms have produced substantial effects in the intended directions, but with some side effects that may not have been anticipated.

The following paragraphs summarize the findings from our study that address the specific questions raised at the beginning of the chapter.

1. To what extent do the courts find liability only where negligence is present and award damages commensurate with the loss suffered? Damage awards are strongly influenced by the plaintiff's economic loss and by the law defining and sometimes limiting compensable damages. Our data do not permit an accurate estimate of awards for pain and suffering. The data on the issue of liability are also limited, but clearly refute the extreme charge that juries compensate without regard to fault in cases of severe injury. Overall, plaintiffs win less than one case in three. The more severe the injury, the more likely it is that the verdict will favor the plaintiff, but this may simply reflect the fact that severe injuries are indeed more likely to result from negligence than from simple bad luck. The system does tend to penalize the most obvious error, not necessarily the most serious or most common one, which distorts the deterrent signal sent to medical practitioners.

2. Do outcomes generated by the out-of-court settlement process bear any relation to court outcomes? The answer is yes: settlements average 74 percent of the potential award at verdict. The 26 percent difference is plausibly explained by discounting for the probability that the plaintiff will win and for the anticipated costs of going to verdict. But if there is indeed uncertainty as to whether negligence occurred—which is inevitable as long as medicine is not a precise science—then discounting the award to reflect this uncertainty, which is the result of the settlement process, may result in an appropriate fine for deterrence purposes.

Claims that have a higher probability of winning at verdict also have a higher probability of receiving some compensation in settlement, but the correspondence is far from perfect. Some 39 to 53 percent of claims that are dropped would in fact have won if pressed to verdict, while 57 to 77 percent of claims actually settled would have won at verdict. Much of this discrepancy—the much higher mean award and much lower rate of the plaintiff winning some positive amount at verdict than at settlement—is attributable to the fact that the cases that are actually litigated to verdict constitute a small, atypical subset, "self-selected" to that stage of disposition precisely because the outcome was unpredictable to the litigants, the potential award was large, and the evidence for the plaintiff was weak. Thus we get a very biased impression of the operation of the malpractice system from observing the minority of more visible cases that are litigated to verdict rather than the great majority of cases that are settled out of court.

3. Is compensation unfairly distributed? The answer is probably not, if fairness means distribution in direct relation to the severity of the injury. Although half of the payment dollars are concentrated on 3 percent of claims, this is a reasonably accurate reflection of the fact that most claims involve fairly minor injuries, with most of the economic loss concentrated on the few severely injured claimants.

4. Why is the system so costly to operate? Do costs distort the disposition process? Because the data files contain no information about the plaintiff's litigation expense and limited information about that of the defense, conclusions about the causes and effects of litigation expense are necessarily based on indirect inference. Both theory and evidence suggest that the fundamental cause of expenditure on litigation is uncertainty about the outcome in court—both liability and damages—and about the parties' ability to influence that outcome. Claims involving permanent disability, where the range of possible awards is largest, are more likely to go to court, whereas claims involving obvious error are much more likely to settle out of court.

Litigation expense apparently does influence whether a claim is paid, how much is paid, and how far it is likely to proceed in the disposition process. The fact that small claims are more likely to be dropped and less likely to proceed to verdict is evidence that fixed costs make prosecution of cases with small stakes relatively less worthwhile. The fact that settlement size tends to be higher in cases with relatively large costs of defense (multiple defendants or a physician defendant) and lower in cases with relatively large plaintiff costs (court congestion) implies that although cases will tend to settle for the expected court award, deviations from that norm occur as a result of anticipated litigation expense, which affects the parties' relative bargaining power.

Should this influence of litigation costs on claim disposition be viewed as a distortion? That depends on the benchmark we use and the source of the costs. In a hypothetical world where the courts could freely observe the truth, expenditure on litigation would be pure waste and its effects a pure distortion. But in the real world, where the courts cannot costlessly observe the truth, at least some of the expenditure on litigation must be viewed as an investment in ferreting out the information necessary to make a more accurate decision and is therefore not pure waste. To the extent that the plaintiff's costs are high when his case is weak and the defendant's costs are high when his case is weak, a bargaining process that yields a lower settlement when plaintiff costs are high and a higher settlement when defense costs are high is consistent with adjusting the penalty to reflect the probability that negligence has occurred. Thus to the extent that settlement size departs from the expected court award on account of the expected litigation costs, there is not necessarily a distortion of the optimal deterrent signal in a world of imperfect information. But in cases where litigation costs are high for reasons unrelated to the need for information — for example, dilatory tactics by the defense, naming of spurious defendants by the plaintiff — such costs do indeed distort claim disposition and hence distort the deterrent signal.

5. What has been the impact of tort reforms? Tort reforms designed to reduce large awards appear to have achieved their intended effect. Perhaps not surprisingly, modification of the collateral source rule to admit evidence of collateral compensation, but without mandating offset, has had only a weak effect, if any. Statutory regulation of contingent fees has not simply reduced the fee and thereby increased the net recovery of the plaintiff. On the contrary, fee ceilings appear to have discouraged attorneys' efforts and hence have resulted in lower settlements, fewer cases litigated to verdict, and more cases dropped without payment.

6. What are the lessons for claim reserving? For the insurance company that must decide what size of reserve to establish when a claim is filed, setting the reserve equal to the expected value of the case (probability of a plaintiff verdict times expected verdict) is a good first approximation. This should be adjusted upward if defense costs are relatively high (for example, because of multiple defendants), and adjusted downward if the plaintiff faces high costs (for example, as a result of court congestion in the absence of prejudgment interest). The potential verdict can be predicted on the basis of the economic loss, the severity of the injury, the plaintiff's age, and rules limiting damages by caps or collateral source offset.

More generally, the statistical model we used could be applied to any set of closed-claim data to obtain current parameter estimates of the effect of case characteristics on disposition in the jurisdiction of interest. These parameters can then be applied to individual claims as they are filed, to predict the likely payment and stage of disposition, and such estimates can form the basis for the claim reserve. They obviously do not replace actuarial assessment of particular characteristics of individual claims or claimants, but computer-based estimates can provide an invaluable benchmark against which to check subjective estimates.

To some these may seem simple and unexceptional results, hardly in need of proof. But public debate at the time of the malpractice crisis revealed that they are far from self-evident to quite a few people, including many medical and legal practitioners. These results provide some basis for considering the need for and the likely effects of reforms of the current system, which are the subject of Part III.

APPENDIX

Evidence from Studies of Other Tort Claims

To what extent does medical malpractice resemble or differ from other types of personal injury litigation? Can the conclusions of this analysis be more widely generalized to the tort system as a whole? Two studies of jury verdicts in Cook County, Illinois, and in San Francisco for the period 1960–1980 shed some interesting light on these questions (Peterson and Priest, 1982; Shanley and Peterson, 1983). Professional malpractice (predominantly medical malpractice) accounted for only 7 percent of civil jury trials but 13 percent of total dollars awarded in San Francisco, and for 3 percent of trials and 6 percent of dollars in Cook County. Malpractice plaintiffs win less frequently than plaintiffs in any other type of case. In San Francisco, for example, the plaintiff win rate ranges from 35 percent for malpractice to 69 percent for worker injury cases, with an average of 59 percent on all cases. The malpractice plaintiff win rate rose from 27 percent for the 1960–64 period to 43 percent for the 1970–74 period, and then fell back to 32 percent for the 1975–79 period (Table A.1). But when malpractice plaintiffs do win, they win larger awards: the median (most typical) award ranges from $15,000 for automobile accidents to $75,000 for malpractice (1979 dollars), with an overall median for all types of cases of $21,000. The average ranges from $46,000 for automobile accidents to $280,000 for malpractice claims (Table A.2). For all types of case, the average exceeds the median because of the few very large awards.

To some extent, the relatively high awards for malpractice reflect the fact that malpractice claims tend to involve more severe injuries. Using the Cook County data, Peterson found that based on the raw

Table A.1 Trends in the percentage of plaintiff victories for specific case types in San Francisco County

Year	Increasing percentage					Decreasing percentage			
	Auto accident	Common carrier	Injury on property	Street hazard	Mal-practice	Worker injury	Contract business	Product liability	Intentional tort
1960–64	60	57	46	40	27	67	74	57	52
1965–69	64	59	47	45	35	72	71	55	38
1970–74	65	63	47	52	43	70	71	54	49
1975–79	75	64	54	45	32	65	56	52	44
1960–79	65	60	48	46	35	69	66	54	45

Source: Shanley and Peterson (1983).
Note: Numbers are percentage of all cases tried to civil juries in which liability is found against at least one defendant (including defaults and admitted liability).

Table A.2 Trends in median plaintiff awards in San Francisco (in thousands of 1979 dollars)

Year	Malpractice		Intentional tort		Contracts/ business		Product liability		Worker injury	
	Mean	Median	Mean	Median	Mean	Median	Mean	Median	Mean	Median
1960–64	89	45	61	22	65	34	70	19	102	50
1965–69	217	111	62	19	108	25	138	51	128	53
1970–74	319	88	67	16	181	45	103	36	134	60
1975–79	457	70	339	20	237	44	219	57	140	62
1960–79	280	75	179	19	164	37	137	37	125	55
Change, 1960–64 to 1975–79 (%)	513	156	556	91	365	129	313	300	137	124

Source: Shanley and Peterson (1983).

data, malpractice awards are on average 3.7 times larger than awards for injuries on property (slip and fall, for example), but that this differential is reduced to a factor of 2.3 after controlling for type of injury and other case characteristics. Thus the predicted median award for a seriously disabling injury such as leg amputation is $330,000 if the defendant is a private property owner, $754,000 if the defendant is a physician, $761,000 for a work injury, $678,000 in a product liability action, and only $199,000 in an automobile accident (1979 dollars).

Several factors may contribute to the tendency of juries to award more for the same injury, depending on the identity of the defendant. Both Peterson (1984) and Wittman (1983) found evidence of higher awards against corporate defendants. I have found that awards tend to rise with the limits of the defendant's insurance coverage. Using data on malpractice claims closed in 1970, I estimate that the elasticity of the award with respect to the limits of the defendant's insurance coverage was 0.5 to 0.9 for verdicts and 0.14 for settlements. Thus the fact that most private individuals do not carry the millions of dollars of coverage commonly purchased by physicians and corporate defendants may explain, at least in part, why the same injury receives almost four times as much compensation if the cause is medical malpractice as opposed to an automobile accident. Indeed, the analysis by Rolph and his colleagues (1984) of automobile accident claim files confirms that the limits of insurance coverage constrain payments to automobile claimants in out-of-court settlements, presumably reflecting similar constraints on jury verdicts.[18] Thus the tendency of physicians to seek virtually complete coverage may be one factor fueling the size of malpractice awards.

There are other important differences between the disposition of automobile tort claims and that of malpractice claims. Lawsuits are filed in only 20 percent of automobile claims, and only 1 percent are litigated to verdict, whereas suits are filed in 58 percent of malpractice cases and 7 percent are litigated to verdict. In part this reflects the lower stakes of automobile claims: the median economic loss was $300 (1977 dollars). But more important, it probably reflects the greater complexity and hence greater cost of proving a medical malpractice claim, which effectively bars claims with very modest loss. This is evidenced by the higher rate of attorney representation on malpractice claims — 58 percent for malpractice claims closed prior to suit and 98 percent for claims in which a suit was filed, compared to 29 percent for automobile claims closed prior to suit and 22 percent for automobile claims in which suit was filed.

The automobile data do support the conventional wisdom that the ratio of recovery to economic loss declines with the size of economic loss.[19] This results primarily from the fact that compensation for pain and suffering increases less than in proportion to economic loss, although the larger the economic loss, the higher is the probability of receiving compensation for pain and suffering. Note, however, that these findings are based primarily on settlements and hence are probably influenced by litigation costs, as described earlier; they do not necessarily prove bias in court dispositions.

4

The Frequency and Severity
of Malpractice Claims

THE DRAMATIC INCREASE in malpractice claims in the last two decades has been ascribed to many causes. As the use of medical services increased following the introduction of the Medicare and Medicaid programs in 1965 and the concurrent growth in private health insurance, the exposure to iatrogenic injury likewise increased. Medical procedures have become more complex and invasive, raising the risk of serious injury. Increased specialization has allegedly broken down the traditional relationship of trust between patients and physicians, making patients more willing to sue.

However, the fact that similar developments have affected all lines of tort liability suggests that changes unique to medical care alone may not account for the growth in claims. The increase in tort litigation has been attributed to a pervasive increase in litigiousness. But even if an attitudinal change has occurred, it is neither sufficient nor necessary to explain the rise in claims. If plaintiffs and attorneys respond to economic incentives, a greater willingness to sue is unlikely to be sustained unless it is validated by more frequent or larger payoffs. And in fact, the payoff to suit has increased as a result of pro-plaintiff trends in common law doctrine, which have raised compensable damages, eroded traditional defenses and extended the scope of liability, and reduced the plaintiff's costs of proving negligence.[1]

In response to the malpractice crisis, many states enacted changes in tort law applicable to medical practitioners. These reforms include measures to constrain the scope of liability, reduce the size of awards, limit the time allowed to file suit (the statute of limitations), limit contingent fees of plaintiff attorneys, and discourage "frivolous" suits by introducing pretrial screening panels, arbitration, or both. After 1976 the frequency of claims leveled off in general and even fell in some states, notably those with the highest frequency in 1975. Severity has continued to increase, but less rapidly for states with relatively high awards in 1975. But the deceleration of claim frequency was not confined to medical malpractice, and more recent evidence indicates that it was short-lived. Thus it remains an open question as to how far the tort reforms have brought the growth in claims under control.

This chapter provides empirical evidence on the contribution of various factors to the diversity in the frequency and severity of malpractice claims across states and over time. Specifically, I report estimates of the effects of medical, demographic, and legal characteristics, trends in litigation in general, and changes in common and statutory law, using data on claims closed in 1970 and 1975–78 (Westat, 1973; NAIC, 1980). A better understanding of the determinants of the number and size of claims is an essential precondition to evaluating proposed reforms and their likely effects. To the extent that variation in claims is caused by variation in the frequency and type of medical treatments, tort reform may be inappropriate or ineffective. But if variation in claims is caused primarily by variation in incentives created by the legal system, then tort reforms that affect these incentives will affect claim costs. The optimal design of such reforms is a crucial issue to be considered later in the book.

Although policy analysis is primarily concerned with the efficiency and efficacy of alternative policies, a related issue of growing interest is the way in which laws evolve. Thus, two secondary questions will be addressed briefly: what determined the extent of tort reform in different states, and what can we infer about the determinants of policy enacted through legislatures rather than the courts?

Trends in Malpractice Claims

Physicians have been liable for malpractice suits since the fourteenth century in England and the late eighteenth century in the United States. But until recently such suits were rare events. The earliest comprehensive data, derived from an American Medical Association (AMA) survey of physicians, showed that in 1956 roughly 19 percent of physicians in active private practice had had at least one claim during their lifetime. This implies a risk of one claim per 269,960 patient visits, or one claim per 65 physicians per year.[2] A second survey conducted in 1963 showed essentially no increase in claim frequency. This finding generated the optimistic conclusion that "apparently, the efforts . . . to develop claims prevention programs have been effective" (AMA, 1963, p. 980). No comprehensive data on the size of awards (severity) are reported in these surveys. Sandor (1957) reported that the largest sum awarded by a trial court was $230,000 in 1955, and that in California the average physician paid between $300 and $400 for his malpractice coverage. In 1983 dollars, this is equivalent to a maximum award of $867,790 and an average premium between $1,132 and $1,509 — far short of the actual average premium in 1983 of $7,100.

Claim frequency appears to have risen dramatically in the late 1960s. A survey of claims closed in 1970 indicates a frequency of one claim per 37 physicians by 1968, or an increase of 76 percent over the rate at the beginning of the decade.[3] Frequency continued to rise in the early 1970s. The leading writer of malpractice insurance, the St. Paul Fire and Marine Insurance Company, had one claim pending per 23 insured physicians in 1970; by 1975 this had increased to one claim per 8 physicians. These St. Paul data understate the national average because they exclude such relatively litigious states as California, Washington, D.C., Florida, Illinois, and New York. In California, where both frequency and severity increased at an average annual rate of almost 20 percent between 1969 and 1974, one in three physicians had a pending claim in 1975.[4] This surge in malpractice claim frequency in the late sixties and early seventies culminated in the insurance crisis of 1975. Thereafter frequency leveled off or actually fell in many states, but has now resumed its upward trend. The St. Paul Insurance Company reports that since 1977, claim frequency on a reported basis has increased at an average annual rate of 12 percent.

These patterns in malpractice litigation parallel to some extent trends in other areas, notably product liability and liability of owners, landlords, and tenants. The only countrywide data available for comparing trends in different lines of tort litigation are those on claims incurred, by policy year, reported by the Insurance Services Office (ISO).[5] The advantage of these incurred-claim data over the closed-claim data (which are used in the subsequent analysis in this chapter) is that incurred claims include claims closed, claims reported but still open, and the insurer's estimate of claims not yet filed ("incurred but not reported"). Incurred claims therefore present a more current picture of trends in claim filings and are not distorted by changes in the rate of disposition of claims. There is a disadvantage of incurred-claims data, however: because of the lags in filing and closing claims, the statistics on incurred frequency and severity incorporate a mixture of hard data and insurers' projections.[6] The element of projection is larger and the estimates consequently less reliable for lines of insurance with a long "tail" (lag in filing and disposition of claims), such as medical malpractice and product liability, and in more "immature" (recent) policy years. Projection is also relatively more important for severity than for frequency, because of the lag in closing claims. Since projections are based on past experience, they are accurate only as long as trends are stable over time.

Frequency.   Figures 4.1 and 4.2 show trends in frequency and severity for the lines and policy years for which data are available. There are two series of data on frequency of claims against physicians and surgeons. The first, which reflects the information available to the ISO as of April 1975, shows a mild increase in frequency from 1966 to 1970, followed by a rapid acceleration in the early 1970s. The average exponential growth rate over the entire period is 12 percent, but the average for 1971–1973 alone is 19 percent. The

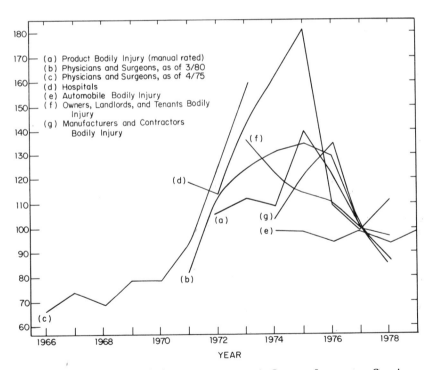

Figure 4.1 Frequency of claims (1977 = 100). Source: Insurance Services Office (unpublished data).

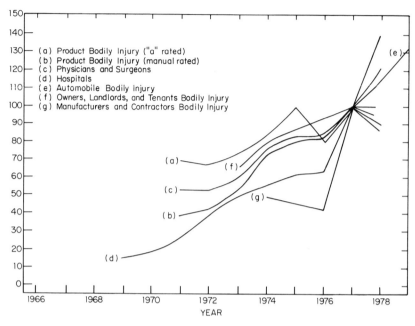

Figure 4.2 Severity of claims (total limits; 1977 = 100). *Source:* Insurance Services Office (unpublished data).

second series reflects information available as of March 1980. It shows an increase for policy years 1971 to 1975, followed by a decrease, such that the average exponential growth rate for the period 1971–1978 is −0.3 percent. Thus the earlier projections greatly overestimated claim frequency for the late 1970s. Claims against hospitals, for which only the 1980 estimates are available, show a similar but more extreme mid-decade peak than claims against physicians and surgeons.

Product liability bodily injury claims and manufacturers' and contractors' bodily injury claims show similar but less extreme mid-decade peaks. Automobile bodily injury and physical damage claims were essentially stable throughout the period, with average annual trends of −0.5 percent and −0.9 percent, respectively, for the period 1973–1980.[7] Thus, although trends in medical malpractice claim frequency appear to have been more extreme than in other lines, the experience was not unique. To some extent the appearance of greater volatility of medical malpractice claims may be an artifact of less reliable data, because of the long tail of this line.

Severity. For all lines, the steady upward trend in claim severity throughout the decade outpaced the general rate of inflation. From 1971 to 1978 the average incurred cost per claim against physicians and surgeons increased at 12.4 percent per annum, compared to 18.9 percent for claims against hospitals. Comparable trends for product liability bodily injury and physical damage are 19.4 percent and 12.1 percent, respectively, and 14.1 percent and 15.6 percent for automobile bodily injury and physical damage. This steady upward trend in severity after the mid-1970s may misrepresent the true trend in compensation for a given injury, for two reasons. First, an increase in compensation will tend to induce the filing of more small claims, which tends to pull down average severity. Second, if the frequency of filing is increasing (even with no change in mix), claims closed in each successive year include an increasing proportion of small claims, again pulling down average severity.[8] Severity per paid claim therefore understates the underlying trend in compensation when compensation or frequency is increasing and, conversely, overstates the true trend when compensation or frequency is decreasing. The evidence from jury verdicts in San Francisco and Cook County, Illinois, shows that, after adjusting for inflation, typical or median jury awards have been quite stable, but the few very large awards have risen dramatically, pulling up the average (Shanley and Peterson, 1983). This pattern applies to all lines of litigation and is not confined to malpractice.

Interstate variation. Perhaps as striking as the growth over time is the enormous variation across states in claim frequency and severity in any year. For example, in 1976 the frequency of claims closed per 100 physicians ranged from 0.47 in Maine to 8.81 in California — an eighteenfold range. In the same year, claims per 100,000 population ranged from 1.24 in Maine to 17.72 in California and 21.99 in Washington, D.C.; severity ranged from $4,243 in Maine to $89,147 in Nevada.

Table 4.1 summarizes trends in the frequency and severity of malpractice claims closed.[9] In these data the unit of observation is the state — claims per 100,000 population and average paid claim. The mean is that of the state means, with each state given equal weight. This may differ from the means from the ISO data reported earlier, which are based on countrywide totals and therefore effectively assign each state a weight proportional to the number of claims in that state; thus these means are dominated by the few most populous states.

Between 1970 and 1975 the typical state experienced a growth of claims closed per capita of 29 percent per annum. Frequency fell from

Table 4.1 Medical malpractice claim frequency and severity: state means, levels, and growth rates

	Mean	Median	25th percentile	75th percentile	Minimum	Maximum
Claims per 100,000 population						
1970[a]	2.76	2.56	1.99	3.27	0.35	8.86
1975	10.04	8.98	6.42	12.14	3.34	44.38
1976	7.14	6.47	4.78	8.39	1.24	21.99
1977	6.09	5.81	3.92	7.52	1.72	13.76
1978	6.23	5.81	3.96	7.89	1.40	17.44
Growth rate[b]						
75–70[c]	33.2	28.7	20.8	38.4	8.1	79.7
76–75	−26.3	−27.4	−42.6	−8.7	−70.8	31.1
77–76	−8.9	−9.3	−21.3	3.3	−57.6	121.0
78–77	7.8	2.0	−15.0	26.2	−59.5	124.4
Paid claims per 100,000 population						
1975	3.64	3.10	2.12	4.58	0.96	18.59
1976	2.81	2.67	1.73	3.62	0.37	8.16
1977	2.51	2.37	1.47	3.26	0.43	6.18
1978	2.68	2.37	1.51	3.44	0.52	6.57
Severity ($)						
1975	19,793	16,719	11,186	25,429	2,789	62,120
1976	24,505	21,612	14,640	29,643	4,243	89,147
1977	29,945	25,335	19,525	39,101	3,816	102,317
1978	36,766	32,550	16,961	49,096	5,267	160,161
Growth rate[b]						
76–75	67.4	33.8	−12.2	83.3	−92.6	575.0
77–76	60.8	33.6	−23.5	78.0	−75.0	1,053.0
78–77	67.9	25.0	−30.6	76.5	−80.0	1,534.0

a. 1970 sample incomplete.
b. Growth rate $= [(\text{Claims}_t / \text{Claim}_{t-1}) - 1] \times 100$.
c. $[(\text{Claims}_{75} / \text{Claims}_{70})^{1/5} - 1] \times 100$.

1975 to 1977 and then leveled off in 1978. Year-to-year changes were highly erratic across states, but in general the claim level in states starting at a relatively low level grew more rapidly, with the result that the range between the most and least litigious states narrowed (from 3.3 versus 44.4 claims per 100,000 population in 1975, to 1.4 versus 17.4 in 1978).[10]

Between 1975 and 1978 severity grew by 30 percent a year for the typical state. The mean exceeds 60 percent, reflecting extreme changes in a few states. However, year-to-year changes are even more volatile for severity than for frequency, ranging from −90 percent to +1,000 percent. This reflects the small number of claims in some states — in 1976, 35 states had under 100 paid claims — and the huge range of potential awards. As in the case of frequency, severity grew most rapidly in states where the initial level was low. The mean of the state means grew more rapidly than the countrywide mean, because the claim level in the majority of small states grew more rapidly than in the few states that account for most of the claims. These averages probably overstate somewhat the trend in compensation because with the decline in frequency of filings and lengthening of the lag in disposition, successive years would include relatively fewer small claims.

Theoretical Analysis of Claim Frequency and Severity

The relationships of primary interest from the perspective of economics and policy — the deterrent effect of tort sanctions on quality of care and the effect of laws on number of claims filed — cannot be estimated directly because there are no data on injuries and claims filed. But some information can be gleaned from the available data on claims closed, which provide an incomplete and lagged reflection of injuries and claims filed. Before turning to the results of the analysis, I outline in this section the theoretical model underlying the empirical estimates to show how feedbacks and lags complicate measurement of effects using closed-claim data.

Frequency of claims. To establish a claim for medical malpractice, a plaintiff must show that he sustained damages resulting from medical treatment that violated the "due" standard of care. The frequency of claims filed thus depends on the rate of iatrogenic injury, the standard of due care, and other factors affecting the payoff to suit. Since the mid-1960s, the unprecedented increase in the quantity and complexity of medical care delivered has certainly increased the potential for iatrogenic injury overall, but considerable disparity among states remains. As a consequence of advances in medical technology, physicians have a vastly increased capacity to do good — and to do harm. The actual frequency of injuries depends on the normal risk of the procedures performed and on the incentives of medical providers to practice with care. A physician's expectation of being sued for malpractice if he is negligent is one factor affecting these incentives.

Only a fraction of the total number of iatrogenic injuries are potentially actionable under the negligence system, and in general the courts defer to the customary practice of the profession in defining the standard of care in medical and other professional liability cases. In recent years, however, the courts have expanded the liability of medical providers by rejecting traditional defenses and recognizing new grounds for action. For example, the abolition of the locality rule substituted a statewide or national standard for a local standard as the norm of acceptable practice; the abolition of immunity for charitable and government institutions has exposed voluntary and government hospitals to suit; the doctrine of *respondeat superior* has been used to extend the liability of hospitals for the actions of their employees; the doctrine of informed consent has set new standards for the responsibility of physicians to inform patients of potential risks of treatment; and finally, the courts have occasionally asserted the right to override medical custom and apply a cost-benefit calculation to individual cases.[11] If the standards applied by the courts are continually changing, the frequency of claims will be higher, the more frequent the upgrading of standards; the longer the delay in adapting medical practice to new standards (which in turn depends on the incentives for physicians to adapt); and the longer the statute of limitations.

As we have seen, only a fraction of the stock of *potential* claims are actually filed. The propensity to file depends, among other things, on the expected payoff to filing, net of costs. The expected payoff in turn depends on the standard of care and of compensable damages applied by the courts, and the costs of filing depend on the availability and price of legal services and on the rules of procedure and evidence. Between 1950 and 1980 the number of lawyers per capita in the United States increased 70 percent, which some have alleged has contributed to the surge in all lines of litigation, including malpractice. At the same time, changes in common law have eroded traditional defenses against malpractice claims and effectively reduced plaintiffs' litigation costs. These changes include abolition or modification of the locality rule;[12] allowing medical texts as evidence of customary practice; and expansion of the doctrine of res *ipsa loquitur*, which shifts the burden of proof to the defendant. In an attempt to contain these trends, many states since 1975 have shortened statutes of limitations, reinstated some form of locality rule, and limited the application of *res ipsa*. Other states have introduced arbitration or pretrial screening panels, which may lower costs and hence raise the net payoff to filing.[13] Given these factors affecting claims *filed*, the frequency of claims *closed* in any year depends on the rate of filings in several prior years and on lags in disposition, which may exceed ten years but average around two years.

It is important to note that the short- and long-run effects of a change in law on claim frequency may differ. If the law has been stable for a long period, physicians will have adjusted their mode of practice, taking into account the expected costs of malpractice suits if they violate prevailing standards of due care. Imagine now that this equilibrium is disturbed by pro-plaintiff legal developments, such as those of the 1960s, which reduce plaintiffs' costs and expand liability and compensable damages. Incidents that were previously not actionable or financially not worth filing become worth filing under the new standards. The increase in claims is greater, the longer the statute of limitations, which determines how many years of prior practice may be affected by current changes.[14] Over time medical practice adjusts to the higher risk of suit. The new equilibrium of claim frequency may be higher or lower than the old equilibrium, but it could be higher even if the frequency of *injuries* has fallen simply because a larger fraction of the potential claims are filed. But claim frequency will certainly be lower in the long run than during the transition phase, after the backlog of claims that became worth filing in response to the change has worked its way through the system and after physicians have adjusted to the new standards.

Average severity.   The potential severity per paid claim (including awards and out-of-court settlements) depends on the economic loss incurred by plaintiffs and on the standards of compensable damages applied by the courts. The trend over time in common law has been to extend the categories of compensable damages to include more intangible (general) damages, such as loss of consortium. To reverse this trend, many states since 1975 have modified basic tort damage rules for cases of medical malpractice by measures such as the following: dollar ceilings, either on the total award or on general damages; modification of the collateral source rule, to admit evidence and, in some states, mandate offset of compensation from other sources against the tort recovery; elimination of the plaintiff's *ad damnum*; and periodic payment of future damages.

The predicted effects of these factors on potential verdicts does not carry over immediately to observed severity per paid claim, because changes in these factors may induce changes in the mix of claims actually filed. For example, consider the effect of an increase in norms of compensation. The observed average severity could rise or fall in response to an increase in compensation, because such an increase raises the expected net payoff on all potential claims. This induces the filing of claims with true damages or probability of winning too low to have been worth filing prior to the increase. Thus differences in average severity across states understate differences in standards of compensation since the mix of claims will differ, with fewer minor claims in states with conservative standards of compensation.

Similarly, the effects of pro-plaintiff changes in standards of compensation or burden of proof are hard to tease out from observed data. Observed severity of claims may increase or decrease, depending on the number and characteristics of marginal relative to inframarginal claims. The long-run increase in claim frequency will be less than the short-run increase, with relative magnitudes depending on the statute of limitations and how physicians adjust. This has the important implication that even if one could accurately measure the effect of past changes in law on claim costs, one might not be able to generalize the conclusions to other states or time periods.

In summary, one can expect medical, demographic, and legal factors to affect the frequency and severity of claims closed. But several of these variables may have both direct and indirect channels of influence, and may affect both the frequency of injury and the propensity to file. Distinguishing these separate effects is not possible with the data available, but we can measure overall effects. With this caveat, let us turn to the evidence.

Empirical Evidence

Data. The data on claims are drawn from two surveys of claims closed by insurance companies in 1970 and 1975–78. The 1970 survey is a weighted random sample of claims closed by 26 insurers that accounted for 90 percent of the market. Because the number of paid claims is very small in some states, severity is not calculated for 1970. The 1975–78 survey covered all insurers writing malpractice premiums of one million dollars or more in any year since 1970.[15] These data on claims closed reflect claims filed on average two years earlier.

Several variables were constructed to measure the effects of common law doctrines and statutory reforms. An index variable (1970

LAWS) which takes values 0 through 4 measures the number of the following common law doctrines recognized prior to 1970 (Dietz, Baird, and Berul, 1973): abolition or expansion of the locality rule, informed consent, abolition of charitable immunity, and *respondeat superior*. Data on the statute of limitations, before and after any changes, and on other post-1975 tort reforms were compiled by a survey of the relevant statutes. To test for the deterrent effects of high malpractice insurance costs, I used two variables: the rate filed by the ISO for general practitioners, for basic limits of coverage, effective March 1975; and the percentage increase recommended by the ISO in April 1975. Data on demographic, medical, and other legal character-istics were obtained from several sources.[16] All variables are defined in Table 4.2.

Ideally, we would like to measure the net effects of medical, demo-

Table 4.2 Mean, standard deviation, and definition of all variables

Variable	Mean	Standard deviation	Definition
% Urban	66.80	15.10	% population in places ≥ 25,000 population in 1970
% Old	.10	0.02	% population over 65
Physicians per capita	1.21	0.41	Nonfederal physicians in patient care, per 100,000 population
1970 Laws	2.48	0.79	Number of doctrines applied by 1970: locality rule expanded or rejected; charitable immunity rejected; res ipsa applied; informed consent applied
1970 Stat. lim.	7.76	3.55	Statute of limitations for adults, pre-1975; = 10 if unlimited dis-covery period
OLT severity	7.80	.28	Severity per paid claim, liability of owners, landlords, and ten-ants ($ logarithm)
No-fault	0.32	.47	= 1 if state adopted no-fault auto-mobile law; = 0 otherwise
1975 Stat. lim.	3.52	3.54	Statute of limitations for adults, post-1975; = 10 if unlimited dis-covery period
Lawyers per capita	1.83	1.62	Lawyers per 100,000 population
% ABA	58.67	10.36	% of lawyers belonging to Ameri-can Bar Association, 1975

Table 4.2 (continued)

Variable	Mean	Standard deviation	Definition
Ad damnum	18.14	17.22	Ad damnum eliminated (months pre–Dec. 1978)
Cap	10.22	16.00	Cap on awards (months pre–Dec. 1978)
Collateral source	5.36	13.52	Mandatory offset of collateral compensation (months pre–Dec. 1978)
Fee limit	12.22	17.11	Limit on contingent fees (months pre–Dec. 1978)
Share	64.60	13.21	Market share of leading insurer, 1974
% Medical society	.60	.13	% of physicians belonging to state or local medical society, 1975
1975 Premium	5.73	1.79	ISO rate for general practitioners, as of March 1975 ($ logarithm)
ISO increase	1.45	1.15	% rate increase recommended by ISO, April 1975
Informed consent	.48	.50	= 1 if informed consent applied by 1970, = 0 otherwise
Respondeat superior	.66	.49	= 1 if respondeat superior applied by 1970, = 0 otherwise

graphic, and legal characteristics on malpractice litigation. This is not an easy task, however, because these characteristics are themselves highly correlated. To help identify net contributions, the estimates are performed stepwise, including first only medical and demographic factors (physicians per capita, population over age 65, and degree of urbanization), then adding characteristics intended to measure the cost and availability of legal services (lawyers per capita and membership in the American Bar Association), and finally adding specific laws see Table 4.3). Table 4.4 converts the coefficient estimates from the final equation in Table 4.3 to elasticities, which measure the percentage change in an outcome variable — frequency, severity, or total claim cost — in response to a percentage change in an explanatory variable. In Table 4.3 the data from all years are pooled and the coefficients are estimated under the assumption that the effects of each variable are the same in all years. Since the effects of the laws are in fact likely to vary over time, Table 4.5 reports these coefficients for each year separately.[17]

Table 4.3 Malpractice claim frequency and severity: medical, demographic, and pre-1975 legal variables

Explanatory variable	Claim frequency per 100,000 pop. ($\log(F/1-F)$)			Severity per claim (log.)			Total claim cost per 100,000 (log.)		
	Eq. (1)	Eq. (2)	Eq. (3)	Eq. (1)	Eq. (2)	Eq. (3)	Eq. (1)	Eq. (2)	Eq. (3)
% Urban	0.012	0.012	0.014	0.015	0.013	0.012	0.034	0.030	0.032
	(3.31)	(3.18)	(3.85)	(3.94)	(3.41)	(3.11)	(5.66)	(5.02)	(5.50)
Physicians per capita	0.516	0.610	0.543	0.356	0.170	0.026	0.327	0.156	0.087
	(4.23)	(3.66)	(3.33)	(3.15)	(1.03)	(0.16)	(1.45)	(0.51)	(0.29)
% Old	2.99	3.32	0.774	1.81	1.25	0.391	6.62	5.65	2.59
	(1.32)	(1.42)	(0.34)	(0.99)	(0.70)	(0.21)	(1.98)	(1.65)	(0.75)
1970 Laws	—	—	0.143	—	—	0.069	—	—	0.215
	—	—	(2.81)	—	—	(1.38)	—	—	(2.80)
1970 Stat. lim.	—	—	0.011	—	—	0.016	—	—	0.025
	—	—	(0.98)	—	—	(1.59)	—	—	(1.44)
OLT severity	—	—	−0.089	—	—	0.163	—	—	0.072
	—	—	(1.31)	—	—	(1.35)	—	—	(0.58)
No-fault	—	—	−0.143	—	—	0.102	—	—	0.104
	—	—	(1.56)	—	—	(1.57)	—	—	(0.85)
Lawyers per capita	—	−0.030	−0.024	—	0.051	0.065	—	0.043	0.048
	—	(0.80)	(0.62)	—	(1.20)	(1.59)	—	(0.42)	(0.50)
% ABA	—	0.003	0.005	—	−0.008	−0.005	—	−0.008	−0.003
	—	(0.84)	(1.25)	—	(2.53)	(1.85)	—	(1.47)	(0.65)
R^2	0.239	0.246	0.333	0.314	0.347	0.410	0.308	0.292	0.371

Note: t-statistics are in parentheses. Coefficients constrained across years 1970 and 1975–78 for frequency, 1975–78 otherwise. Weighted generalized least squares estimates.

Table 4.4 Partial derivatives and elasticities derived from Tables 4.3 and 4.5

Explanatory variable	Claim frequency per 100,000 pop.		Severity per claim		Total claim cost per 100,000 pop.	
	Partial derivative $\left(\dfrac{\partial F}{\partial X}\right)$	Elasticity $\left(\dfrac{\partial F}{\partial X}\dfrac{X}{F}\right)$	Partial derivative $\left(\dfrac{\partial LnA}{\partial X}\right)$	Elasticity $\left(\dfrac{\partial A}{\partial X}\dfrac{X}{A}\right)$	Partial derivative $\left(\dfrac{\partial LnT}{\partial X}\right)$	Elasticity $\left(\dfrac{\partial T}{\partial X}\dfrac{X}{T}\right)$
% Urban	.0009[a]	.86[a]	.012[a]	.80[a]	.032[a]	2.16[a]
Physicians per capita	.036[a]	.61[a]	—	—	—	—
1970 Laws	.330[a]	.33[a]	.069	.17	.215[a]	.53[a]
1970 Stat. lim.	—	—	.016	.12	.025	.19
No-fault	−.0096	−.043	.102	.03	—	—
Informed consent	.018[a]	.121[a]	.102	.05	.210[b]	.10[b]
Lawyers per capita	—	—	.065	.12	—	—
Respondeat superior	—	—	—	—	.243[b]	.16[b]

a. Significant at $p = .05$.
b. Significant at $p = .10$.

Medical and demographic factors. The number of physicians per capita, which is a measure of exposure to iatrogenic injury, is a significant determinant of claim frequency. For a state with the mean density of physicians per capita, an increase of 100 physicians adds an additional 3.6 claims. In percentage terms, the 40 percent increase in physicians per capita between 1960 and 1978 could account for a 24 percent increase in claims over this period—a small fraction of the total increase.

It is of some policy interest to try to identify whether particular types of medical care have higher risk of suit. In aggregate country-wide data, surgeons appear to have a much higher claim frequency than nonsurgical specialists. If it is implausible that surgeons are negligent much more often than nonsurgeons, this suggests that surgeons are at a higher risk of being sued, perhaps because surgical injuries are more severe or more obvious. Unequal risk of suit for a given quality of care would distort the expected cost of different procedures to physicians and hence could distort medical choices and the quality of care. But in these data the proportion of physicians in surgical specialties does not appear to contribute to variation in the frequency of claims per capita. However, the high correlation (0.85)

Table 4.5 Year-specific effects of laws on frequency (F), severity (A), and total claim cost (T)

Explanatory variable	Dependent variable	1970	1975	1976	1977	1978	All years constrained[a]
1970 Laws	F	0.116	0.168	0.239	0.159	0.123	0.143
		(1.35)	(2.51)	(3.14)	(2.14)	(1.41)	(2.81)
	A	—	0.167	0.031	0.048	0.066	0.069
		—	(1.72)	(0.35)	(0.60)	(0.92)	(1.38)
	T	—	0.077	0.391	0.340	0.229	0.215
		—	(0.72)	(3.38)	(3.41)	(2.16)	(2.80)
1970 Stat. lim.	A	—	0.028	−0.025	0.013	0.035	0.016
		—	(1.43)	(1.38)	(0.79)	(2.47)	(1.59)
	T	—	0.009	0.054	0.020	0.068	0.025
		(0.35)	(2.00)	(0.89)	(2.77)	(1.44)
No-fault	F	—	−0.201	−0.06	−0.07	0.003	−0.143
		—	(1.81)	(0.50)	(0.58)	(0.02)	(1.56)
	A	—	0.205	0.180	−0.005	0.103	0.102
		—	(1.74)	(1.66)	(0.05)	(1.15)	(1.57)
	T	—	0.114	0.128	0.036	0.130	0.104
		—	(0.68)	(0.71)	(0.23)	(0.77)	(0.85)
Informed consent	F	0.202	0.265	0.404	0.314	0.338	0.272
		(1.54)	(2.51)	(3.38)	(2.83)	(2.57)	(3.51)
	T	—	0.132	0.560	0.340	0.246	0.210
		—	(0.80)	(3.11)	(2.07)	(1.48)	(1.75)
Respondeat superior	T	—	0.225	0.378	0.278	0.305	0.243
		—	(1.24)	(1.77)	(1.49)	(1.67)	(1.85)
Cap	A	—	−0.008	−0.014	−0.009	−0.001	−0.008
		—	(1.26)	(2.28)	(1.54)	(0.23)	(2.03)
Collateral source	A	—	−0.011	−0.035	−0.027	−0.009	−0.021
		—	(0.84)	(2.96)	(2.66)	(0.87)	(2.61)
Ad damnum	T	—	−0.088	−0.035	−0.050	−0.048	−0.073
		—	(3.38)	(1.27)	(1.98)	(1.76)	(3.17)
Fee limit	A	—	0.006	−0.020	−0.013	0.002	−0.007
		—	(0.52)	(1.85)	(1.46)	(0.16)	(1.03)
	T	—	−0.013	−0.011	−0.012	0.011	−0.016
		—	(0.77)	(0.61)	(0.76)	(0.60)	(1.21)

Note: Numbers are coefficients from adding law variables to Eq. (3) in Table 4.3. t-statistics are in parentheses.
a. Coefficients are constrained to be equal in all years.

between surgical and nonsurgical specialists per capita hampers the measurement of separate effects.[18]

Similarly, there were no discernible effects of different types of treatment or quality of care, although it is widely believed that one reason for the increase in malpractice claims is developments in medical technology, which permit increasingly complex and invasive procedures. I used two measures of the complexity of medical treatments: hospital staff (average full-time equivalent) per patient day, which could also indicate quality of care; and the ratio of hospital cost per day to the average manufacturing wage, which is a proxy for the capital intensity of hospital facilities. Neither of these variables adds overall explanatory power, after controlling for number of physicians.[19] It appears that the high correlation between physician density and these indicators of complexity precludes measuring separate effects. The measured effect of physician density reported here is therefore a gross effect, which compounds the effects of increased number and different mix of medical treatments associated with higher physician density.

Claim frequency and severity are unrelated to the percentage of the population over age 65. Since hospital admission rates for the elderly are roughly twice as high as for persons under 65, and the rate of negligent injury per admission is roughly twice as high for the elderly, the absence of any significant difference in claim frequency implies that the probability of an elderly person's filing a claim, given a potentially actionable injury, is roughly one-fourth that of persons under 65. This lower propensity to sue on the part of the elderly is presumably in part a response to lower compensable damages. The finding of no overall difference in claim costs for the elderly implies that on average the higher rate of injury offsets the lower rate of suits and awards. Thus a pro rata contribution by Medicare to the costs of malpractice insurance is appropriate, at least from an actuarial standpoint.

Although the concentration of medical services in urban areas contributes to the higher claim frequency in these areas, it is far from the sole cause. After controlling for physician density, urbanization is the most significant and the most powerful predictor of frequency. A 10 percent increase in the measure of urbanization of a state is associated with an 8.6 percent increase in claims per capita and an 8.0 percent increase in severity. The higher frequency in urban areas is in part a response to the inducement of higher verdicts awarded by urban courts. As discussed earlier, the higher observed severity in urban areas understates the true difference in compensation, to the extent that higher potential verdicts induce the filing of more minor claims which pull down observed average severity.

Attempts to identify more precisely the characteristics of urban environments that influence claim frequency and severity were unsuccessful. In particular, the fact that the measured effect of urbanization is essentially unaffected by including number of lawyers and specific laws implies that the relatively high density of lawyers and the existence of pro-plaintiff laws do not account for the litigiousness of urban areas. Other variables that proved insignificant were the percentage of the population on welfare, the unemployment rate, and court delay.[20] Per capita income also had no significant effect on claim frequency or severity, after controlling for the number of physicians and lawyers. Thus the high simple correlation between income and both frequency and severity of claims is apparently a byproduct of the medical and legal environment found in high-income states rather than a direct effect of income on awards and on the propensity to sue.

In an attempt to measure the deterrent effect of tort sanctions on physician behavior, I tried including the 1975 level and the percentage increase in malpractice insurance premiums. No significant effect was found, but this may well be because any negative deterrent effect is swamped by the reverse, positive effect of claims on premiums. Measurement of the deterrent effect requires better data on patterns of practice and injury rates.

Cost of legal services. There is a strong correlation between number of lawyers per capita and claim frequency and severity.[21] This has led some to blame the rise in tort litigation, including malpractice claims, on the increasingly abundant supply of lawyers. The argument might be persuasive on theoretical grounds if an increase in the number of lawyers tended to be associated with a lower price of legal services. If so, an increase in the number of lawyers would be expected to raise claim frequency but would not necessarily affect severity. More claims would be filed, but both the plaintiff and defense would respond to the lower price by buying more legal effort per case, with offsetting effects on the outcome.

The evidence here tends to refute the hypothesis that the density of lawyers contributes directly to higher malpractice claim costs. Once we control for medical and demographic characteristics of areas in which lawyers are relatively numerous, lawyer density has no net effect on claim frequency. Severity is weakly positively related to lawyer density. Taken at face value, the estimates imply that a 10 percent increase in lawyers per capita is associated with a 1.2 percent increase in average severity. However, even this low elasticity is almost certainly an overestimate because of the effect running in the opposite direction: lawyers tend to locate in areas where claim frequency and severity are high and hence the demand for their services is high. The observed correlation between claim severity and lawyer density is therefore an upward-biased measure of the net contribution of lawyers to severity.[22]

At the time of the malpractice crisis, the surge of malpractice litigation was widely blamed on lawyers displaced from automobile litigation by the passage of no-fault laws.[23] This argument is unpersuasive a priori because most of the automobile tort thresholds were set so low as to constitute little bar to litigation, and thus it is unlikely that there would have been any significant spillover effects on malpractice litigation. But to provide empirical evidence, an indicator variable was included to identify states that enacted some form of automobile no-fault law prior to 1975. The evidence is inconsistent with what would have been expected if no-fault had indeed increased the supply of lawyers to malpractice litigation—that is, an increase in frequency but minimal effect, if any, on severity. Even if the coefficients are taken at face value, the size of the effect is minimal: they imply that states that adopted no-fault had 11 percent higher claim severity and 13 percent lower claim frequency, with no significant net effect on total claim cost per capita.

If, as is commonly alleged, professional associations can raise wage rates by restricting competition, then attorney wage rates would be higher in states where a high percentage of attorneys are members of the American Bar Association (ABA), and claim frequency should be lower. Contrary to this hypothesis, frequency is unrelated to ABA membership. Claim severity is lower in states where membership in the ABA is relatively high, but the magnitude of the effect is trivial. In light of this evidence, it seems more likely that ABA membership itself has little influence on litigation but rather reflects unobserved factors, such as a relatively conservative legal environment, that tend to be associated with low awards.

Pre-1975 laws. Specific laws do indeed appear to make a difference and do not merely reflect demographic factors. States that adopted the four pro-plaintiff common law doctrines considered here (abolition of the locality rule and of charitable immunity, expansion of informed consent and of *respondeat superior*) prior to 1970 had significantly higher frequency and severity of claims through the mid-1970s than states that had not adopted these doctrines at that time. On average over the period 1975–1978, states that recognized all four doctrines by 1970 had 53 percent higher claim frequency per capita, 28 percent higher severity, and 86 percent higher total claim cost per capita than states that recognized none of the doctrines.[24] Of the four doctrines, informed consent had the greatest impact.

These estimates probably overstate the net causal effect on claims of these specific laws because of correlation with other unmeasured differences in legal doctrine and of reverse causation; that is, these doctrines may have been adopted in states which, for other reasons, had a relatively high claim frequency. Nevertheless, the hypothesis that the laws had a net positive effect is supported by the pattern of the coefficients over time (see Table 4.5). The effects peaked in 1976 and declined thereafter. Claims closed in later years would include an increasing fraction filed after 1970, for which the indicator of doctrines recognized by 1970 is an increasingly inaccurate measure of applicable law since the doctrines became more widespread over time.

To test whether trends in malpractice litigation merely reflect trends in litigation in general, measures of the frequency and severity of claims for two other lines — liability of owners, landlords, and tenants (OLT) and of manufacturers and contractors — were included. The correlations were surprisingly low; only the most significant, OLT severity, is included here. States with relatively high awards for OLT tend to have high malpractice severity but relatively low malpractice claim frequency. The negative relation between malpractice claim frequency and *observed* OLT severity may reflect the filing of more low-valued claims in response to an increase in standards of compensation.

Effects of the post-1975 tort reforms. These data on claims closed during the period 1975–1978 cannot show the full, long-run effects of reforms enacted in that same period because many of the claims would have been filed before the effective dates of the reforms and hence would be unaffected. Nevertheless, if the reforms significantly reduced the expected payoff to filing, then the number of claims filed, especially claims with low potential recoveries, might be expected to fall immediately. Since minor claims account for a large fraction of the total and are settled more quickly, a reduction in claims filed could reduce claims closed within a year. Thus whether the post-crisis tort reforms contributed to the observed reduction in frequency between 1975 and 1977 is an important empirical question.

Some error in measuring those reforms and their effects is inevitable, because statistical analysis requires reducing the diverse and complex statutes to a few, quantifiable dimensions. The laws are measured here in terms of number of months in effect prior to December 1978 (the latest date in the claims files). For example, if a state enacted a cap on awards in January 1975, this variable would be assigned a value of 48. Because of the lag in realizing the full impact of a change, one would expect the coefficients to increase in magnitude and significance over time as the fraction of claims closed subject to the new laws increased. Table 4.5 reports individual-year coefficients where these approach conventional statistical significance in any year.

Several of the measures designed to reduce awards appear to have had their intended effect. States enacting a cap had 19 percent lower awards two years later $(0.008 \times 24 = 0.192)$. States mandating the offset of compensation from collateral sources had 50 percent lower awards within two years, whereas laws that admit evidence of collateral compensation without mandating offset had no discernible effect. Elimination of the plaintiff's *ad damnum* appears to have reduced total claim cost, although for frequency and severity individually the effect is not statistically significant. Limits on contingent fees show some sign of reducing severity and total claim costs, but the significance level is low.

States with long statutes of limitations were expected to experience higher claim frequency in times of changing legal standards.[25] The measured effect is indeed positive, but the statistical significance is low. Severity is significantly higher, however, in states that had long statutes of limitations. A plausible explanation for this finding is that claims filed long after the incident involve above average stakes, because delay increases the costs of filing and thus eliminates proportionately more minor claims. Because the sample of paid claims is under 100 in many states, one or two very large claims can dominate average severity. The effect of the pre-1975 statute on claims closed is greatest in 1978, reflecting claims filed in the peak filing years of 1973–75.

There is no evidence in these data that the post-1975 reductions in statutes of limitations had any effect. However, since these changes will operate with an even longer lag than other tort reforms, less impact is expected to be evident in 1975–78 closures. In fact, there may be an initial perverse effect if filings are accelerated in response to a shortening of the statute.

Regressions not reported here failed to show any significant effect on claim frequency or severity of any of the following post-1975 laws: voluntary or mandatory pretrial screening panels; arbitration; restrictions on informed consent; restrictions on the use of *res ipsa*; periodic payment of future damages.

There is no evidence that the tort reforms contributed to the post-1975 reduction in frequency. Contrary to the expectation that the impact of the reforms would increase over time, the coefficients tend to be largest in 1976. This finding casts doubt on how much of the observed effect is attributable to the laws per se, rather than to changes in attitude or other unmeasured factors that accompanied (and contributed to) changes in the law. If so, the observed effects could be short-lived.

It must be emphasized that these findings are rough estimates of short-run effects. The intrinsically small sample size, combined with interstate variation in the details of each law, creates severe measurement problems. Further, these data are too early to detect full long-run effects, especially of changes in the statute of limitations. Nevertheless, it is reasonably safe to conclude that although the laws limiting awards had an immediate effect on severity, neither these nor the other tort reforms can explain the dramatic drop in frequency between 1975 and 1977. Many commentators have inferred from the upturn in frequency since 1978 that the tort reforms did not have any longer-run effect. But this inference is too hasty; it may well be that frequency is lower than it would have been if no changes had been enacted. Measuring the long-run effects of the changes must thus await more recent, comprehensive data, which would permit testing whether the reforms have slowed, if not halted, claim growth in states that adopted them.

Determinants of the Post-1975 Tort Reforms

Legislatures in every state adopted some program of tort reform in response to the 1975 crisis. To provide some evidence on how public policy is formed and why different states reacted in different ways, this section analyzes the determinants of this legislation. Again, there is no simple, accurate solution to the problem of reducing the great variation in number, stringency, and timing of laws to a few measurable dimensions. Here I consider four measures: an aggregate of the total number of laws passed out of a possible twelve, each weighted by the number of months in effect;[26] limits on contingent fees; the reduction in the statute of limitations; and the number of years of the new statute of limitations.

The growing body of theoretical and empirical literature on the evolution of the law assigns a primary role to the size of interest groups most affected and their costs of organizing to exert political influence. In the case of malpractice tort reforms, the groups with most at stake are the medical and legal professions and the insurance industry. Standard public choice theory would predict that tort reforms would be more comprehensive or would be passed earlier, or both, in states in which the medical profession and insurance industry were relatively strong and the legal profession relatively weak. The incentives of physicians to lobby for legislation would be higher, the higher the absolute level of insurance premiums and the higher the percentage increase in 1975, because sudden large increases cannot readily be passed on through higher fees. My expectation was that public support of tort reform would be stronger, the more severe the crisis, as measured by the frequency and severity of claims in 1975. I also included the number of pro-plaintiff common law doctrines recognized by 1970, to test whether common law and statutory law tend to reflect similar or opposing forces.

Table 4.6 reports the results. For two of the dependent variables (number of laws and limits on contingent fees) three equations are given, each including a different measure of the severity of the crisis: the 1975 level and proposed increase in insurance premiums, the actual frequency of claims closed in 1975, and the predicted frequency.

Contrary to expectations, the number of physicians per capita and their cohesiveness, as measured by membership in state or local medical societies, apparently had little impact on the total number or the timing of tort reforms, although these variables did increase slightly the likelihood of a limit on contingent fees. By contrast, a high density of lawyers per capita did significantly reduce the number of reforms enacted and, in particular, reduced the likelihood of a limit on contingent fees.

Fewer laws were passed in states in which a single carrier dominated the insurance market, which suggests that the presence of multiple insurers with a stake in the market contributed to the extent and promptness of tort reform. But if this interpretation is correct, it is surprising that the number of insurers had no significant effect on the statute of limitations. A long statute of limitations is a major source of insurance risk, which is of more concern to insurers than the overall level of claim costs because higher claim costs may raise the demand for insurance.

States with a high degree of urbanization tended to adopt more numerous and early reforms. Urbanized states also reduced their statutes of limitations by a greater amount, and the revised statutes were absolutely shorter. States with relatively pro-plaintiff common law made more numerous and early changes in statutory law, including limits on contingent fees. Since these tort reforms tend to

Table 4.6 Determinants of post-1975 tort reforms

Explanatory variable	Number of laws (post-1975 laws)			Limit on contingent fees			Post-1975 stat. lim. Eq. (1)	Change in stat. lim. Eq. (1)
	Eq. (1)	Eq. (2)	Eq. (3)	Eq. (1)	Eq. (2)	Eq. (3)		
Physicians per capita	−0.310	−1.348	4.559	18.290	14.236	27.003	4.177	−4.111
	(0.04)	(0.18)	(0.51)	(1.29)	(0.94)	(1.51)	(1.34)	(0.09)
1970 Laws	3.151	2.763	3.541	9.549	8.522	10.208	0.337	−0.930
	(2.21)	(1.84)	(2.14)	(3.34)	(2.87)	(3.09)	(0.53)	(1.05)
% Urban	0.217	0.159	0.174	0.110	0.001	0.033	−0.174	0.176
	(2.23)	(1.64)	(1.70)	(0.566)	(0.001)	(0.16)	(4.04)	(2.92)
% Medical society	0.085	−1.399	5.367	23.529	19.151	33.778	−5.061	9.916
	(0.01)	(0.12)	(0.41)	(1.05)	(0.82)	(1.29)	(1.02)	(1.44)
1975 Premium	0.469	—	—	1.184	—	—	0.465	−0.699
	(0.78)			(0.98)			(1.74)	(1.87)
ISO increase	1.714	—	—	2.852	—	—	−0.442	0.022
	(1.78)			(1.47)			(1.04)	(0.04)
Share	−0.236	−0.206	−0.223	−0.199	−0.139	−0.174	−0.002	0.006
	(2.88)	(2.46)	(2.51)	(1.21)	(0.84)	(0.99)	(0.06)	(0.12)
Lawyers per capita	−1.502	−2.358	−1.35	−4.869	−6.725	−4.544	−1.07	−0.277
	(1.07)	(1.56)	(0.80)	(1.73)	(2.25)	(1.34)	(0.17)	(0.32)
1975 Acutal claims per capita	—	38.755	—	—	94.593	—	—	—
		(1.14)			(1.40)			
1975 Predicted claims per capita	—	—	−33.046	—	—	−60.940	—	—
			(0.57)			(0.53)		
C	3.254	11.141	3.245	−44.963	−26.488	−43.557	13.769	−9.867
	(0.28)	(0.92)	(0.24)	(1.91)	(1.10)	(1.58)	(2.65)	(1.36)
R^2	0.395	0.350	0.318	0.389	0.362	0.319	0.365	0.310

Note: t-statistics are in parentheses.

restrict plaintiff rights, this suggests significant differences in the relative power of the various interest groups in affecting law made through the courts and the legislature, with defense interests having more impact on the legislature and plaintiff interests having more impact on the courts.

None of the measures of the extent of crisis — the level and proposed increase in insurance premiums, frequency or severity of claims — appear to have had a significant effect on the extent of tort reform. Of these measures, the proposed premium increase in 1975 apparently had the greatest impact. This is not surprising: in the long run high premiums can be passed through in higher fees for medical services, but in the short run fees are constrained by fee ceilings, especially for Medicare and Medicaid. A large, sudden premium increase, like the one that occurred in 1974–75, is therefore much more onerous to physicians than the same increase spread over several years.

Conclusions

Although trends in malpractice litigation have paralleled trends in other lines, this analysis of the contribution of medical, demographic, and legal factors to malpractice litigation indicates that factors specific to medical care and malpractice law have played a significant role. The growth in medical services since the mid-1960s has certainly contributed to, but does not fully account for, the increase in claims and persistent diversity among states. Factors affecting the expected net payoff to suit play an important role. In particular, the pro-plaintiff trend in common law doctrines in the sixties had a major effect on malpractice claims through the mid-seventies. By contrast, the increased number of lawyers and no-fault automobile laws do not appear to have had a significant independent effect. Of the post-1975 tort reforms, dollar caps and mandatory offset of compensation from collateral sources significantly reduced claim severity, but none of the others had a discernible impact. However, these estimates of the effect of the post-1975 tort reforms based on claims closed in the period 1975–1978 must be viewed as rough measures of their short-run impact.

Two important questions remain unanswered. The first is to identify the characteristics of urban environments that generate higher claim frequency and severity. Urbanization is the single most powerful predictor of both frequency and severity of claims. Higher awards by urban courts are probably one factor inducing the higher claim frequency. Other factors that were examined but do not account for urban litigiousness include complexity of medical facilities, per capita income, welfare, and unemployment rates. It may be that more impersonal physician-patient relationships in urban areas make patients more willing to sue. But this remains unquantified — and perhaps unquantifiable — speculation.

The second unexplained puzzle is the post-1975 decline in claim frequency. It apparently cannot be attributed to the tort reforms — which does not mean that these reforms will not reduce or at least slow the growth of frequency in the longer run. It is possible that the post-1975 decline in frequency was a temporary lull resulting from a transitory change in attitude associated with the 1975 crisis. It is also possible that the preceding peak as the aberration, reflecting the backlog of potential claims that became worth filing as a result of the pro-plaintiff shift in common law in the 1960s combined with long statutes of limitations. By the late 1970s this backlog had worked its way through the system, and things may have returned to a more normal trend.

It is also possible that more potential claims are forestalled because hospitals are increasingly willing to initiate compensatory action before a claim is filed, giving payment refunds to patients whose complaints about poor hospital service are found to be justified.

Finally, it is also plausible that the increased exposure to suit has made physicians and hospitals more careful; there is ample evidence of greater attention to injury prevention, especially by hospitals. The AMA (1983) estimates that hospital expenditure on risk management now totals almost $1 billion per year. Thus the tort system may indeed deter injuries, as intended, although we cannot measure this influence precisely. Sorting out which of these hypotheses are correct must await more comprehensive data.

II

ISSUES IN MEDICAL MALPRACTICE INSURANCE

MEDICAL MALPRACTICE reached public awareness not because of the thousands of patients who are injured each year as a result of malpractice, but because of a breakdown in the market for malpractice insurance. The acceleration of claim frequency and severity in the early seventies caused little concern until insurance premiums exploded in 1974–75, with insurers seeking premium increases of up to 500 percent. For example, surgeons in Los Angeles saw their rates triple overnight, from $12,000 to $36,000. In some states the crisis in price became a crisis in availability: most traditional insurers restricted coverage and some withdrew totally from the market. A 1975 survey showed that physicians in 16 states were having difficulty obtaining the coverage that most view as an essential precondition of practicing medicine.

The resolution of this crisis has involved significant changes in malpractice insurance markets. To resolve the immediate availability problem, legislatures in most states moved to mandate the formation of a joint underwriting association (JUA) or some other form of compulsory pooling arrangement. These mechanisms—similar to assigned risk pools for automobile insurance—compel insurers to provide malpractice insurance as a condition of continuing to write other lines of insurance in the state. In some states the mandatory pool still remains a major source or even the sole source of coverage. In others, the voluntary market was preserved by switching from the traditional type of coverage (an occurrence policy) to a more restricted form (a claims-made policy), which provides less real insurance and leaves the physician exposed to greater risk. Dissatisfied with these developments, some physicians have formed their own insurance companies. These "bedpan mutuals" have flourished and now write more than 40 percent of premium volume nationwide. Whether they will be able to survive a new surge in claims remains an open question.

Although malpractice premiums remained level or even fell in the late 1970s, there are signs that a new storm may be building. Rate increases of 20 and 30 percent a year have been sought since 1982. Insurers' loss ratios (the ratio of claim plus expense costs to premiums) are rising again; in June 1983 they exceeded 150 percent. Such negative underwriting results are tolerable only as long as the difference is made up by investment income. A significant decline in investment earnings or in stock prices could trigger another round of large premium increases.

These events raise several important issues. The huge premium increases and sudden contraction of the insurance market in the mid-1970s led many to question whether private insurance markets are indeed able to ensure the availability of malpractice insurance at stable and competitive prices. What caused the last crisis? Have the solutions adopted at that time resolved the underlying problem sufficiently to prevent a recurrence? And are they efficient? Several of these solutions — physician-owned mutuals, the claims-made policy — imply a contraction of the market in risk spreading, with physicians apparently bearing more risk. This shifting of risk from the insurance industry to physicians is *prima facie* surprising, since theory suggests that joint-stock companies should still be the more efficient bearers of risk. Insurance regulators, dissatisfied with the workings of private markets, have actively intervened to control insurance rates and types of coverage. Has such regulation improved the performance of the market? What, if any, is the appropriate role for government intervention?

A more basic question is whether liability insurance in general and the rating features of malpractice insurance contracts in particular interfere with deterrence. Insurance protects the tortfeasor from the penalties meted out by the tort system. With complete insurance, the cost of injuries is not internalized to the physician, and the tort system is frustrated in its potential role of correcting incentives for injury prevention. At the limit, with full liability insurance, litigation to determine fault is a pure waste of resources; the negligence system is reduced to an excessively costly system of compensation.

In principle, however, liability insurance need not interfere with deterrence if insurance premiums adjust to reflect the insured's quality of care. As a theoretical proposition, if the price of insurance coverage accurately reflects the insured's probability of loss — perfect experience rating — insurance does not interfere with incentives for care. In practice, perfect experience rating is prohibitively costly, and most lines of insurance adopt a second-best solution: the insured retains some financial stake in the loss through a deductible, a coinsurance percentage, or a premium that is merit-rated on the basis of claim experience. This financial exposure preserves some, albeit reduced, incentives for loss prevention. But such forms of risk retention appear to be relatively uncommon in medical malpractice insurance contracts. There are no deductibles or coinsurance, and merit rating is rarely applied. Thus, key issues in evaluating the operation of the malpractice system are the following: Do the terms of malpractice insurance contracts provide appropriate incentives for injury prevention, consistent with the deterrent function of the tort system? If not, why not? Could government intervention improve the situation?

In this section on insurance issues, Chapter 5 describes the malpractice insurance market, Chapter 6 analyzes the causes of the crisis of 1974–75 and the viability and efficiency of the solutions adopted at that time, and Chapter 7 deals with the efficiency of malpractice insurance contracts and rating practices. The analysis throughout focuses on insurance for physicians and surgeons because of lack of data on hospital insurance.

5

The Malpractice Insurance Market

PROFESSIONAL LIABILITY INSURANCE protects the physician against the legal expense of defending and paying claims arising out of professional practice. Medical malpractice insurance is not like automobile liability insurance or homeowners' insurance, with which most people are familiar: the physician cannot simply call up his local insurance agent, or choose from twenty or more companies listed in the yellow pages. Typically, there would be at most two or three companies writing a significant volume of business in his area, of which one may be a physician-owned company. If there is a major stock company, it is often writing insurance through a program sponsored by the local medical society. Premiums are high, sometimes in excess of $50,000 a year, depending on the physician's locality, medical specialty, and the limits of coverage he chooses. At least as burdensome as the absolute level of premiums has been their erratic and unpredictable escalation over the last two decades.

The purpose of this chapter is to describe some of the peculiar features of medical malpractice insurance, to show why it is a particularly risky line for insurers to write, and to show how several of the unusual institutional features of this market are in fact a response to the peculiar risks.

The Nature of the Malpractice Risk

Medical malpractice meets none of the ideal conditions of an insurable risk. The ideal insurance risk is one where the insurer is able to pool a large number of homogeneous but independent, random events. Under these conditions, by the law of large numbers, the outcome for the pool is predictable with virtual certainty, even though the outcome for each individual may be highly uncertain. Medical malpractice lacks all these properties of large numbers, independence, and risk beyond the control of the insured.

First, the pool of potential policyholders is relatively small. In 1975 there were 50,000 physicians in active practice in the continental United States. But this figure grossly overstates the pool of homogeneous risks because individual physicians differ enormously in their expected claim cost, depending on factors such as their specialty, geographic location, type of practice, and personal characteristics. A crude indicator of the diversity in exposure among physicians is the spread in their insurance premiums. In 1975, premiums paid by a representative nationwide sample of physicians ranged from $500 to over $50,000.[1]

The pool of claims, which provides the basis for estimating claim severity, is even smaller than the exposure base for estimating frequency. In 1976 there were 17,683 claims closed, of which 7,262 closed with payment to the plaintiff. But claims are concentrated in only a few states. Of the 7,262 paid claims, 4,647, or almost two-thirds, occurred in the seven states that each had more than 300 claims.[2] New Hampshire had only 3 paid claims, and thirty-five states had fewer than 100. The small sample problem is exacerbated by the huge range in awards, from zero to several million dollars. Because of the highly skewed distribution of awards, with 50 percent of dollars paid on 3 percent of claims, the rare multimillion dollar claim can enormously increase total losses or average cost per physician in a small insurance program.

The diverse and unpredictable nature of medical malpractice losses is illustrated by some of the statistics we have already encountered. In 1975 there was an eighteenfold range among states in the frequency of claims per 100 physicians, from 1.2 in Maine to 17.4 in California. Average claim severity ranged from $10,000 in Maine to $40,000 in California. For small states, there is great year-to-year volatility. Between 1975 and 1976 the change in claim frequency ranged from −40 percent to +150 percent, and changes in severity per claim show even greater volatility. For example, in North Dakota, with fewer than 20 paid claims, the average increased from $6,801 in 1975 to $40,259 in 1976; in Tennessee, with roughly 70 paid claims, the average increased from $10,482 in 1975 to $56,548 in 1976. Obviously, with fluctuations of this magnitude in average claim cost, there is great uncertainty as to what constitutes an actuarially fair insurance premium. Actuarial credibility can be increased by averaging over states and years, but at the cost of treating as homogeneous risks that may in fact be quite different.

The second condition of risk-free insurance that is violated by medical malpractice is independence of losses. Multiple claims against an individual physician are not independent, to the extent that they arise out of systematic characteristics of his practice. Information about defective practices uncovered in prosecuting one claim can and have been used to prosecute other claims.

Even more problematic, claims against physicians as a group are not independent. Each patient's incentive to file a claim and the size of awards are influenced by sociolegal trends—attitudes of juries, changes in legal doctrines—which affect all insureds alike. This common sociolegal risk is not reduced by pooling a large number of policyholders. Although sociolegal risk affects all lines of liability insurance to some degree, it contributes more to the medical malpractice risk as a result of the long tail in claims. Because of the inherent lag in discovering some types of iatrogenic injury, accommodated by discovery rules and long statutes of limitations, several years may elapse between the occurrence of an injury and the filing of a claim, and the additional delay from filing to final disposition averages two years but may exceed ten. The longer this lag from injury to claim disposition, the greater is the impact of nondiversifiable, sociolegal risk, relative to more readily diversifiable individual risk.[3]

Third, the probability of loss is partially within the control of the insured, creating problems of moral hazard and adverse selection. Moral hazard occurs when insurance reduces incentives to prevent loss, thus increasing the likelihood of the loss insured against. Adverse selection occurs when, in ignorance of differences among policyholders, an insurer attracts those of above-average risk. This may result if low-risk policyholders drop out of the market rather than paying rates designed to cover average risk, or are bid away by another insurer offering lower rates with selective underwriting. With adverse selection, an insurer who raises rates may attract the worst risks and end up with higher claim costs and lower profits. Thus many of the features of the malpractice insurance market can be understood as responses to the problems created by the small pool, the long tail, moral hazard, and adverse selection.

Types of Coverage

Prior to 1975 malpractice insurance policies were typically written on an occurrence basis. An occurrence policy written on January 1,

1970, covers any claims arising out the physician's practice during 1970, even if filed many years later. The adoption of the occurrence policy for professional liability was a natural development from its use for the major liability lines, such as automobile and homeowners' liability, where the occurrence and the manifestation of injury typically coincide, leading to minimal lags in the filing of a claim. In professional liability, however, delay in the manifestation of certain injuries has led courts to adopt long statutes of limitations and discovery rules to protect the interests of victims. Since the price of an occurrence policy is set at the outset of the policy year, but claim costs may not be known for many years because of delay in claim reporting and disposition, the occurrence insurer bears all risk arising from sociolegal and financial trends affecting future claims.[4]

Since 1975 some carriers have replaced the occurrence policy form with a claims-made policy. A claims-made policy covers all claims filed in the policy year arising out of incidents occurring in that year or at any time since the retroactive date specified in the policy. Potential claims or incidents reported by the policyholder are usually also covered, even if not yet filed by the potential plaintiff. The typical claims-made policy guarantees the availability of an endorsement to cover claims incurred but not filed during the policy year. This is crucial when the policyholder terminates regular coverage, as a result of retirement or nonrenewal for any reason. However, since the availability but not the price of the reporting endorsement is guaranteed in advance, a claims-made policy effectively transfers from the insurer to the policyholder the risk associated with the long tail in claims. Regulators in several states disallowed the claims-made policy, at least initially. I shall discuss the efficiency of this type of policy in the next chapter.

Sources of Coverage

Prior to 1975 the state or local medical society in 34 states sponsored an insurance program that guaranteed coverage to all members in good standing. Such programs still exist in many states. Typically, physician representatives participate actively in underwriting, determining the premium rate structure and handling claims. While large states such as California had more than one sponsored program, most states had a single dominant program. As a result, malpractice insurance markets were highly concentrated: in 1974 the median market share of the leading writer in each state was 52 percent (Steves, 1983).

Outside of medical society programs, the only alternative source of coverage in 1974 was an individual policy. But even prior to the crisis, individual policies had declined from more than 70 percent of the market in the early 1960s to under 30 percent by 1973, and they have since continued to decline. By 1974 at least one leading carrier still active in the group market was refusing to write any new individual policies and only renewed old policies as an accommodation to agents concerned about retaining the policyholders' other coverages, such as homeowner's or automobile liability. As I shall argue later in the chapter, the demise of the individual market is attributable to the problems of small risk pool, adverse selection, and regulation in this line of insurance.

To the extent that it exists, the individual market relies heavily on the rating services of the Insurance Services Office (ISO). As the leading rating bureau for all lines of property-casualty insurance, including medical malpractice, the ISO performs those insurance functions that are subject to significant economies of scale: it develops a classification scheme and policy forms, collects loss data from member companies, adjusts the data for trends, computes advisory rates, and handles rate filings and other dealings with insurance regulators. Insurance companies can purchase these ISO services on a piecemeal basis. For example, even the largest companies typically purchase ISO rates and rating services in states where they write individual rather than program coverage (U.S. Senate, 1975). It would probably not be an exaggeration to say that, at least in small states, the existence of an individual market is dependent on the existence of the ISO.[5] It is estimated that as of 1973 over half the total market was reported to the ISO, although only 25 percent of premiums were actually written at ISO rates. Since 1975 the role of ISO has diminished considerably. Nevertheless, because of its pooling activities, the ISO has been challenged as a noncompetitive influence in medical malpractice and in other lines of insurance. Evidence pertinent to this question will be presented later in this chapter.

Since 1975 many physicians and hospitals have formed their own mutuals or "captive" companies, which have grown at the expense of the joint stock companies and now account for more than 40 percent of medical malpractice premium volume nationwide. Thirty of the physician-owned mutuals were created by medical societies, and an additional ten were formed independently. Coverage through physician-owned programs is now available in 36 states.

Physicians unable to obtain coverage from any of these sources may obtain it through the mandatory assigned risk pools (joint underwriting associations) or from so-called surplus lines or nonadmitted carriers such as Lloyd's of London, which specialize in high-risk insurance at high rates.

The Rating Structure

The ISO rating structure was used extensively in the individual market and often was adopted with only minor modifications in the group market. The primary bases of rating are limits of coverage (for example, $1 million per occurrence, $3 million total for the policy year), medical specialty, and geographic location. Territorial rates for a base class and basic limits of coverage are multiplied by specialty differentials and excess limit factors to obtain rates for other medical specialties and higher limits of coverage. Most states, with the exception of the largest, constitute a single territory. The ISO classification of medical specialties was expanded from two classes in 1962 to five in 1967 and seven in 1975. Since 1969 the ISO has used two sets of excess limits factors, one for medical and one for surgical specialties. For example, the markup for $1 million/$3 million coverage would be 1.69 times the basic rate for $25,000/$75,000 coverage for physicians, and 1.79 times for surgeons. Because these differentials are applied multiplicatively, the eightfold range between the lowest rated class (physicians doing no surgery) and the highest (surgical specialists) applies to ISO rates countrywide.

Detailed data on rates under the numerous group programs are not available. However, an analysis of premiums paid by a nationwide sample of physicians over the three-year period 1974–1976 shows that although only a small fraction of the market was nominally written at ISO rates, even in group programs the rates followed a rigid, multiplicative pattern similar to the ISO's both in structure and differentials, with the exception that group programs appear to have compressed rates for high-risk surgical specialties relative to lower-risk medical specialties (Danzon, 1980a).

Aside from the rating factors already mentioned—coverage limits, specialty, and territory—in 1975 there was apparently very little rating on the basis of individual exposure or experience. The ISO manual applies surcharges for specific procedures, such as x-ray or shock therapy, and for partnerships and employees. There is no rating on the basis of volume of business, as is common in some other lines of professional liability, except for a crude adjustment for part-time practice. Deductibles, coinsurance, or surcharges for individual claim experience were not part of the basic rating structure.

Since 1975 the rating structure has remained basically the same, although the growth of the mutuals and decreased influence of the

ISO have resulted in more variation in specialty differentials among states. Some mutuals have adopted merit rating programs, but individual surcharges are applied to no more than 1 or 2 percent of physicians.

Although this rating structure is extremely rigid, to some extent it reflects the fact that the small pool of policyholders and the instability of loss experience over time preclude drawing finer classifications with actuarial credibility. Moreover, moral hazard and the potential for multiple, nonindependent claims against an individual physician no doubt contribute to the prevailing view that no price is high enough for the bad risk—hence the tendency to deny coverage totally rather than surcharging premiums.

Competition in the Malpractice Insurance Market

Medical malpractice insurance markets are highly concentrated. Although the market share of the top four firms countrywide is only around 40 percent, in most states one or two firms write 90 percent of the policies for physicians. Traditional theory of the effect of market structure on performance would infer that competition would be weak. In addition, the role of the ISO in publishing advisory rates has been challenged as anticompetitive in malpractice and other insurance lines.

The high degree of concentration derives primarily from the operation of sponsored group programs. Group programs grew to dominate the market because they offer several advantages over writing individual policies. First, there may be economies of scale in marketing. Second, group programs create a sizable ongoing data base for a relatively homogeneous group, which increases actuarial efficiency. Third, as in group health or life insurance, insuring a group that is formed for purposes other than obtaining insurance provides some protection against adverse selection. The insurer relinquishes control over underwriting in return for the guarantee inherent in writing a share of the market that is large in both absolute and percentage terms.[6] For example, one major carrier requires that at least 60 percent of active physicians in the state be covered through the program. Fourth, cooperation between medical societies and insurers reduces the cost of obtaining regulatory approval of rates. Although rate filings must still be supported by actuarial data, the consent of the insured is usually a sufficient condition for automatic approval.[7] Finally, efficient liability insurance requires input from physicians in underwriting, reviewing claims, and monitoring the legal defense effort. These activities are discussed in detail in Chapter 7.

In addition to these cost advantages, group programs promote competition. The medical society has proprietorship over the data base and can solicit bids from competing carriers. The evidence of this competition for the Southern California Physicians program prior to the huge rate hikes of 1975 (Munch, 1978) is inconsistent with the allegations made at the time, that those rate hikes implied lack of competition. Medical society ownership of the data base thus undermines the potential monopoly power that an established carrier would enjoy if it had sole access to the loss experience of a particular group of policyholders.[8] The rates charged by the sponsored programs in turn constrain rates that can be charged by carriers in the individual market. If the ISO files rates that are substantially in excess of program rates, they are likely to be disapproved by regulators and would create a risk of adverse selection for carriers using those rates.

The argument that concentration is not indicative of lack of competition and that group programs tend to constrain ISO rates is supported by an analysis of premiums paid by physicians from 1974 to 1976 (Danzon, 1980a). These data show no systematic relationship between premiums and concentration. However, this absence of overall effect conceals offsetting effects among specialties. Relative to the individual market, group programs apparently offered 3 to 8 percent lower premiums to surgical specialties and 10 percent higher premiums to nonsurgical specialties. There are two possible explanations of why group programs offered a more compressed specialty rate structure than that recommended by the ISO. First, the ISO rate structure may be actuarially more correct, in which case the programs appear to be effecting a subsidy from low-risk to high-risk specialties. Alternatively, the more compressed program structure may be correct, and the ISO structure a rational adjustment to the risk of adverse selection in the individual market. Unfortunately, the available data are inadequate to distinguish these hypotheses.

Conclusions

Medical malpractice insurance is characterized by a small pool of policyholders, huge variance in potential claims, nondiversifiable sociolegal risk, and potential for adverse selection and moral hazard. The market is highly concentrated at the state level, in part because of medical society–sponsored group programs and physician-owned mutuals. However, both this high concentration and the advisory functions of the ISO rating bureau appear to promote rather than impede competition.

6

The 1975 Insurance Crisis: Causes and Solutions

IN 1974–75 the malpractice insurance crisis broke, with premium increases of up to 500 percent in some states and commercial carriers withdrawing from the market entirely in others. Medical malpractice was said to be uninsurable, and Congress debated the need for a federal insurance or reinsurance program (U.S. Senate, 1975). In response to these events, most states enacted laws to control malpractice claim costs and to ensure the availability of insurance through joint underwriting associations (JUAs). These measures were adopted with little time for empirical analysis to resolve conflicting views about the causes of the crisis. Nevertheless, the crisis abated. In the late 1970s premiums remained stable or even fell in some states, but they are now rising again, at alarming rates in some areas.[1] In most states the voluntary market has reemerged but with substantial changes, notably a contracted role for the joint stock companies and the occurrence policy. In other states—Massachusetts, New York, Rhode Island, South Carolina—there is continued regulatory intervention to hold down rates, and the mandatory JUAs remain a major source and sometimes the sole source of coverage.

Such dramatic volatility of price and supply is not expected in competitive insurance markets. Although other liability lines—notably product liability and municipal liability—also experienced large rate increases in the mid-1970s, the contraction of availability was less severe than for medical malpractice. This chapter examines the disruption of traditional malpractice insurance markets. The purpose is twofold: first, we need to understand the causes and solutions of the last crisis in order to evaluate whether such disruptions are likely to recur; and second, the appropriate role of government needs to be determined. More specifically, is the continued regulatory control over rates warranted by a lack of competition, and are the mandatory JUAs necessary to assure availability?

The first section of the chapter examines how far the huge premium increases of 1975 can be explained by prior trends in claim costs. Since the lag in rates behind rapidly rising claim costs turns out to be important, several possible explanations of this lag are examined, namely, deficiencies in the data available at that time, federal price controls under the Economic Stabilization Program in effect from August 1971 to April 1974, rate regulation at the state level, and the systematic tendency of competitive pricing to produce underwriting cycles. The second section measures the contribution of developments in financial markets in 1974 to the huge rate increases. The third section examines why the crisis in price became one of availability and evaluates the solutions adopted, including the growth of medical mutuals, the claims-made policy, and residual market mechanisms. In the final section I summarize the findings and discuss policy implications.

Trends in Claims and Premiums

Most of the analysis presented here of claim trends and of recommended and allowed rate increases is based on unpublished data from the Insurance Services Office (ISO). Although less than half of physicians' malpractice insurance was written at ISO rates in 1974, these rates nevertheless provide a reasonable picture of marketwide trends since both competition and regulation prevented great divergence between ISO rates and those of independent insurance writers (Danzon, 1980a).

In the Spring 1975 rate review, the ISO estimated a trend of 10.2 percent per annum in severity (cost per paid claim) and a 12.1 percent per annum trend in claim frequency, combining to produce a trend in total claim costs of 23.5 percent. Compounded over the five years between 1969 and 1974, this trend implies that if 1969 rates were adequate, 1974 rates should have been 187 percent higher.[2] Actual rate increases effected between 1970 and 1974, when compounded, produce an average rate increase of 125 percent above 1969 levels. Therefore a 28 percent increase (2.87 ÷ 2.25 = 1.28) was required to compensate for the preceding lag in rates behind costs through 1974. Further projecting the 23.5 percent trend for the 1975 policy year yields 58 percent as the required increase in 1975 rates over 1974, assuming that 1969 rates were adequate.

By 1975, however, it was clear that 1969 rates were inadequate. The projected loss ratio (the ratio of expected claim costs plus allocated loss adjustment expense to premium) on 1969 policies was 1.67 compared to a target loss ratio of 0.66.[3] Thus a 153 percent premium increase (1.67 ÷ 0.66 = 2.53) was required to restore the actual to the desired loss ratio. These estimates imply that by 1975 a 300 percent premium increase was deemed necessary, composed of the following three components:[4]

(1) Due to inadequacy of 1969 rates: 153.0%
(2) Due to lag of rates behind costs, 1969–1974:   27.7%
(3) Projected cost increase, 1974 to 1975:   23.5%
    Needed rate increase by 1975:   300.0%
    Indicated increase using ISO methodology: 170.3%
    Average recommended increase: 197.0%

How reasonable were these ISO estimates? The 1975 estimate of ultimate losses for the 1969 policy year was not excessive: as of 1981, the 1969 loss ratio was 1.71, compared to the 1975 estimate of 1.73. As of 1978, the average rate of increase in claim frequency between policy years 1970 and 1975 was estimated at 16.5 percent, compared to the 1975 estimate of 12.1 percent. The use of a severity trend based on *paid* claim costs would tend to understate the trend in *incurred* claim costs at a time when frequency is increasing.[5] Thus only the desired loss ratio of 0.66 may be challenged as excessive, because of investment income.

CAUSES OF THE 1969–1974 RATE INADEQUACIES

Granted that the 1969 rates were inadequate, why was the adjustment to adequate levels not spread out over the subsequent five years, rather than being concentrated in 1974–75? At the time the most commonly cited factor was ignorance, allegedly resulting from lack of data and unanticipated changes. This explanation is not entirely plausible, because comprehensive data bases were kept by the insurers, by medical-society-sponsored programs, and by the ISO. Nevertheless, let us review the evidence on this point, together with three other possible contributing factors: federal price controls, state regulation, and competition.

   Ignorance.   There is no evidence that trends in severity were underestimated prior to 1975, or radically revised upward in 1975. The severity trend for each year from 1970 through 1975 was as follows: 11.7 in 1970, 8.3 in 1972, 14.3 in 1973, 11.3 in 1974, and 10.2 in 1975. The 1975 treatment of claim frequency represented more of a departure from previous practice. Before 1975 the ISO did not incorporate a frequency trend in the rate-making formula, although there is evidence suggesting that the increase in frequency did not go unnoticed.[6] Nevertheless, a frequency trend was explicitly incorporated into the rating formula for the first time in the 1975 rate review, which raised the trend factor from 10.2 percent (severity only) to 23.5 percent (frequency times severity). Other things being equal, this raised the indicated rate increase using the ISO methodology from 78 percent to 170 percent.[7] Thus a change in the rate-making methodology contributed to the sharp premium increases in 1975, but the lag in making this change cannot be explained by prior ignorance.

The Economic Stabilization Program. From August 1971 through April 1974, insurance rates were subject to the price controls of the Nixon administration's Economic Stabilization Program (ESP). Insurance was subject to special provisions, similar to those applied to other sectors of the economy, permitting limited pass-through of cost increases, with constraints on profit margins.[8] How binding were these controls? Effectively, any rate increase that could be justified on the grounds that past rates were inadequate was exempt from control. Thus the main cause of the 1975 rate increase — past rate inadequacies — was not prevented by the ESP. Other features of the controls were potentially binding: the 20 percent of the premium dollar allocated to general expense and profit was subject to a maximum increase of 2.5 percent; the remaining 80 cents of the premium dollar could only be adjusted for inflation at some fraction of the indicated trend; and modifications of the traditional rating formula were prohibited. Although this might have prevented the introduction of a frequency trend in the rating formula prior to 1974, since controls were lifted prior to the April 1974 review, it cannot explain why such a trend was not introduced at that time.

Although the maximum increases allowed under ESP were less than those indicated by the standard ISO rating formula, the limited evidence available suggests that the controls were not binding constraints. For example, for Rhode Island physicians and surgeons, in October 1972, standard ISO methodology indicated that a 187 percent increase was needed; the allowed increase under ESP was 132 percent; but the ISO only filed for a 50 percent increase. In May 1973 the indicated rate increase for optometrists was 289 percent, the allowed increase was 169 percent, and the filed increase was 100 percent; in January 1974 the indicated rate increase was 270 percent, the allowed increase was 180 percent, and the filed increase was 75 percent. If typical, this evidence implies that either competition or regulation imposed constraints more binding than those of the Economic Stabilization Program.

State regulation. Table 6.1 shows the number of states (of a total of 48) in which the ISO filed rate increases, the average recommended increase, and the average approved increase in 1973, 1974, and 1975.[9] Between 1973 and 1975, a rate increase was filed in an increasing number of states, and the average requested increase almost quadrupled. Of the states where an increase was filed, some increase was granted in 62 percent in 1973, 84 percent in 1974, and 62 percent in 1975; the percentage of the requested increase actually approved fell from 91 percent in 1973 to 67 percent in 1975. Although the average approved increase (in states permitting some increase) rose from 49 percent in 1973 to 146 percent in 1975, regulation became more binding over this period because (1) the allowed percentage, although larger in absolute terms, represented a smaller *fraction* of that filed, and (2) since the filed increase was greater, the absolute gap between the approved and filed rates widened.

To summarize, as of 1973, 11 states had approved rates that were 49 percent below recommended ISO rates; 18 had rates that were 5 percent too low; and the remainder appeared adequate. By 1975, 18 states had approved rates that were 161 percent below the recommended ones and the remaining 30 states had rates that were 70 percent too low. Thus the rate inadequacy had increased both in percentage and, a fortiori, in absolute terms. This understates the impact of rate regulation to the extent that it omits any measure of delay between filing and approval of a requested rate increase, which in some cases could be as long as two years, and it omits any measure

Table 6.1 Filed and approved malpractice insurance rate increases, 1973–1975

ISO rate filings	1973	1974	1975
Number of states in which			
ISO filed rate increase	29	32	48
Average increase filed	52%	92%	197%
Number of states in which			
increase was approved	18	27	30
Average increase filed	54%	82%	218%
Average increase approved	49%	66%	146%
Number of states in which			
increase was denied	11	5	18
Average increase filed	49%	163%	161%

Source: Insurance Services Office, unpublished data.

of the degree to which rate filings were held below indicated levels on the presumption that a small increase might be allowed whereas a large increase would be rejected outright.[10] The fact that no increase was filed in 19 states in 1973 and in 16 states in 1974 even though some increase would have been permitted under the Economic Stabilization Program is further evidence that federal controls were not binding.

Competition.   Identifying state regulation as the focus of rate control does not necessarily identify it as a causal factor. Regulators reflect pressures from their constituents (see, for example, Peltzman, 1976). The regulatory response to an ISO rate filing is influenced by the degree of opposition from affected parties (in this case, the medical profession) and by the rates charged on comparable policies (in this case, rates for the sponsored program, which were determined by negotiation between the insurance carrier and the medical society). As long as the carriers of sponsored programs kept rates low, ISO rates would be effectively constrained both by the risk of adverse selection, if substantially higher rates were filed, and by the tendency of regulators to reject rates for one carrier that are greatly in excess of rates for another. By 1975 the competitive constraint on the ISO to keep rates low was weakened because the carriers of the sponsored programs were filing huge rate increases in many states, in the face of opposition from the medical profession.[11] Regulation became one forum for opposing these increases.

Prior to 1975, competition for group programs was apparently an important factor in holding down rates. The early 1970s witnessed the aggressive entry of new carriers into the group market. For example, the Argonaut entered the market in 1971, took over programs in Pennsylvania, Massachusetts, Florida, northern California, and New York, and by the end of 1974 was writing policies for 30,000 physicians. The Travelers greatly expanded its market share in 1973 by taking on programs in northern and southern California, Arizona, and New Mexico. The experience of the southern California program illustrates the effect of competition: between 1969 and 1975 estimated claim costs in this program increased roughly 705 percent while premiums increased only 73 percent, apparently as a result of competition for the program and competition between the program and carriers offering individual coverage to physicians with no prior claim experience. Assuming that 1970 rates were adequate, by 1976 a 352 percent catch-up premium increase appeared necessary, given the data available at the time.[12]

Obviously, competition cannot explain why carriers would be

willing to write at rates known to be inadequate. The tendency for insurance prices to lag and then lead claim costs and hence to produce cycles in underwriting profits is not confined to that period or to medical malpractice. Since the huge 1975 premium increases, malpractice insurance rates have either declined or remained stable while the combined loss ratio (claim costs plus all expenses, relative to premium) has risen from 94 percent in 1977 to more than 170 percent in 1983. Because medical fees are sticky in the short run, infrequent large premium increases are more costly to physicians than an equivalent series of small increases. This erratic pattern of premium increases is therefore puzzling, and remains an important subject for future research.

Financial Factors

It was widely alleged at the time that the malpractice premium increases of 1974–75 were an attempt by insurers to recoup their huge stock market losses. This charge is *prima facie* implausible. Recoupment of past losses is feasible only in a monopolistic or cartelized market with barriers to entry, and neither of these conditions characterized the malpractice insurance market in 1975. As we have seen, there was significant price competition among the stock companies and in fact new entry occurred on an impressive scale, primarily by medical mutuals, often at rates comparable to those of the stock companies they replaced. Since the formation of new companies took time, there was ample opportunity for the stock companies to back down from their initial rate filings, if these filings had included an above-competitive markup figured on an erroneous presumption that these companies enjoyed monopoly power.

Nevertheless, although the recoupment hypothesis is not plausible, events in financial markets did contribute in a more subtle way to the huge premium increases by raising the competitive supply price of malpractice insurance. The experience of the property liability insurance industry in the early 1970s was unprecedented in the volatility of both underwriting and investment results and their positive correlation. The Dow Jones Index fell from a high of 1297 in 1973 to a low of 578 in 1974. Table 6.2 shows the effect of the decline in value of common stocks on the balance-sheet position of stock companies of the property liability insurance industry. Stock insurers reported a capital loss of $3.9 billion in 1973 followed by a further loss of $6.1 billion in 1974, cumulating to more than 16 percent of mean assets. (In fact this understates the capital loss because the decline in the market

Table 6.2 Underwriting and investment results of stock property-liability insurers (millions of dollars)

Year	Investment income[a] (1)	Mean assets (%) (2)	Capital gain or loss (3)	Mean assets (%) (4)	Under-profit or loss[b] (5)	Earned premium (%) (6)	Total return (1) + (3) + (5) (7)	Capital and surplus (8)	Return on capital (7) ÷ (8) (9)
1966	896	2.87	−1448	−4.65	102	0.70	−450	12,007	−3.7
1967	987	3.03	1315	4.03	10	0.07	2312	13,580	17.0
1968	1101	3.06	1178	3.28	−201	−1.17	2078	14,887	13.9
1969	1238	3.27	−1730	−4.97	−396	−2.07	−888	12,699	−7.0
1970	1439	3.57	−189	−0.47	−154	−0.72	1096	14,014	7.8
1971	1785	3.88	1632	3.55	679	2.85	4096	17,308	23.7
1972	2068	3.84	2656	4.93	915	3.44	5639	21,398	26.4
1973	2491	4.13	−3932	−6.52	226	0.78	−1215	20,056	−6.1
1974	2891	4.72	−6142	−10.03	−1761	−5.60	−5012	14,831	−33.8
1975	3143	4.83	3426	5.27	−2880	−8.34	3689	18,451	20.0
1976	3629	4.73	3242	4.23	−1406	−3.43	−1019	23,021	−4.4
1977	4648	5.07	73	0.08	804	1.65	5525	27,062	20.4
1978	5724	5.27	1338	1.23	1335	2.41	8397	32,510	25.8
1979	7601	5.97	3204	2.51	−365	−.60	10440	39,170	26.7
1980	8836	6.02	4945	3.37	−1956	−2.98	11825	47,499	24.9

Source: Best's Aggregates and Averages.
a. Interest, dividends, and rents.
b. Before federal income tax.

value of the bond portfolio, which constituted 52 percent of total assets in 1974, is hidden by the accounting convention that bonds are carried at amortized book value rather than market value.)[13] At the same time, underwriting losses reached unprecedented levels of $1.8 billion, or 5.6 percent of earned premium, in 1974 and $2.9 billion, or 8.3 percent of earned premium, in 1975. This represents a loss four times as large as the largest underwriting loss of the previous decade (2.1 percent of earned premium in 1969). The adverse underwriting and investment results of 1974 combined to wipe out 26 percent of capital, ignoring losses on bonds.

How much of the 1975 malpractice premium increase can be attributed to these adverse financial developments? To address this question, I developed a model to show how the fair insurance premium — that which yields a competitive return on capital — is affected by such financial variables as the supply price of capital, tax rates, the return on assets, and the premium/capital ratio. I then use the model to show how changes in the values of these parameters in 1975 might have affected insurance premiums (see Appendix B). The results of these calculations are summarized in Table 6.3.

Using the baseline or pre-crisis parameter values implies that for every $100 of expected losses plus expenses, the fair premium was $79. Equivalently, the fair combined loss ratio is 1.26. The accounting "profit" margin, defined as the difference between premiums and undiscounted losses plus expenses, is negative because the lag between premium collection and payout on losses permits the insurer to earn investment income. In competitive markets, this investment

Table 6.3 Effect on fair premium of changes in parameter values

	Baseline value	Hypothetical 1975 value	Fair premium (dollars) (baseline = $79)	Change in fair premium (%)
Cost of capital (r_e)	0.11	0.22	90	+13
Rate of return on assets (r_a)	0.08	0	117	+47
Tax rate on investment income (t_i)	0.3	0	70	−12
Tax rate on underwriting profit (t_u)	0.46	0	88	+10
Capital/premium ratio (k)	0.7	0.25	76	−4

income will accrue to policyholders in the form of a lower premium, except for the profit margin paid to equity owners as a return for bearing underwriting risk.

Let us consider now how this fair premium, per $100 of expected losses, may have changed as a result of financial developments.

Rate of return on assets.   Nominal yields on bonds rose in 1974–75, so there is no reason to attribute the 1974–75 premium increase to a decline in the expected return on assets. Nevertheless, to illustrate the potential effect, Table 6.3 calculates the fair premium under the assumption that expected returns fell to zero ($r_a = 0$). The fair profit margin increases from -21 percent to $+17$ percent, which implies an increase in the fair premium of 47 percent.

Effective tax rates.   Since underwriting losses can be set off against underwriting or investment profits in other lines for tax purposes, the after-tax cost of underwriting losses depends on these profits and their effective tax rate. A sequence of underwriting and investment losses reduces the value of the tax shield and increases the after-tax cost of underwriting losses. For the stock companies in Table 6.2, the underwriting loss of $1.8 billion in 1974 offset the cumulative underwriting gain of the previous three years. Capital losses in 1973 and 1974 more than offset positive investment income in those years. But even under the extreme assumption that the expected value of the underwriting tax shield fell to zero ($t_u = 0$), this would only account for a 10 percent increase in the fair insurance premium, or a reduction in the profit margin from -21 percent to -12 percent.

Cost of capital.   The decline in stock values and increase in bond yields in 1974 suggests an increase in the cost of capital to industry as a whole. Some additional increase in the cost of capital for malpractice insurance is plausible as a result of increased risk from several sources. First, a disproportionate increase in the size of the largest awards would tend to increase the variance and positive skewness of the insurer's loss distribution, thereby raising the risk of insolvency for a given mean loss ratio. Second, the covariance among policyholders increased, to the extent that the growth in malpractice claim costs reflected changes in medical practice, tort law, and the sociolegal environment, which increase nondiversifiable risk. Third, the volatility of financial markets in the early 1970s no doubt increased the variance of investment returns. Fourth, positive correlation between underwriting losses and investment losses apparently increased in the early 1970s, thereby reducing the diversifiability of underwriting risk.

Finally, the catastrophic capital losses increased the premium/

capital ratio, a rough indicator of financial strength, from 1.28 in 1972 to 2.17 in 1974 for stock insurers in the aggregate. (The true increase is even larger because book values do not reflect the fall in market values of bonds.) For the seven companies writing malpractice insurance in California, which included several of the leading malpractice carriers nationwide, the ratio was 4.3 by December 1974. With high premium/capital ratios and great uncertainty as to loss costs, the risk of bankruptcy (or, for the multiline firm, the risk of loss of capital implicitly assigned to medical malpractice) would be substantial. Specifically, at the 4 : 1 premium/capital ratio of some major carriers by December 1974, a 25 percent error in setting premiums could eliminate all capital of a single-line firm. On the basis of past experience, an error of that magnitude was far from unthinkable.[14]

The contention that the events of 1974–75 increased risk and thereby raised the cost of capital to the insurance industry is supported by the fact that in August 1975, the A. M. Best Company downgraded the financial ratings of 24 percent of the 1,000 liability insurance companies it lists. It should be noted, however, that even a large increase in the cost of capital has a minimal effect on the fair malpractice insurance premium. For example, if the cost of capital had doubled, from 11 percent to 22 percent, this implies only a 13 percent increase in the fair premium.

The Availability Crisis and Its Solutions

These events — the lag in premiums behind rising claim costs and the erosion of capital — explain the filing of rate increases of several hundred percent in 1974–75. But these events alone cannot account for the short-run crisis of availability — the total withdrawal of commercial carriers from some states and the contraction of the voluntary market in others. Nor can these events account for the long-run institutional changes that occurred. Medical mutual companies were formed in several states, and by 1981, 10 of the 20 largest carriers were either physician-owned or hospital-owned companies. The claims-made policy form has been widely adopted in place of the traditional occurrence policy. A residual market mechanism, most commonly a joint underwriting authority (JUA), was established in most states; 15 states set up patient compensation funds, which assume liability for all awards above a specified threshold, typically $500,000.

The replacement of commercial carriers with physician-owned companies and the replacement of the occurrence policy with the claims-made policy represent a contraction in the market for risk spreading. Such a contraction is *prima facie* surprising, since many of the factors that increased the expected cost and risk of malpractice insurance should raise the demand as well as the supply price of insurance. On the basis of theory, the predicted response to the developments of 1974–75 would be an increase in the price but not necessarily a contraction in the quantity of insurance written, assuming that commercial insurers were still the lowest-cost bearers of risk because of their advantages in diversification. This was in fact the outcome in some states; but in other states commercial carriers withdrew from the group program entirely, leaving the majority of physicians in the state without coverage, while carriers in the individual market ceased accepting any new policyholders. In Rhode Island, physicians responded with an antitrust suit alleging conspiracy and boycott (*Barry v. St. Paul*).

This total collapse of the voluntary commercial malpractice insurance market in some states must be attributed in the first instance to regulation. The massive increase in the intervention of state insurance commissioners in 1975 was documented earlier in the chapter. Of the 48 states in which the ISO filed a rate increase in 1975, in 18 no increase was allowed, and in the remaining 30 the approved increase averaged 70 percent less than the requested increase. Denial of requested rate increases or approval of the claims-made form, or both, were directly responsible for the withdrawal of the group carrier in New York, northern California, Maryland, Massachusetts, Rhode Island, and South Carolina, for example.[15]

In most lines of insurance, regulation of rates to levels that are inadequate to cover all individuals in a rating class tends to result in selective underwriting by insurers rather than total withdrawal. The voluntary market contracts, leaving higher-risk individuals, for whom the regulated rates are inadequate, to seek coverage in an assigned risk pool or the surplus-lines market. In medical malpractice, the use of selective underwriting as a means of preserving some voluntary market in the face of inadequate rates may have been limited by the role of medical societies, which generally opposed this type of underwriting. Just how important a factor this was cannot be documented with the available data; however, the evidence presented earlier suggests that in some states the approved rates would have been considered inadequate for the great majority of policyholders.

Although regulation may have been the precipitating factor in the crisis of availability, regulatory action in part reflects the preferences of the regulator's constituents. The medical profession supported regulatory attempts to force the insurance industry to write at lower rates. In some states this was successful: the established carriers did continue to write at rates below those initially requested. In states where rates were pushed so low that the carriers opted for total withdrawal, it must be presumed that the medical profession found the alternatives more attractive than the high occurrence rates at which the traditional market could be preserved. In discussing these alternative solutions, I shall attempt to show why they were in fact preferred.

Physician-owned companies. In many states physicians established their own companies, in the form of mutuals or reciprocals. Hospitals opted for self-insurance, captive (wholly owned) insurers domiciled offshore or special pooled trusts, thereby avoiding state insurance regulation. These provider companies are inferior bearers of risk, relative to the large, multistate, multiline stock companies they replaced, for two reasons. First, since the policyholders own the company, the mutual form concentrates the risk to policyholders and to owners of capital, in the event of insolvency, on a single group of individuals. Second, these companies are typically small and undiversified across lines and states.[16] In fact, to offset these disadvantages, some of the mutuals have gone public and are diversifying into other states and other lines of insurance.

The spectacular growth of mutuals since 1975 can be plausibly attributed to their comparative advantage in two areas: reducing claim costs and resolving pricing uncertainty. Malpractice claim costs may be lowered by reducing either the occurrence of injuries or the payout on claims that are filed. Strengthening incentives for injury reduction requires that the insurer be able to monitor individual policyholders, underwrite selectively, and use individual rating. Loss control through an optimal legal defense strategy requires that policyholders monitor the insurer's legal defense effort. The mutual form may offer an advantage in the information available to insurer and policyholder, thereby reducing their costs of monitoring each other and the costs of loss control. However, this information exchange was also possible in the sponsored programs underwritten by commercial carriers because physician policyholders participated actively in underwriting, rate setting, and claim handling. It seems more likely, therefore, that the key advantage of mutuals is that the incentives to utilize such information are greater when the policyholders are also the residual claimants to profit and residual bearers of loss.

The identity of policyholders and residual claimants in a mutual is also an advantage when there is great uncertainty as to the fair price.

Given the long statute of limitations, volatile legal and financial environment, and evidence of a large number of unfiled claims, honest estimates of the fair price of an occurrence policy in 1975 could differ widely. Uncertainty as to the impact of tort reforms enacted at that time contributed to nondiversifiable risk and hence to pricing uncertainty.[17] Because of their depleted capital position, the stock carriers made conservative estimates. If premiums include a markup for risk, the expectation is that ex post there will be a net transfer from policyholders to equity owners. There are mechanisms for sharing this pricing risk between policyholders and insurers, such as retrospective rating of premiums or payment of dividends, both of which are common in workers' compensation insurance. But ex post adjustment of price is a relatively unattractive means of resolving pricing uncertainty in medical malpractice because of the very long tail of malpractice claims. With this lag, the fair rebate could not be determined for up to ten years after writing a policy. Disagreement could be anticipated as to the appropriate interest over that term, and furthermore, such a policy reduces the insurer's incentives for optimum investment in legal defense. These issues are resolved if policyholders are also residual claimants to profit, and hence get to keep the difference if claim costs turn out to be less than premiums. Moreover, some mutuals can effectively raise prices retroactively by assessments or contributions to capital. Such assessable mutuals, which can add capital if necessary to avoid insolvency, can afford to set lower premium rates initially.

The claims-made policy. The traditional occurrence policy covers all claims arising out of incidents that occurred in the policy year, regardless of when the claims are filed. The claims-made policy, which covers only claims filed during the policy year, effectively shifts the risk associated with future claims from the insurer to the policyholder. Although the policy guarantees the availability of an endorsement to cover claims incurred but not filed during the policy year, the price of this future coverage is not fixed in advance.

The claims-made policy offered distinct advantages as a solution to the malpractice insurance crisis. It provided a way around the price controls imposed by insurance regulators, because the premium for the first-year claims-made policy is only a fraction of the premium for an occurrence policy or a mature claims-made policy. Switching to claims-made thus permitted a more gradual transition to the higher premium levels. In addition, because the insurer is less at risk with claims-made, the impaired capital and surplus positions could sustain a larger volume of business on a claims-made basis than on an occurrence basis.

But even in the long run, claims-made may be the optimal type of policy for many physicians, although it provides less real insurance. First, claims-made facilitates individual rating and may therefore reduce moral hazard. The reason is that the policyholder reveals information about his expectation of future claims from past policy years by the limits he selects for current coverage, in addition to his expectation of claims from the current year. Only the latter is revealed by the demand for occurrence coverage.[18] Second, because the insurer assumes less risk, the cost of capital and the amount of capital required as a buffer fund should be lower. Both these factors should reduce the cost of claims-made relative to occurrence coverage.[19] Third, with coverage limits set in nominal dollar terms, in times of rapid inflation of awards the occurrence policy forces the policyholder to buy too much coverage for claims closed in early years in order to have adequate coverage for claims closed in later years.

Finally, claims-made coverage creates the option of not predicting or establishing reserves for future liability arising out of current practice (liability incurred but not reported), but paying out of future income. The physician who does not establish reserves to cover the cost of future coverage faces more uncertainty as to his income net of liability costs. However, the more inelastic the demand for medical services, the greater is the share of liability insurance costs passed on to patients and health insurers, and hence the less the variability in the physician's net income. Because of the reimbursement practices of health insurers, the demand for physicians' services is likely to be more elastic in the short run than in the long run. The real cost to the physician of the risk assumed in a claims-made policy may be less than the cost of paying a stock insurer to assume the risk of estimating and reserving for future claims under an occurrence policy, when claim trends and the return on financial assets are highly uncertain. Thus, effectively, claims-made is pay-as-you-go insurance. To some extent this means that patients in later years pay for claims incurred by earlier patients. But this may be appropriate, since the cost of these claims depends in part on the legal standards adopted at the later date, when the claims are closed (see Chapter 10).

In conclusion, given the fair cost of occurrence coverage at a time of great pricing uncertainty, the claims-made policy may be preferable to physicians because it offers several advantages that offset the greater assumption of risk for future claims. From a social standpoint, there are no overwhelming allocative or distributive objections to the claims-made policy, and no public policy grounds for its disallowance by insurance regulators.

Joint underwriting associations. The residual market mechanisms differ in detail, but their common feature appears to be cost shifting. Typically, all writers of personal liability insurance, including automobile and homeowners' liability, are required to participate in the medical JUA as a condition of writing other lines in the state. Although JUA rates are intended to cover costs, in many states the enabling legislation provides that losses may be recouped by assessment on policyholders in other personal lines or written off against taxes, thereby effecting a cross-subsidy to physicians. In a minority of states, the assessment is to be on policyholders of the JUA. Most JUAs were authorized initially for a limited period. As of 1984, 13 remained in operation (Alliance, 1984), each writing a substantial fraction of the market in its state because rates have continued to be regulated at levels that are inadequate to attract voluntary carriers. As a result of this rate inadequacy, at least 6 of these JUAs (in Massachusetts, New Hampshire, New Jersey, New York, Rhode Island, and South Carolina) have incurred liabilities in excess of assets. The assessments on other insurers that would be necessary to restore the financial health of these JUAs would represent a significant subsidy to medical negligence.

Conclusions

The major cause of the huge 1974–75 premium increases was the rise in claim costs over the preceding five years and the failure of premiums to keep pace. This lag appears to be better explained by competitive pressures on rates than by lack of data on the adverse claim trends or by price controls under the Economic Stabilization Program. Financial factors also contributed to raising the fair or competitive price of insurance in 1974, in particular, the depletion of insurance capital which raised premium/capital ratios to abnormally high levels — above 4 : 1 for some leading malpractice insurers, compared to a traditional ratio of 2 : 1 or less.

The direct cause of the availability crisis was intervention by state insurance commissioners to hold rates below levels perceived as adequate and to deny the conversion to a claims-made form. The crisis was resolved in part by a switch to the mutual form of ownership and to the claims-made policy, which offer a preferred set of incentives and allocation of risk. It was also resolved in part by the subsidy implicit in residual market mechanisms.

What are the lessons for public policy? The evidence strongly suggests that regulatory control over malpractice insurance rates is neither necessary nor useful. The case for regulation presupposes a lack of competition; but as we have seen, the market over the last two decades has been characterized by far more active competition than might be anticipated, given the high level of concentration. This is largely because of the role of medical societies, who own the data on their claims experience and hence can solicit competitive bids from potential new entrants. Moreover, the ability of physicians to form mutuals and the ability of hospitals to self-insure provides an additional competitive check on commercial carriers. Thus regulation is not necessary as a substitute for competition. Where regulators have intervened to control rates, the result has been the typical response to price control: a contraction of supply.

There is no evidence that private markets will fail to provide malpractice insurance, provided rates are not controlled. JUAs remain a necessary source of supply only in states where rates continue to be regulated. Thus there is no public-policy case for a JUA on a permanent basis. At most, a JUA should be retained on a standby basis, although even the need for standby authorization is debatable if rates are not controlled. In any case, a JUA should be self-supporting. To subsidize malpractice insurance through a JUA is to subsidize medical negligence, undermining the fundamental deterrent function of the tort system.

There remains the question of policy toward the physician-owned carriers in the event of insolvency. At this point the risk is hard to estimate. Such carriers are reportedly abnormally highly leveraged after reinsurance (Steves, 1983), and over the six-year period 1976–1982 their underwriting profit (before investment income) averaged a negative 44.8 percent, compared to a negative 20.2 percent for the stock carriers.[20] Mutuals do have the ability to request a contribution to surplus, should insolvency become imminent, and some have already done so. However, if a requested contribution to surplus were to result in rates above those available from stock carriers, it remains to be seen how many of their members would defect.

The regulation of insurer solvency poses a difficult policy dilemma. The evidence shows that insolvencies can be deterred by imposing high capital requirements, but only at the cost of reducing competition (Munch and Smallwood, 1980). The reason is that high capital requirements act as a barrier to the entry of small firms, which are precisely those most likely to become insolvent. Some of the physician-owned carriers have circumvented state solvency regulations by obtaining special authorizing legislation, and avoiding regulation is certainly one factor motivating hospitals to domicile their captive companies offshore.

On balance, however, I would not favor more vigorous attempts to regulate the solvency of the mutuals. Physician policyholders have a great stake in being covered so that they will probably take whatever steps are necessary to assure the solvency of their companies. Needless to say, it is not helpful when requested rate increases are disallowed, as has occurred in New York. But if the insolvency of a mutual should become imminent, the question will arise whether to bail out its policyholders through the state guaranty fund. In such a case, the rules applicable to any insurer should apply: if, and only if, the mutual was previously an assessable member of the fund should it be eligible for a bailout.

APPENDIX A

The ISO Rate-making Process as of 1975

In essence, the ISO rate-making process derives estimates of the ultimate loss cost of the most recent policy years and of recent trends in policy year experience. These figures are then multiplied to project losses for the current policy year. Deriving these estimates involves several steps.

Loss development.   Losses incurred (losses paid and reserves on outstanding claims) on past policy years are reported at successive 12-month intervals, that is, as of 27, 39, 51 (and so on) months after the beginning of the policy year. A one-year development factor is the ratio of losses reported at successive 12-month intervals. The one-year development factors from the three most recent policy years are averaged. The ultimate development factor is then the product of these one-year development factors. Thus if all claims are closed by 10 years after the first policy is written, incurred losses on policies written in calendar year 1973, evaluated as of March 1975, must be multiplied by the product of eight one-year development factors. Development factors for frequency of claims and total losses are then applied to the most recently available reported experience for preceding policy years to obtain developed frequency and developed losses for each policy year.

Estimation of trends.   Trends in frequency and severity of claims, by policy year, are estimated by fitting an exponential curve through the developed experience for the five most recent policy years, where experience to date is developed to ultimate experience as described above. The product of the estimated trends in frequency and severity yields the estimated trend in total loss costs.

Projected loss ratio and the final premium.   A premium rate that becomes effective January 1, 1975, will cover medical practice occur-

ring in the two subsequent calendar years. Losses are therefore projected to the midpoint of this two-year period, that is, 12 months after
the rate becomes effective. For the 1975 rate increase, a weighted
average of projections based on policy years 1972 and 1973 was used,
with weights of 0.3 and 0.7 respectively. This weighted-average projected loss ratio is compared to the target loss ratio for medical malpractice (0.66). The indicated rate increase is then whatever factor is
necessary to reduce the projected loss ratio to the target ratio.

This procedure will tend to overestimate trends in claims if sociolegal changes affect calendar-year rather than policy-year claims. A
given increase in claim frequency in one calendar year then affects
all prior policy years and their development factors. The development procedure that uses the product of one-year development factors will project increases in policy-year costs of some multiple of the
true increase. Thus this methodology tends to produce cycles in projected claim costs.

APPENDIX B

Model of the Fair Insurance Premium

Let

r_e = competitive supply price of capital

r_a = rate of return on assets

t_i = tax rate on investment income

t_u = tax rate on underwriting profit

P = premium per policy

L = expected loss and expense costs per policy

K = equity capital

N = number of policies written

g = reserves/premium ratio

k = capital/premium ratio = K/PN

The "fair" insurance premium is that which yields an expected return equal to the competitive cost of capital, r_e, where

$$r_e = [r_a(1 - t_i)K + (1 - t_u)(P - L)N + r_a(1 - t_i)gPN]/K.$$

Solving for the fair premium, P:

$$P = \frac{L(1 - t_u)}{1 - t_u + r_a(1 - t_i)(g + k) - kr_e}.$$

Baseline parameter values. In order to calculate the effect of 1975 changes in specific parameters, we must select baseline values against which to measure.

Taxes. In principle, underwriting income is taxed at the standard corporate rate (46 percent in the early 1970s). Investment income is taxed at a variety of rates. Interest income and 15 percent of dividend income are taxed at the full corporate rate; 40 percent of capital gains are taxed at the corporate rate; tax-exempt bonds, which in recent years have constituted roughly 40 percent of insurance investment portfolios, bear the implicit tax rate equal to the difference between their yield and that on taxable bonds of comparable risk (in the last decade, roughly 30 percent less).

Effective tax rates tend to be lower because underwriting losses can be used to shield investment income or underwriting profits in other years. We may assume that a company will invest in taxable securities until any dividend exemption and tax shield from underwriting losses are exhausted, and then invest in tax-exempt bonds, bearing an implicit tax rate of 30 percent, since this is less than the corporate rate on taxable investment income. As upper-bound estimates I use the corporate rate for the tax rate on underwriting profits and losses $(t_u = 0.46)$, and for the tax rate on investment income I use the implicit rate on tax-exempts $(t_i = 0.3)$.

Return on assets (r_a) and equity (r_e). There is great diversity in the composition of insurance company portfolios and hence in their actual yields. As a baseline case, we may assume that the firm invests policyholder-supplied funds in minimum-risk assets, that is, government bonds with maturity matched against the expected payout structure on claims. Such a firm will have a minimum supply price of equity capital, embodying a risk premium due solely to underwriting risk. The firm that chooses a more risky investment portfolio will earn higher yields on policyholder-supplied funds on average. In competitive markets, however, the differential over the risk-free yield should accrue to shareholders, not policyholders, as a return for incurring the higher risk. I use $r_a = 0.066$, the average yield on 10-year U.S. bonds for the period 1970–1973. For the period 1969–1973, the median return on equity of the insurance industry was 11.7 percent. I use $r_e = 0.11$.

Reserves/premium (g). The amount of investable reserves per premium dollar depends on the lag between premium collection and payment of claim and other expenses. In 1974 medical malpractice loss reserves were on the books for about five years. This must be adjusted downward to allow for the facts that roughly 20 percent of the premium dollar goes to general expenses, which are paid within the first year, and that premiums are not collected immediately. I therefore assume $g = 4$.

Capital/premium (k). For the years 1970–1973, the ratio of policyholders' surplus to net premium written for stock property-casualty insurers averaged around 0.7, before falling to 0.46 in 1974. I therefore use $k = 0.7$.

7

Insurance versus Prevention: The Optimal Trade-off

MANY COMMENTATORS doubt the deterrent value of tort liability in general and medical malpractice liability in particular, because physicians are typically insured against the penalties meted out by the tort system. To quote an administrator of one of the physician-owned carriers, "Jurors incorrectly believe they are punishing the physician, when, in fact, it all lands on the shoulders of the insurance company and is, in turn, passed back to the medical community overall." (Sweetland, 1984, p. 81). Some have questioned whether insurance against liability for negligence should be disallowed as contrary to social policy, just as punitive damage awards are uninsurable in some states. Others simply accept the idea that insurance destroys deterrence, and propose reforms with the sole objective of more efficient compensation, abandoning any attempt at deterrence.[1] But in a rigorous analysis of the effect of liability insurance on incentives for prevention, Shavell concludes that "liability insurance does not have an undesirable effect on the working of liability rules . . . the terms of insurance policies sold in a competitive setting would be such as to provide an appropriate substitute (but not necessarily equivalent) set of incentives to reduce accident risks. In other words, it is not socially beneficial for the government to intervene" (1982a, p. 121).

This chapter addresses the role of liability insurance and its effect on prevention in the context of medical malpractice. The first section introduces the concepts of risk aversion and moral hazard, which create the tension between insurance and prevention. In the second section I discuss the socially optimal trade-off between insurance and prevention and the optimal form of insurance contract, to provide a benchmark against which to evaluate actual contracts, which are described in Part 3. Part 4 describes institutional factors in the health care system that may distort the insurance-prevention trade-off chosen by physicians, relative to the social optimum. In the final section I summarize the findings and discuss policy implications.

Risk Aversion, Insurance, and Moral Hazard

So far we have considered the functioning of the tort system in a world of risk neutrality: patients are indifferent or neutral to the risk of injury, and physicians are neutral toward the risk of liability, if fully compensated. The risk-neutral individual is concerned only with the expected dollar value of alternative options. Returning to the example of Chapter 1, the risk-neutral patient would be indifferent between facing a 1 in 100 chance of incurring a $5,000 loss and buying full insurance for $50, a price that is "actuarially fair" or just equal to the expected loss insured against. But the risk-neutral individual would, in theory, not buy insurance in the real world, where insurance premiums include a "load" or markup over actuarial cost to cover the overhead expenses of the insurance firm. The widespread purchase of insurance despite significant loading charges suggests that most people are risk-averse, that is, are willing to pay a premium to substitute a sure income prospect for a risky one with equal expected value. In the previous example, the risk-averse patient might be willing to pay $60 for an insurance policy even though the expected loss is only $50. Thus a liability rule that imposes risk on risk-averse physicians creates a real social cost. Allowing liability insurance against this risk creates a positive entry in the social ledger.

On the other hand, since injuries are costly to patients, liability insurance may create a negative entry in the social ledger if it undermines incentives for injury prevention. Ideally, insurance should protect individuals from losses beyond their control.[2] In reality, people insure against losses that are partially within their control. For example, the probability of an automobile accident depends partly on weather conditions and mechanical failures, but partly on whether the insured himself pays attention. The probability of a malpractice claim depends partly on unpredictable effects of treatment and on whims of patients and courts, but also on the care of the physician. Thus the individual may view insurance and prevention as alternative means of protecting himself against loss.[3]

This tendency for insurance to reduce incentives for loss prevention is called moral hazard. Visiting the physician more frequently if one has health insurance, not locking a door if one has theft insurance, not installing a smoke detector — or even committing arson — if one has fire insurance are all examples of moral hazard. Although some may make value judgments about such behavior, the term is used here simply to refer to a rational response to incentives to treat insurance as a substitute for prevention; it carries no ethical connotations.

Since liability insurance is desirable in that it protects physicians from risk, but may be undesirable if it reduces incentives for prevention, the question arises: How much insurance is optimal, from the standpoint of economic efficiency? Will the invisible hand of competition guide private insurance markets to offer and physicians to choose insurance contracts that are socially optimal? The next section first defines the optimal levels of insurance and prevention, when both are available, and then considers how insurance contracts should be designed to achieve this optimal mix.

Optimal Insurance Contracts with Moral Hazard

Once we recognize risk aversion and the possibility of compensating some but not necessarily all losses through insurance, the objective of efficient social policy toward injuries can be stated as the minimization of the sum of four types of costs (Calabresi, 1970):

Minimize utility value of:

    insured losses (compensation)
  + uninsured losses
  + prevention costs
  + overhead (costs of litigation, insurance overhead)

I shall assume that the policy tools available include the liability rule (standard of care and the structure of damage awards) and the level of liability insurance coverage. I shall also assume that the liability rule and structure of awards are optimally set and focus on how liability insurance affects the incentives for prevention and hence the costs of injuries and the burden of uninsured risk.

The socially optimal level of prevention is that which, at the margin, balances the (utility) value of the reduction in injury costs (compensated + uncompensated losses + overhead) against the (utility) cost of loss prevention. If all losses can be fully insured at actuarial cost, the problem reduces to the familiar one of minimizing the dollar value of injury plus prevention costs. But when compensation through insurance uses real resources, because of litigation or claim adjustment expense, or when there are uninsurable losses, such as pain and suffering, the optimal level of care is higher and the optimal number of injuries lower than if all losses could be insured and compensated at actuarial cost.

In practice, of course, the level of care is not dictated but is chosen by medical providers on the basis of their training, preferences, incentives, and constraints, including those created by the rule of liability and the terms of the providers' liability insurance coverage. The socially optimal insurance policy is defined by weighing the benefits of additional coverage — reduction in uninsured risk to patients and providers — against the increased injury costs if insurance induces moral hazard and departure from the optimal level of prevention.

Insurance creates moral hazard when the insured bears the full cost of any preventive measures he takes but does not realize the full benefits of lower expected loss. Consider a homeowner deciding whether to install a lock on his front door. If the odds of a theft of goods worth $1,000 are 1 in 100 without a lock but only 1 in 1,000 with a lock, then the expected benefit of installing a lock is the reduction in probability times the size of the loss,[4] or $9. Thus if the lock costs less than $9, it is worth installing, and the rational individual has every incentive to do so if he is not insured. If he is fully insured, however, and if his premium is essentially unaffected by his own precautions, he has no incentive to install the lock. He bears the full cost of the lock, but the benefits, in terms of reduction in thefts, are captured by his insurer initially or are passed on to all policyholders, in the form of lower premiums. Similarly, the patient who visits the doctor more frequently because he is insured is responding to incentives to "free ride" at the expense of other policyholders in his insurance plan: he captures the full benefits of the additional visit but bears only a fraction of the costs, if his premium is group-rated or community-rated. And likewise, the insured physician is more likely to cut corners when taking a history, or to take on a case that he is not really qualified to treat, if his insurance will cover any mishaps.

Of course, policyholders as a group ultimately bear the full cost of moral hazard, since insurance premiums must rise to cover the added costs. Each policyholder individually has a reduced incentive to take care, but policyholders overall would face lower total costs of insurance plus prevention if the insurance policy preserved individual incentives to take cost-effective precautions. The added prevention costs would be more than offset by the premium reduction made possible by the reduction in losses. In other words, policyholders are better off if insurance contracts restrain moral hazard.

Moral hazard is eliminated if each insured realizes the benefits of his own care in the form of a premium reduction commensurate with the lower risk of loss. An insurance premium that adjusts to reflect the expected loss implicit in the insured's level of care is said to be perfectly experience-rated. Perfect experience rating does not mean that the insurer raises the premium after each loss to recoup the loss; that would be tantamount to no insurance. Perfect experience rating requires that the premium be adjusted to reflect the expected future losses. In the previous example, the homeowner's insurance premium with perfect experience rating would be $10 without a lock, $1 with a lock. Because the change in premium internalizes to the insured the reduction in expected losses, his incentives to install the lock are identical with and without insurance: it is worthwhile if the lock costs less than $9.

Perfect experience rating eliminates moral hazard: precautions that are cost-effective without insurance are cost-effective with insurance. Insurance still provides protection when a loss occurs, but incentives to invest optimally in loss reduction are preserved.[5]

OPTIMAL FIRST-PARTY COVERAGE
The characteristics of optimal insurance coverage have been extensively analyzed in the first-party context, such as health or fire insurance, where the policyholder insures against losses to himself (Mossin, 1968; Arrow, 1970; Zeckhauser, 1970; Ehrlich and Becker, 1972). If insurance could be costlessly administered (zero load) and perfectly experience-rated, and if losses were purely monetary, the optimal policy would provide full coverage. Full insurance coverage eliminates all risk, and with perfect experience rating, incentives for prevention are preserved. When the insurance premium includes an expense load, the optimal policy provides full coverage above a deductible (Mossin, 1968).[6]

In practice, perfect experience rating is not feasible: an insurer cannot costlessly monitor each policyholder's activities and adjust the premium to reflect the implied risk of loss. Some relevant information is available and is routinely used. Fire underwriters inspect premises and give discounts for installation of sprinklers; health and life insurers may relate premiums to health-related habits and characteristics, such as smoking, exercise, blood pressure, and weight; automobile insurers give no-claim bonuses; malpractice insurers inquire about the physician's specialty, practice, and prior claim history. But constantly updating information and premiums is prohibitively costly.

When perfect experience rating is infeasible, it becomes cost-effective to limit coverage in order to deter moral hazard. The optimal policy includes a copayment or retention by the policyholder — an upper limit on coverage, a deductible, a coinsurance percentage, or a premium that depends on past loss experience — thereby preserving his financial stake in prevention. The form of the copayment varies, depending on how the insured can influence the loss. If his care affects the probability but not the size of the loss, then the optimal policy includes a deductible but provides full coverage of losses in excess of the deductible. On the other hand, if the insured can affect the size of the loss, then the optimal policy will provide either an upper limit of coverage (indemnity insurance) or a coinsurance rate (the insured bears some fraction of all losses).

These principles derived from economic theory are borne out in practice by standard health insurance contracts. The loss in this case is the insured's expenditure on health care, which is partially within his control, partially in the hands of his physician and of fate. Three risk-sharing features are common. Most policies include a deductible, to deter the filing of small claims, and a coinsurance percentage, to preserve incentives to limit total expenditure. The coinsurance percentage is typically larger for elective services, such as outpatient psychiatric care, than for services such as emergency surgery, which are less within the control of the insured and thus less prone to moral hazard. A maximum reimbursable fee for each procedure of medical condition and a limit on total expenditure in any year further constrain moral hazard by the policyholder and limit risk to the insurer.

Incomplete coverage preserves some, albeit diluted, incentives for prevention. In the previous example, if the homeowner has a 50 percent coinsurance rate on his policy, he pays half of any losses and thus retains half of any reduction in expected loss. It would pay him to install a lock if it cost less than $4.50 — his share of the expected loss reduction of $9.00 — although from a social standpoint it is cost-effective to install a lock if it costs less than $9.00. Thus copayment reduces but does not fully eliminate moral hazard. Some cost-effective prevention measures are not taken, and since coverage is incomplete, there also remains some uninsured loss. But some sacrifice of both risk spreading and loss reduction is a second-best optimum in the real world, where perfect experience rating is prohibitively costly.

Since a trade-off between risk spreading and prevention is inevitable, the question is where to draw the line. This depends on the risk aversion of those exposed to loss and on the feasibility of loss reduction. Optimal coverage is higher, the more risk-averse the insured, hence the greater the disutility of an uninsured loss. Optimal coverage approaches complete coverage if the cost of prevention is either very high or very low (Shavell, 1979). The reason is that if the cost of prevention is very high (the risk is largely beyond the control of the insured), then a reduction in coverage buys very little in terms of loss reduction in return for the increased exposure to risk. If the cost of prevention is very low, then a small departure from complete coverage suffices to eliminate moral hazard, so again a high level of coverage is optimal.

In the first-party context, policyholders are insuring against losses to themselves. Assuming that no one else is affected, insurance contracts that provide policyholders higher levels of utility and hence higher profits to insurance carriers are also socially optimal. Competition in insurance markets will thus tend to lead to the evolution of socially optimal contracts, and there is no case for government intervention.[7]

OPTIMAL LIABILITY COVERAGE

If the malpractice system operated in practice according to the stylized model outlined in Chapter 1, there would be no liability insurance because it would be cheaper to prevent than to insure those injuries that would be judged negligent. The insurance premium must cover all losses for which the physician is liable. But under the Hand negligence standard, the courts find liability only when the damages exceed the costs of prevention. Therefore it would be cheaper for the physician to be nonnegligent and hence avoid all liability than to be negligent and insure against the resulting liability.

The conclusion, that there is no demand for liability insurance under a negligence standard, presupposes that courts enforce an efficient due-care standard with perfect accuracy, and that this is known to physicians and patients. The demand for insurance can arise either out of errors of commission or omission by claimants or courts, or out of damage awards that are too low. If courts set the standard too high, holding physicians liable for some injuries where the cost of prevention exceeds the expected benefits (type 2 errors or invalid claims), it is cheaper for the physician to insure than to prevent these injuries, and this is socially optimal. But if victims sometimes fail to file or courts to find liability in all true instances of negligence (type 1 errors), or if liability payments are too low, then it is cheaper for the physician to insure than to avoid some instances of negligence, and this is not socially optimal. Thus the valid demand for liability insurance under a negligence rule is for insurance against the risk that is beyond the physician's control — errors by victims or by courts.[8] In particular, if the courts set the standard too high relative to the efficient standard, it is cheaper for physicians to insure against losses than to try to prevent them. The standard may be correct on average, with random errors, or it may be systematically too high for some or all physicians. For example, if a common standard is set for all physicians, it will be systematically too high for physicians of below-average skill or training, who face above-average prevention costs, and for physicians who treat patients of above-average risk. These physicians will prefer above-average levels of coverage.

If the insurer had costless information that would enable him to distinguish between true incidents of negligence and erroneous imputations by the courts, then matters would be simple: the optimal liability insurance contract would cover the physician fully against all invalid claims but provide no protection against valid claims. This would provide full insurance while preserving optimal deterrence. But obviously, if the information needed to write this optimal policy were publicly available, there would be no need for the courts to adjudicate negligence.

Casual evidence suggests that type 1 errors dominate the demand for insurance. In medical and other lines of professional liability, the courts defer to the customary practice of the professional "in good standing" as the standard of due care, rather than applying the Hand cost-benefit calculus in each case. This creates a bulwark against type 2 errors for above-average physicians, but a presumption of type 2 errors and consequent incentive to insure for those of below-average competence. Thus if type 2 errors predominated, we might expect that a substantial fraction of physicians would not buy insurance, which is not the case. On the other hand, if the estimates presented in Chapter 2 are correct, that at most 1 in 10 incidents of negligence give rise to a claim and of these fewer than 50 percent are compensated, this implies that type 1 errors are very common. This type of error gives all physicians an incentive to buy insurance and to be negligent some of the time.

The practical issue is, therefore, What are the characteristics of the optimal liability policy when the insurer cannot costlessly monitor the physician's care ex ante or discriminate valid from invalid claims ex post? Because the terms of malpractice coverage affect patients as well as physicians, the physician's private optimum may differ from the social optimum. Let us first consider the physician's private optimum.

Damage coverage. Assume initially that courts adjudicate all claims costlessly, but with some error. The only expense incurred by a liability defendant is the damage payment to a successful plaintiff. Many of the results that are familiar from first-party insurance contracts apply. Some copayment is optimal, both on account of the load and to control moral hazard. Assuming that physicians can affect the probability and size of loss, copayment should include a deductible and coinsurance. Because court and claimant error is the risk being insured against, and the optimal policy with perfect information would provide full coverage of invalid claims but zero coverage of valid claims, it may be optimal for the insurer to utilize additional information and relate copayment to the probable validity of the claim. In particular, if courts are better informed than claimants, such that valid claims have a higher probability of winning, then copayment should be higher on claims the plaintiff wins than on claims the plaintiff loses. But if court error is significant, it may pay for the insurer to invest in further information and levy a surcharge or fine incorporating this additional information, rather than having a simple deductible or coinsurance rate on all paid claims.

The optimal level of coverage is higher, the higher the ratio of invalid to valid claims and the higher the cost to the insurer of drawing this distinction ex post. This is because the higher the relative frequency of invalid claims, the smaller is the loss reduction bought by an increase in exposure.[9] Thus if patients and courts are totally unable to distinguish between valid and invalid claims, optimal coverage is highest for those specialties where the normal risk of adverse outcome, given nonnegligent care, is relatively high — plausibly, surgical specialties. But note that if court decisions are sufficiently random to make full coverage the optimal policy, then the negligence rule of liability has no individual deterrent value, and we may well question whether it is worth retaining.

These conclusions are derived from the principles of first-party insurance, where the policyholder insures against loss to himself and thus the policy that maximizes his utility is also socially optimal. This presumption may not apply to liability coverages, where the policyholder insures against claims for compensation by injured third parties. If tort awards do not fully compensate victims, liability costs would not convey the full social cost of injuries to physicians. Physicians would tend to overinsure and practice with insufficient care, from a social standpoint. However, private choices of liability insurance will also be socially optimal provided the structure of tort awards is optimally designed, to convey to defendants the victim's interest in prevention (see Chapter 9). Given such an optimal structure of tort awards, there is no case for government intervention, despite the patient's interest in prevention and the problem of moral hazard. Competitive liability insurance markets will tend to devise insurance contracts that are preferred by physicians, given their liability exposure which, by assumption, reflects the patient's interest in prevention. As we have seen, we can expect the preferred policies to protect the physician against invalid claims but to penalize him for valid claims. Such policies are also socially optimal because, by the definition of the efficient due-care standard, invalid claims are for injuries not worth preventing.

Legal defense insurance. The analysis thus far has ignored the fact that the outcome of a claim, once filed, can be greatly influenced by the legal efforts of plaintiff and defendant in court and in out-of-court settlement. The need to provide for legal defense alters the optimal liability insurance contract considered so far. For several reasons, it is efficient to provide legal defense insurance together with damage insurance. This prevents duplicative monitoring of the physician's care, which would be necessary if damages and legal defense insurance were provided in separate policies, and eliminates the need for the damage insurer to monitor the legal defense insurer.

This solution, of combining legal defense and damage coverage in a single liability insurance policy, exposes the physician to moral hazard with respect to the insurer's legal defense effort, unless the insurer bears the full loss. But this would require that the physician have full coverage, which would undermine his incentives for injury prevention. Further, if the physician's copayment on damage coverage is to be related to valid claims only, which I have argued is optimal, physicians must monitor the drawing of the distinction between valid and invalid claims. In the absence of such monitoring, the insurer's incentive is to declare all claims valid and hence subject to copayment. Thus, where both the insurer and the physician can affect the probability or size of loss—the insurer through legal defense, the physician through injury prevention and sometimes his cooperation in legal defense—no simple copayment structure can simultaneously provide both parties with correct marginal incentives.

Because of the need to preserve the insurer's incentive to defend claims, the optimal level of copayment by the policyholder is lower on a liability policy than on first-party coverage with comparable policyholder moral hazard.[10] For example, a deductible undermines the insurer's incentive to fight claims that can be settled for less than the deductible. In the case of medical malpractice claims closed in the period 1975–1978, defense expenditure on the 51 percent of claims that closed without payment averaged $3,075, and for the 64 percent of claims that closed for under $3,000, legal expense exceeded damages paid (NAIC, 1980). This may minimize total insurance losses by deterring other potential claims. An insurance contract with a deductible might increase physicians' incentives for care, but it would also reduce the insurer's incentive to fight small claims. Thus with a deductible, the number of small claims filed and closed with payment might rise sufficiently to offset any saving in injury prevention.

Note that the legal defense insurance contract that maximized the physician's utility would also be socially optimal provided patients were aware of the terms of the physician's coverage and its effect on their likely recovery, in the event of a claim. In this case market forces would internalize to physicians all consequences of their choice of liability coverage. For example, if the physician chose a policy with no deductible, to encourage legal defense against small claims, the patient would perceive that as an individual claimant, he might be worse off as a result of legal defense effort that reduced his expected award. He could trade off this reduction in expected compensation, if he were injured, against the gain from the lower cost of liability insurance to physicians, and hence the lower costs of health care. However, to the extent that such prescience on the part of patients is implausible, there is no presumption that the type of legal defense coverage chosen by physicians will be socially optimal. Moreover, once we recognize that litigation expenditures affect court outcomes and have precedent value affecting other cases, unconditional conclusions about the social efficiency of liability rules and insurance arrangements are approximate at best.[11]

Evidence on Malpractice Insurance Contracts

Evidence from malpractice insurance markets is only partially consistent with what we might expect, based on the theoretical discussion so far. Two features distinguish medical malpractice markets from many other lines of insurance. The first is the active role of physicians on the supply side of the market, both in the sponsored programs written by stock carriers and in the mutuals. Physician participation in claim handling is consistent with the need for policyholder monitoring of the insurer's legal defense effort. Thus there is plausibility in the claim often made by mutuals that they have greater in-house expertise in distinguishing invalid claims, and are willing to take a harder line in defending them. This may indeed be one factor contributing to the mutuals' growth in market share.

The second striking feature of medical malpractice insurance is the rare use of explicit copayment. Deductibles and coinsurance are not used. In cases where companies do impose a surcharge for multiple claims, the structure of these merit-rated programs is consistent with the argument advanced earlier that the risk being insured against is that of invalid claims, so that insurers would attempt to distinguish valid from invalid claims. For example, one mutual company levies a surcharge of $2,500 per claim for more than one claim *paid* over $10,000 (or considered indefensible) in a three-year period. Another mutual imposes a two-year surcharge of 10 percent of premium for one "transgression," 20 percent of premium for two transgressions, and would probably terminate the policyholder after more than two. A transgression is defined by physicians on the board, on the basis of a review of claims and characteristics of the policyholder's practice. One company abandoned an attempt to introduce merit rating based on *all* claims, rather than paid claims only, because of opposition from physicians. A subjective review process is also used in screening applicants, rather than a mechanical rule based on claim history.[12]

A review of the rating structure tends to understate the degree of risk retention by physicians for several reasons. First, to the extent that some companies use claim history as a basis for screening applicants and are able to offer lower rates, a financial incentive to prevent claims is preserved. Second, and probably far more important, there is an implicit deductible in the uninsured costs a physician incurs if he is sued. The costs of time, worry, embarrassment, and loss of reputation are hard to quantify, but the fact that professional liability policies typically preserve the insured's right to refuse to settle indicates some degree of exposure.[13] A rough measure of these costs may be obtained from amounts awarded in countersuits by physicians against unsuccessful claimants for malicious prosecution. As of 1981, compensatory awards ranged from $2,000 to $35,000 (Taub, 1981) — a nontrivial implicit deductible.[14]

Nevertheless, the typical medical malpractice insurance policy seems to provide more complete coverage and less incentive for loss prevention than does the typical liability policy in other contexts. Deductibles are common in professional liability policies of attorneys, architects and engineers, corporate officers and directors, and accountants; in product liability policies (U.S. House of Representatives, 1979a); and in workers' compensation. Merit rating or experience rating on the basis of prior claims are also common in automobile liability and workers' compensation insurance.

Institutional Factors Affecting the Demand for Insurance

It has been shown that insurance interferes with the deterrent function of the tort system unless premiums are experience-rated or physicians retain a stake in the loss. The empirical evidence suggests that neither of these conditions are met in malpractice insurance: individual merit rating and other forms of risk retention such as deductibles, coinsurance, or surcharges are rare. This section examines several institutional factors that may help to explain the apparent lack of demand for risk retention in medical malpractice insurance.

Are claims random? It was argued earlier that the optimal liability policy with perfect information would penalize the physician for valid claims arising out of true incidents of negligence but not for invalid claims reflecting court error. It is commonly argued that merit rating of malpractice premiums would be either infeasible or unfair since claims are random, either because physician negligence is random or because courts are random in their determination of liability.

The limited evidence available does not support this thesis. In a study of claims against 8,000 physicians in California over a four-year period, 46 physicians (0.6 percent) accounted for 10 percent of all claims and 30 percent of all payments. This is inconsistent with a purely random distribution of claims and awards (Rolph, 1979). On the contrary, statistical analysis of these data indicates that for purposes of predicting a physician's claims rate, four years of data on his past claim experience provide as much information as knowing his specialty. Similar conclusions emerge from data on the claim experience of the Maryland insurance program (Rolph, 1979). These data suggest that, at least in the group programs, more merit rating is feasible than in fact occurs, and one must look to other factors to explain why this potential is not exploited.

High-risk patients. Another common argument is that some physicians are sued more often, not because they are negligent more often but because they treat difficult cases or high-risk patients. Penalizing these physicians by surcharging their policies is said to be inequitable and inefficient, in that it would make all physicians unwilling to treat high-risk patients. This argument implicitly presupposes that courts do not adequately recognize differences among patients and consistently set standards too high for patients with above-average risk of an adverse outcome.

Even if differences in patient mix rather than differences in quality of care account for the above-average claim experience of some physicians, this alone cannot explain the lack of merit rating. Competitive pressures should lead insurers to offer policies that reflect measurable differences in claim costs, regardless of their cause. Physicians would accept such policies and be willing to treat high-risk patients if they could charge higher fees to cover the additional malpractice exposure. Such a solution is potentially efficient; it is also equitable in the sense that patients who have a higher likelihood of compensation would pay for it in the form of higher fees for medical services.

This hypothetical solution to the problem of high-risk patients may not be feasible in practice, however, if the characteristics that make a patient high-risk cannot be readily verified. Although the physician may correctly identify patients who pose an above-average malpractice risk, unless he can convince the patient and the third-party payer, he cannot be reimbursed for assuming this risk.[15] If malpractice premiums were merit-rated but medical fees could not be raised for high-risk patients, then physicians would be unwilling to treat them. Consequently, if physicians feel an obligation to treat such patients, they might resist merit rating while accepting rating on the basis of procedures which pose an objectively verifiable higher risk of claim and which thus can be compensated by higher fees. The fact that surcharges for specific procedures, such as x-ray or shock therapy, are more common than surcharges for adverse claim experience is consistent with this hypothesis.

Thus in theory, systematic differences in patient risk, due to characteristics that are difficult to document and hence to be reimbursed for, could reduce the demand for automatic merit rating of premiums. This would explain why physicians as a group prefer to have underwriting and individual rating decisions made by their peers, who are more able to distinguish true negligence from judicial error, and it may be a factor that distinguishes the medical profession from other professions. But just how important this factor is empirically cannot be determined without data on the claim histories and practice characteristics of individual physicians.

Passing on costs. The analysis so far has assumed that the physician bears all costs of the insurance premium, the uninsured loss (retention), and prevention. In fact, physicians bear only a small fraction of the costs of malpractice insurance and prevention. Insurance premiums are tax-deductible, as are expenses of legal defense, damage payments, and other out-of-pocket costs if the physician is not insured. Thus if a physician is in a 50 percent tax bracket, 50 percent of malpractice insurance costs are passed on to taxpayers. Of the remaining 50 percent, some fraction is passed on to patients in the form of higher fees for medical services.

The ability of physicians to pass on premium and prevention costs is greatly influenced by the extent to which medical services are covered by health insurance and by the reimbursement practices of health insurers. Currently, 88 percent of hospital care and 63 percent of ambulatory care (primary physician services) are covered by some form of private or public insurance. Because health insurance premiums are largely tax-exempt, whereas a patient's out-of-pocket medical costs are not (unless they exceed 5 percent of income), medical costs that are covered by health insurance appear to be subsidized to the individual patient and physician.

The reimbursement practices of health insurers create incentives that tend to distort the physician's choice of prevention and insurance in two ways. First, malpractice premium costs can be passed on in reimbursable fees more readily than can out-of-pocket (retention) liability costs. Typically, medical care is billed on a fee-for-service basis. Health insurers set an upper limit on the "maximum allowable charge" per procedure, and pay the lesser of the physician's actual fee or the maximum allowable charge, minus the patient's coinsurance percentage. Malpractice insurance costs are more readily incorporated in the maximum allowable charge than are out-of-pocket retention costs. Maximum charges for Medicare patients explicitly allow for the pass-through of average malpractice insurance premium costs, but not an individual physician's out-of-pocket costs.[16] Private insurers typically set the maximum allowable charge for each physician by reference to charges of other physicians in the locality. Thus liability premium costs that are common to all physicians can be passed through, whereas costs specific to a few individual physicians, such as a deductible or premium surcharge, cannot.[17]

Second, the fee-for-service reimbursement system tends to raise the relative cost of physicians' time as an input in care (Danzon, 1982). Whereas additional procedures, such as laboratory tests and x-rays, can be reimbursed in full, the cost of additional physician time, beyond that implicitly covered by the allowable charge, is borne by the patient or the physician. Although insurers' fee schedules recognize different categories for some procedures, depending on the complexity of the case, this flexibility is far from perfect; fees for many procedures are fixed, regardless of time spent. Under some health insurance programs, the physician may bill the patient for more than the insurer's allowable charge, in which case the patient bears the cost of the additional time. Under programs with assignment, the physician cannot bill the patient in excess of the insurer's allowable charge, so the physician bears the cost of any additional time. Thus the fee-for-service system permits more complete insurance coverage of additional tests than of additional time. This effectively subsidizes tests, relative to the physician's time, and, to the extent that time and tests are substitute inputs in injury prevention, it raises the cost of prevention relative to insurance.

I have analyzed elsewhere the effect of cost shifting on the physician's choice of insurance, uninsured retention, and prevention (Danzon, 1983b); the results are summarized here. The analysis assumes that the physician is risk-averse and maximizes his utility. It is not intended to imply that physicians are motivated solely by utility maximization; norms of practice and concern for the patient surely play a role. The purpose of the simplified model is merely to show how reimbursement and tax rules may distort the physician's trade-off between insurance and care, and create incentives to adopt inefficient methods of prevention.

The results of the formal analysis confirm what intuition might lead one to expect.

1. If all costs are passed through at a uniform rate, the choice of insurance and prevention is undistorted if insurance is actuarial and losses are fully compensated. When insurance contains a load, the insurance/prevention mix is affected, but the direction is ambiguous a priori.

2. If the physician can pass on insurance costs more readily than retention costs, he will buy more insurance coverage than if there were no pass-through. He will opt for complete coverage even if premiums contain a load, if his share of any uninsured costs exceeds his share of premium costs times the load.

3. If the physician bears a higher fraction of the cost of his own time than of other prevention inputs such as tests, he will substitute tests for time, where possible. This "tax" on the physician's own time may explain the common perception that the malpractice system tends to encourage high insurance premiums and excessive tests — defensive medicine — rather than deterrence of negligence.

4. Full coverage, in the absence of experience rating, will reduce prevention.

Professional politics. We have seen that physicians play an unusually important role in the malpractice insurance market, through mutuals and group programs sponsored by medical societies. Collective influence may contribute in two ways to potentially inefficient levels of coverage and lack of retention. First, if average premium costs can be passed on as higher allowable charges but out-of-pocket malpractice expenses cannot be, physicians as a group have an incentive to opt collusively for less copayment than they would do individually. Second, if high-risk individuals dominate in physician-sponsored programs or companies, the policies offered may reflect the preferences of a relatively high-risk group within the profession, who prefer a policy with more complete coverage and less individual rating than would the majority of physicians.

The earlier discussion of the optimal policy implies that surgeons would prefer a higher level of coverage than nonsurgeons, if surgeons are at higher risk of invalid claims because surgery entails a higher rate of obvious iatrogenic injury. And there is some evidence that physician-dominated insurance programs favor surgeons. The 1974–76 evidence (Danzon, 1980a) that sponsored programs compressed specialty differentials is suggestive of a cross-subsidy to surgical specialties. One mutual explicitly subsidizes the highest-risk specialties.[18]

But the extent to which physician-dominated companies or programs can effect a subsidy from low-risk to high-risk physicians is limited by the availability of alternative sources of coverage for the low risks. Firms writing in the individual market may not be effective competition to group programs because individual writers face higher marketing costs, higher costs of accurate actuarial information and of meeting regulatory requirements, and risk of adverse selection. The declining share of the market written as individual policies confirms their comparative disadvantage. But in the absence of barriers to entry by mutuals catering to low risks, one must infer that the typical policies with complete coverage and little individual rating are preferred by the majority of physicians.

On the other hand, the active involvement of medical societies may contribute to efficiency in several ways. First, recall that the ideal liability policy would provide complete insurance against court or claimant error but no insurance against true negligence. There are two ways of distinguishing valid from invalid claims: the first would apply probabilistic inference to the individual's claim record, relative to the norm for the group; the second method would simply use direct review of the evidence by experts. Peer review of claims may be more cost-effective in medical malpractice than in most other lines of insurance, including other professional liability lines, because of the technical nature of the issues. In particular, systematic error may be more likely if optimal practice varies considerably depending on the unique conditions of each individual patient, but the lay jury lacks the expertise to draw such distinctions and therefore applies the average customary standard in all cases. The need for technical expertise, combined with the heterogeneity that makes the standard of custom inaccurate in many cases, will tend to make rating on the basis of peer evaluation preferable to rating on the basis of number of claims. Rating based on peer review is also socially beneficial provided those making the reviews are constrained in their ability to effect cross-subsidies.

Second, the medical society acts on behalf of physicians as monitor of the insurer's legal defense effort. This is necessary because, to the extent that the physician bears some financial loss, or uninsured time and embarrassment costs, the insurer's incentives to defend claims are suboptimal from the standpoint of policyholders. Third, the insurer would have every incentive to designate all claims as negligence rather than as court error if the policyholder is penalized more heavily for negligent claims. Policyholders must therefore monitor the drawing of this distinction, and the medical society performs this role.

Conclusions

If the negligence system operated in practice as it should in theory, insurance would not interfere with deterrence because there would be no demand for insurance. In practice, imperfect information leads to type 1 errors (failure to find liability) and type 2 errors (invalid claims) in applying the negligence standard, and hence to a demand for liability insurance. Because insurers, like courts, lack the information to distinguish valid from invalid claims, liability insurance cannot be perfectly experience-rated. Copayment, which is the standard solution to the resulting moral hazard problem in first-party coverage, tends to encourage moral hazard on the part of the legal defense insurer. Thus in liability insurance, copayment induces a trade-off between loss reduction by injury prevention and by legal defense.

Typical malpractice insurance policies provide virtually complete coverage of monetary losses. This may be optimal for the average policyholder because of the uninsured time and reputation costs of suit, the need to control moral hazard on the part of the legal defense insurer, and the effective subsidy to liability insurance that results from health insurance reimbursement policies. But in the case of liability insurance against losses to third parties, the policy that maximizes policyholder utility may not be socially optimal. Whether actual levels of insurance and prevention are too high or too low, from a social perspective, cannot be determined a priori because there are several possibly offsetting factors to consider. The lack of experience rating of premiums and the high levels of coverage tend to discourage prevention. On the other hand, physicians' ability to pass on prevention costs tends to encourage excessive prevention, at least for preventive services such as laboratory tests, whose cost can be shifted.

The case for limiting the intervention of the medical profession on the supply side of the insurance market is weak. It is possible that this intervention distorts the choice of policy toward one with less risk retention — and hence less incentive for prevention — than might be socially optimal or preferred by the average physician, but the evidence is ambiguous. On the other hand, physician input performs a useful function in screening applicants, discriminating between valid and invalid claims, and monitoring the insurer's defense effort on behalf of policyholders. The more insurer moral hazard can be controlled by monitoring, the more policyholder moral hazard can be controlled by copayment. This may be one reason why mutuals use surcharges more frequently than do stock companies.

An unambiguously useful reform would be one that improved the accuracy of court decisions by means other than expenditure by the litigants. In that case, the system would work in practice as it should in theory, and there would be no demand for liability insurance. It is easier to point to the need for such a reform, however, than to devise it. But since regulatory bodies have no superior information that would ensure a more accurate adjudication of claims or merit rating of insurance than do the parties directly involved, there is no strong case for government intervention, despite the lack of any strong presumption that private arrangements will be socially optimal.

III

REFORMS AND ALTERNATIVES

THE PREVIOUS CHAPTERS have described how the malpractice system should operate in principle and provided some evidence of its operation in practice. In the following chapters I discuss reforms that could make the existing system more cost-effective, as well as more radical alternatives to the present system. Chapter 8 evaluates the practice of judging physicians by the standards set by their own profession. I argue for modifying the standard of custom to allow cost as a legitimate reason for departure from the customary norms of fee-for-service practice. For related reasons, I contend that many of the distortions in medical care that are often called defensive medicine are more likely a result of patients' extensive health insurance coverage. In Chapter 9, I discuss the issue of damages, arguing that the tort norm of full compensation is not optimal from the standpoint of either compensation or deterrence. I then evaluate specific reforms, including caps on awards, scheduled benefits, collateral source offset, and periodic payment of future benefits. In Chapter 10, I advocate a short statute of limitations. Chapter 11 addresses the problem of litigation costs and evaluates the effects of policies such as limits on contingent fees charged by plaintiff attorneys and the use of screening panels and binding arbitration. In Chapter 12, I discuss more radical alternatives to the current negligence-based system, in particular, private contracting over liability and mandatory no-fault compensation, either for all iatrogenic injury or for a subset of designated compensable events. The final chapter reviews the arguments made throughout the book and summarizes the findings and conclusions.

8

The Standard of Care

I ARGUED in Chapter 1 that the economic rationale for imposing a negligence rule of liability is to correct distortions in physicians' incentives that arise from imperfect information. Optimal incentives would in principle be provided if negligence were defined as laid down by Judge Learned Hand in *U.S. v. Carroll Towing*: a defendant is negligent if the loss caused by the accident, multiplied by the probability of the accident's occurring, exceeds the cost of preventing the accident.[1] In most cases of personal liability, the courts dispense with a case-by-case cost-benefit calculus and use the looser but conceptually similar "reasonable and prudent man" standard.

To define the standard of care owed by professionals, however, the courts defer to the customary practice of members of the profession in good standing. The rule elaborated by the New York Supreme Court in *Pike v. Honsinger* (1898) remains largely applicable today (except for the reference to locality):

> A physician or surgeon, by taking charge of a case, impliedly represents that he possesses, and the law places on him the duty of possessing, that reasonable degree of learning and skill that is ordinarily possessed by physicians and surgeons in the locality in which he practices . . . Upon consenting to treat a patient, it becomes his duty to use reasonable care and diligence in the exercise of his skill and the application of his learning to accomplish the purpose for which he was employed. He is under the further obligation to use his best judgment in exercising his skill and applying his knowledge. The law holds him liable for an

injury to his patient resulting from want of the requisite skill and knowledge or the omission to exercise reasonable care or the failure to use his best judgment. The rule in relation to learning and skill does not require the surgeon to possess that extraordinary learning and skill that belong only to a few men of rare endowments, but such as is possessed by the average member of the profession in good standing . . . The rule of reasonable care and diligence does not require the use of the highest possible degree of care and to render a physician or surgeon liable, it is not enough that there has been a less degree of care than some other medical man might have shown or less than even he himself might have bestowed, but there must be a want of ordinary and reasonable care, leading to a bad result (*New York Reports,* 155, p. 201).

The use of custom to define the standard of care has been justified by the inability of laymen to evaluate the technical judgments of specialists: "Courts have recognized the fact that laymen lack the capacity to adequately evaluate a physician's conduct or to adequately determine what a reasonable and prudent man under the same circumstances with specialized training and knowledge would have done" (Meltzer, 1975, p. 308). By contrast, in other areas of negligence law, compliance with customary practice is not an acceptable defense. In Judge Learned Hand's famous dictum in *The T. J. Hooper,* a calling "never may set its own tests, however persuasive be its usages. Courts must in the end say what is required; there are precautions so imperative that even their universal disregard will not excuse their omission."[2]

Of the rare exceptions to reliance on the standard of custom, one of the best known is the 1974 case of *Helling v. Carey.*[3] The plaintiff, a 32-year-old woman, suffered permanent eye damage from angle glaucoma. The defendant, an ophthalmologist, had treated her during the ten years prior to the diagnosis of the glaucoma. During that time he did not administer a pressure test for glaucoma, it being customary practice not to administer such tests to persons under age 40 in the absence of specific reasons because of the low incidence of glaucoma (about one case in 25,000 persons) in that age group. The lower courts found for the defendant, on the ground that his conduct conformed to standard professional practice. The Washington Supreme Court found the defendant liable as a matter of law, noting that the glaucoma test was cheap, safe, and accurate in detecting glaucoma, and should be given to all patients as a matter of course. The

Washington state legislature, under pressure from the medical profession, subsequently enacted legislation to restore the supremacy of professional custom.[4]

The accuracy of the court's cost-benefit calculus and its perception of professional custom may be challenged (Wiley, 1981), but this is not the issue here. The fundamental question of principle posed by this case is whether the courts should have the discretion to override professional custom in defining the due standard of care. Epstein argues for the supremacy of custom in all situations where the harm is suffered by a party with whom the defendant has a consensual arrangement, as in the case of professional liability: "In the consensual situation, custom is only evidence on the ultimate question of the distribution of risks adopted by the parties. Custom must give way to contract whenever the two standards conflict . . . But in consensual situations custom should not yield to any judicial determination of the appropriate standard of care. To put the point another way, if we accept the defense of assumption of risk — a necessary element in any theory of corrective justice — we must then reject the view of Learned Hand in The T. J. Hooper" (1976, p. 110).

The case for deferring to custom is compelling in the context of a competitive market, where all costs of injuries are borne by informed customers in contractual relations with producers. In such circumstances, competitive pressures will tend to generate the level of safety and allocation of risk preferred by those at risk, and there is no presumption that courts can improve on the revealed preferences of the parties involved. Posner justifies the defense of custom in medical malpractice on these grounds: "Because victim and injurer are in a buyer-seller relationship, the potential injurers (doctors) have an incentive independent of the law to provide the level of care for which potential victims are willing to pay . . . The physician implicitly promises to treat the patient with the care customary among physicians in the area. If he does not use that much care he is guilty of malpractice, a tort, but he has also and by the identical conduct violated his contract with the patient" (1977, p. 127).

But the argument that custom reflects the informed choices and hence the revealed preferences of consumers does not necessarily apply in the case of medical care. Because health care is a service, often not subject to repeat purchase, it is difficult for consumers to do extensive comparison shopping for price and quality ex ante, and to monitor performance ex post. In fact the primary justification for holding physicians liable in tort is that consumers lack the information necessary to enter into and enforce efficient contracts. If common, consumer underestimate of risks and inability to detect substandard quality would lead to a customary standard of care that involved excessive utilization of risky procedures and suboptimal care per procedure, relative to what fully informed consumers would prefer and be willing to pay for. Overestimate of risks would, of course, lead to errors in the other extreme. Thus if consumer information is sufficiently imperfect to justify professional liability in tort, by the same token this undermines the presumption that customary norms provide an appropriate standard of care. Imperfect information is more serious in a market for services, where the producer may discriminate among individual clients on the basis of their sophistication, than in a market for a standardized product, where a minority of informed consumers will suffice to "regulate" quality for all.

In addition to imperfect information, the custom standard encounters another, perhaps more difficult problem in the case of medical malpractice. The extensive coverage of health care by first-party, fee-for-service health insurance has led to a systematic divergence between customary practice and socially optimal practice, as the latter would be defined by the Learned Hand calculus. On the one hand, to the extent that insurance undermines consumers' incentives to be cost-conscious, it has further eroded competitive forces that are already weakened by imperfect information. On the other hand, fee-for-service health insurance leads to overutilization of services beyond socially cost-effective levels, because the price to the patient at the point of purchase is less than the full social cost. This is the familiar problem of moral hazard. If the physician acts as a perfect agent for the patient, given the patient's insurance coverage, he will provide services as long as the expected benefit exceeds the private, out-of-pocket cost to the patient. But this private cost is usually only a small fraction of the full social cost. Many of the innovative developments currently under way in health insurance markets — prospective payment, preferred provider and capitation arrangements, and so on — are designed to constrain this excessive utilization induced by traditional fee-for-service reimbursement. But as long as fee-for-service remains the norm, health insurance tends to create a divergence between customary practice, which reflects the private optimum, and the social optimum that would be defined by the Learned Hand calculus.

Because of the technical nature of the issues in malpractice cases, there is no feasible alternative to using customary practice as the benchmark standard of due care. But since customary care will not necessarily be socially optimal care, because of consumer misperceptions and the distortions induced by health insurance, I would argue that courts should retain the discretion to apply a cost-benefit calculus as a last resort.

If courts do apply a cost-benefit test of negligence, the question will inevitably arise as to whether a private or a social measure of costs should be used. Here it seems necessary to draw a distinction. If the allegation is performance of unnecessary procedures, then private cost to the patient should be used. To use social cost would create an unbearable tension between the standards of the courts and health care norms based on market forces, which reflect private costs. Although we may wish to correct the pervasive distortions in health care delivery induced by health insurance, the malpractice system is surely not the place to do so.

But if the allegation is failure to perform a test or to take some preventive measure, then full social cost should be used. If expected benefits to the patient exceed full social cost, they a fortiori exceed private costs. Equivalently, the fact that social costs exceed expected benefits should be recognized as a defense against failure to take costly precautionary measures. The threat of malpractice suits should not be allowed to impede the move currently under way toward a more explicit recognition of the fact that we can no longer afford to provide all possible medically efficacious care — that is, care that yields any benefit, no matter how small, regardless of cost. To facilitate the adoption of more cost-effective norms of medical practice, the courts, in defining the standard of due care, must recognize cost as a valid defense against malpractice actions alleging failure to take additional precautionary measures, such as additional tests or longer hospitalization.

The Locality Rule

A valid objection to the standard of custom is that holding all physicians to a uniform standard reduces the range of quality of service available to consumers. Equal access to equal care may be a goal, but it is not the reality built into current health policy. Moreover, it is in fundamental conflict with the principle of free choice, which holds that individuals should be free to spend their income as they wish. Some consumers will be willing to pay for a higher quality of care than others, and this will be reflected in a range of quality offered by the market, with a corresponding range of prices. If all physicians are held to a common standard, consumers are deprived of the option of choosing a lower-cost, lower-quality option.[5]

In practice, some bulwark against the imposition of uniform standards was maintained by the locality rule, which defines the due-care standard with reference to the customary practice of the locality. In the early form of this rule, exemplified by the quotation from *Pike v. Honsinger* at the beginning of the chapter, the medical expert testifying for the plaintiff must have practiced in the defendant's community. The rule was intended to protect the rural practitioner, who was assumed to be less well-informed and less able to keep abreast of new developments than his urban colleague. Since the turn of the century and particularly in the last two decades, the strict version of the locality rule has been expanded to include similar localities. Now the most common rule is a statewide standard for general practitioners and a nationwide standard for specialists. However, a nationwide standard for all health care seems to be implied by the federal government's move toward uniform reimbursement except for local wage differences.[6]

One rationale for a more widely drawn standard is to enable plaintiffs to use nonlocal physicians as experts, and hence break down the "conspiracy of silence" of local physicians, whose reluctance to testify against one another allegedly blocked meritorious cases. Just how serious this problem was remains debatable. Although a few documented cases exist of pressure to discourage or punish expert witnesses, Waltz and Inbau (1971) conclude that "all that can fairly be said is that there are far fewer known examples of coercion . . . than would be anticipated if such practices were widespread." Consistent with this, the statistical analysis of claim frequency in Chapter 4 found no evidence that states that rejected the locality rule relatively early had significantly higher claim frequency. Nevertheless, there is obvious potential for abuse of a locality rule, to deprive the plaintiff of the expert testimony necessary under a standard of custom. The solution adopted in some states, of codifying a locality rule in terms of "similar communities," offers a reasonable compromise between preserving a source of nonlocal expert testimony and preserving the viability of diverse standards of care in different communities.

The more pressing current problem is to obtain legal recognition of differences in standards of care among different types of providers and, more generally, legal recognition of the legitimacy of weighing cost in the treatment decision. The potential saving that might be offered by lower-cost providers, such as health maintenance organizations or outpatient clinics, cannot be realized if all are held to the standards that have developed under the unrestricted fee-for-service system. I return to the problem of heterogeneous standards in Chapter 13.

Informed Consent

The earliest cases raising the issue of consent are those in which a physician proceeded despite a patient's protests: in one such case the plaintiff was strapped to a mechanical table and given intermittent stretching, in spite of his continuing objections;[7] in another the plaintiff alleged that the defendant caused damage to her elbows by excessive manipulations against her objections, following the removal of a cast.[8] Liability was for the tort of battery. During the 1960s the doctrine developed that the physician had a duty to disclose, and the action became one of negligence for failure to conform to the proper standards of disclosure, to be determined by expert testimony on customary standards.

But in 1972, two cases expanded the doctrine of informed consent to enable an injured patient to recover damages if he can show that such damages resulted from a treatment to which he, or at least a reasonable man in his position, would not have consented if given all the material information, even if the actual performance conformed to the standard of due care.[9] Thus this is one area where courts have been willing to override the custom of the profession in favor of a more general reasonable-man standard. In principle, this provides a mechanism for holding physicians liable for unnecessary treatments and hence is a key doctrine if the negligence system is to deter excessive performance of procedures with low benefits or high risks, which are misperceived by patients.

Risk disclosure is an issue on which it makes most sense to replace custom with a reasonable-man standard. On theoretical grounds, customary disclosure of risks is likely to be suboptimal because physicians have little incentive to reveal risks that will reduce demand for their services. And on practical grounds, evaluating what information a reasonable man would want in order to make an informed choice is an issue within the competence of a lay jury to decide. In principle, the disclosure required should be based on a cost-benefit calculus: disclosure should be required if the costs of giving that information are less than the expected benefits. In practice, of course, this may be difficult to apply. Nevertheless, the burden of proof on the plaintiff is not trivial: he must show not only failure to disclose material information but also that, if given such information, he would not have undergone the treatment. Moreover, his compensation is in principle limited to the marginal damage resulting from the allegedly unnecessary treatment. In other words, if the patient was injured as a result of a procedure performed without his informed consent, but would have suffered slow deterioration of his prior condition without such treatment, then in principle he should only be compensated for the additional loss resulting from the treatment. Although such apportionment may be tricky, it is routinely required in cases where a defendant exacerbates a preexisting condition.[10]

Defensive Medicine

Although many deny that the threat of liability has any impact on patterns of medical practice, because of the insulation provided by malpractice insurance coverage, it is also believed that defensive medicine is widespread. Even in the early 1970s, between 50 and 70 percent of all physicians claimed that they practiced defensive medicine of one sort or another with varying degrees of regularity (Bernzweig, 1973). How can these apparently contradictory criticisms of the tort system be reconciled? How does defensive medicine differ from the intended increase in precautionary measures?

Previous commentators have noted this dilemma. Defensive medicine has been defined as "a deviation from what the physician believes is sound practice, and is generally so regarded, induced by a threat of liability . . . Not all practices motivated for liability considerations result in poor-quality care. It is, therefore, difficult to draw the line between where good medicine stops and defensive practice begins," (Hershey, 1972). However, there seems to be a consensus that the defensive practice of certain medical procedures has been carried beyond the point of good medicine; the most frequently cited examples are excessive use of diagnostic laboratory tests and x-rays, and unnecessary hospitalization. Defensive omissions include the refusal to undertake procedures or to treat patients who the physician believes pose a high risk of suit.

Bernzweig (1973) suggests that "a physician who states that a particular diagnostic test is not medically necessary may really mean that it is not cost-effective, i.e., not worth the additional expense involved." But to define defensive medicine simply in terms of departures from cost-effective care leads to a gross exaggeration of its magnitude. Defensive practices (acts or omissions) must be defined as those that would not have occurred in the absence of the malpractice threat. This is a much smaller quantity than the number that are not cost-effective, if cost-effective is defined in terms of social benefits and social costs. The reason is that even in the absence of the malpractice threat, health care utilization is pushed beyond the point where social benefits equal social costs because of health insurance. Under typical health insurance policies the patient faces a point of purchase price of at most 20 percent of the full billed price, and for many hospital services marginal coinsurance rates are zero. Of course in the long run patients pay the full cost of health care through higher insurance premiums. But the private incentives for utilization are based on the private cost to the patient, relative to the expected benefit. Because private cost is only a fraction of social cost, utilization tends to exceed the socially cost-effective level even in the absence of the malpractice threat. Only any additional procedures performed because of the liability threat can be correctly called defensive medicine.

This distinction between defensive medicine and the "excessive" care induced by health insurance is illustrated in Figure 8.1, which shows the demand and supply of diagnostic laboratory tests. The demand for tests (D) reflects their value to patients. The line labeled "Social Cost" measures the full resource cost of producing and performing tests. If patients paid for tests in full, the quantity demanded would be Q_s. The line labeled "Private Cost" indicates the point-of-purchase price to the patient. With health insurance that pays 80 percent of costs, the height of the private-cost line is 20 percent of the height of the social cost. Faced with this price, the patient—or the physician acting as his agent—increases utilization to Q_p. Thus the difference, $Q_p - Q_s$, measures the increase in tests due to health insurance. The social cost of these additional tests is less than their social benefit (assumed to be equal to the private benefit, as measured by the demand line), and the deadweight loss (excess of costs over benefits) is measured by the large shaded triangle.

If the physician believes that by performing additional tests he can

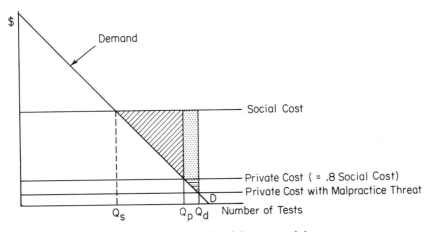

Figure 8.1 Demand and supply of diagnostic laboratory tests.

reduce his probability of being sued or his probability of being found liable, if sued, this can be modeled as a reduction in the price at which he would be willing to supply tests. The line labeled "Private Cost with Malpractice Threat" indicates the patient's 20 percent of this new lower supply price. The quantity of tests increases to Q_d, and the difference, $Q_d - Q_p$, measures the net increment due to defensive medicine. Although the deadweight cost of these additional tests is measured by the difference between their full social cost and their social benefit (the dotted area), only the lower triangular portion of this area is strictly due to defensive medicine. The remainder derives from the distortion in private prices due to health insurance.

The steady growth in clinical laboratory testing in recent years has lent some apparent credibility to the charges of defensive medicine. Bolsen (1982) estimates that the number of tests performed grew 10 to 15 percent a year during the period 1950–1975. What tends to be ignored is that many factors other than increased exposure to liability have contributed to this trend. The percentage of the population with some private insurance for outpatient tests and x-rays increased from 41 percent in 1965 to 74 percent in 1979, and coverage of inpatient tests is even more extensive. Technical advances have increased the diagnostic potential of tests and in some cases produced dramatic reductions in cost. For example, with automated multichannel blood analyzers it is now possible to perform twelve or more tests for less than the cost of performing one by traditional manual techniques.[11] Increased competition in the clinical laboratory industry has reinforced the cost reduction due to technical change.[12] This reduction in the absolute cost of tests implies a fortiori a reduction in their cost *relative* to other health care inputs, which have risen in cost more rapidly than the general rate of inflation. Some substitution of low-cost for high-cost inputs is an efficient response to a change in relative prices.

Finally, as we have seen, the reimbursement practices of third-party payers are likely to encourage an inefficient substitution of tests for the physician's own time. When allowable charges for a physician's time (visits) are subject to stricter controls than fees for tests, as is common under both public and private insurance programs, the physician's incentive is to increase the number of tests relative to his own time, per visit, as one means of circumventing the fee controls (Danzon, 1982). Thus some utilization of tests beyond the private optimum (which exceeds the social optimum, because of insurance) may be attributable to fee controls within the fee-for-service reimbursement system. A similar distortion arises in an inpatient hospital setting (Pauly, 1980), where ancillary services are often more fully insured than physician services. This may be one reason why allegations of defensive medicine routinely refer to excessive tests and other ancillary services rather than to excessive inputs of physician time, whereas the evidence from malpractice incidents and claims cited in Chapter 2 suggests that injury prevention requires more time, not more tests. The pure defensive-medicine incentive may also induce the substitution of tests or additional procedures for more time per procedure if it is easier to document the performance of tests and procedures and use such documentation as evidence of the quality of care in court.

The only evidence on changes in physicians' practice patterns in response to the threat of liability is derived from self-reported responses to a survey of 1,240 physicians (AMA, 1983). Of the respondents, 41 percent said that they prescribe additional diagnostic tests, 27 percent provide additional treatment procedures, 36 percent spend more time with patients, 45 percent refer more cases to other physicians, 35 percent do not accept certain types of cases, 57 percent maintain more detailed patient records, and 2.6 percent drop their liability insurance completely. Obviously, there are many potential biases involved in self-reported responses to a survey designed to estimate liability costs. Moreover, though some of these response patterns may entail costs in excess of benefits, others may yield positive net benefits—for example, spending more time with patients, referring cases to other physicians, and keeping better records. Thus this type of data cannot be used to estimate waste resulting from defensive medicine. The only inference that can legitimately be drawn is that physicians probably do respond: for good or ill, the signals of the tort system do penetrate the insurance screen.

Conclusions

Because of the complexity of the issues in medical malpractice cases, there is no practical alternative to customary norms as the standard of due care. However, the courts should retain the right to override custom in specific cases in favor of a reasonable-man test or an explicit cost-benefit calculus. Because of consumer misperceptions and the distortions induced by health insurance, customary practice does not necessarily reflect the informed preferences of consumers, and one purpose of tort liability is to correct the resulting distortions. To prevent malpractice liability from blocking the progress toward more cost-effective norms of medical practice, different norms for different delivery systems must be recognized. Regardless of customary practice, a defendant should not be held liable for failure to take measures whose social costs exceed expected benefits. The extent of defensive medicine, defined as any net excess of costs over benefits that results from changes in practice patterns in response to the liability threat, has never been accurately estimated. Prevailing estimates fail to net out the unnecessary practices that are a response to extensive fee-for-service health insurance and ignore the benefits that may flow from some additional precautionary measures.

9

Size and Structure of Awards

THROUGHOUT THE 1970S medical malpractice awards surged upward at a rate in excess of the general rate of price inflation and the cost of medical care. Between 1970 and 1975 the average malpractice award increased from $11,518 (Westat, 1973) to $26,565 (NAIC, 1980) — an average annual rate of increase of 18 percent. The upward trend continued to $26,691 in 1976, $34,788 in 1977, and $45,187 in 1978. This represents a cumulative increase of 70 percent over three years and an annual growth rate of 19.3 percent in current dollars, or 12.4 percent in constant dollars after adjusting for inflation.[1] Average indemnity per defendant followed a similar if less extreme pattern, increasing from $17,163 in 1975 to $27,130 in 1978; this represents a 58 percent cumulative increase and an average annual growth rate of 16.5 percent in current dollars, or 9.7 percent in constant dollars.[2]

Shanley and Peterson (1983) found that for most types of tort claims, jury awards increased more rapidly for severe injuries than for minor injuries in the first half of the decade, but this asymmetry may have slowed after 1975. The evidence from the malpractice claim files is partially consistent with this finding. In 1970 there were only 75 awards nationwide over $100,000 or more, and two over $500,000; but between January 1974 and June 1975, there were eleven multimillion-dollar awards in California alone (*Professional Liability Newsletter*, June 1975). Table 9.1 shows that between 1975 and 1978, average indemnity (settlements and verdicts) for severe injuries continued to increase at least as fast as for minor injuries, although conclusions are tentative because of the small number of severe injury claims.

Table 9.1 Average indemnity and year-to-year changes, by severity of injury[a]

Severity of injury	1975	1976	1977	1978
Temporary minor	$5,465	$5,893	$8,273	$8,324
Change (percent)	—	+8%	+40%	+1%
N	1,316	2,265	1,834	2,076
Temporary major	$15,679	$17,143	$15,263	$18,598
Change (percent)	—	+9%	−11%	+22%
N	635	1,145	1,157	1,273
Permanent significant	$54,775	$61,417	$73,599	$89,634
Change (percent)	—	+12%	+20%	+22%
N	239	419	393	527
Permanent grave	$213,777	$234,480	$308,067	$349,203
Change (percent)	—	+10%	+31%	+13%
N	89	126	139	217
Death	$36,420	$48,708	$54,294	$71,768
Change (percent)	—	+5%	+11%	+32%
N	692	1,160	995	1,259

Source: NAIC (1980), pp. 58–60.
a. Includes settlements and verdicts. Related claims have been consolidated as one incident. Claims closed without payment are excluded.

The empirical findings reported in Chapter 4 suggest that tort reforms — in particular dollar caps and mandatory offset of collateral benefits — may have slowed the relentless growth of awards in some states. But while some states are considering more stringent limits on awards, others have ruled such limits unconstitutional.[3] The design of tort awards, for medical malpractice and tort claimants in general, is therefore high on the current policy agenda. This chapter analyzes the optimal structure of damage awards for purposes of compensation and deterrence. Specific changes — dollar caps, periodic payment, and collateral source offset — are then discussed in detail, and the chapter concludes with a list of recommendations.

The Optimal Structure of Tort Awards

A damage award serves two functions in the tort system: it provides compensation to the injured plaintiff and determines the fine to be paid by the negligent defendant, in the absence of insurance. Cook and Graham (1977) and Spence (1977) have shown that the full-compensation principle underlying tort awards is unlikely to be optimal from the standpoint of either prevention or compensation, at least in cases of seriously disabling injuries. Elsewhere I have extended Spence's model to consider the optimal structure of malpractice awards (Danzon, 1984b). The main implications of this extended model are that the optimal award depends on the type of injury, the expense load of the defendant's liability insurance, and the extent to which contractual relations between the parties ex ante transmit consumers' true willingness to pay for safety. There are two issues: compensation and deterrence. Optimal compensation depends only on the type of loss and the expense loading. The optimal compensatory award is the amount of insurance the victim would have purchased voluntarily, at the price implied by the load of the defendant's liability insurance.[4] This is intuitively obvious since the tort system provides compulsory insurance, purchased from the defendant or ultimately from his liability insurer. The tort norm of full compensation is optimal only if the loss is purely monetary and the load is zero. But for a serious injury that affects the utility of wealth, optimal compensation could be more or less than the monetary loss depending on whether disability raises or lowers the marginal utility of wealth, which cannot be determined a priori. Full compensation for pain and suffering is unlikely to be optimal because insurance can only transfer money from the healthy to the disabled state, but money cannot replace the nonpecuniary losses of physical injury. Optimal insurance transfers dollars only to the point where the victim values the marginal dollar as much when disabled as when he is healthy. With a positive load, optimal coverage is lower.

If optimal compensation is less than full, so that the victim is not indifferent to the occurrence of injury, the compensatory award alone may provide insufficient incentives for prevention. This is most obvious in the case of a bachelor with no heirs, who might be willing to pay large sums to reduce his risk of death even though he would not buy life insurance. In a frictionless world where patients correctly perceive the risk of injury ex ante and can costlessly monitor performance ex post, their willingness to pay for injury prevention is internalized to physicians through the fees they are willing to pay for different qualities of service. In that case the compensatory award also suffices for optimal deterrence.

But if patients misperceive risk or cannot observe whether the quality of service delivered is that contracted for, or if contracting costs are high, patients' willingness to pay for risk reduction is not internalized to the injurer. The tort system may correct this potential market failure by levying a fine over and above the compensatory award. At the extreme, with no internalization through markets and a risk-neutral or fully insured (but perfectly experience-rated) defendant, the optimal fine is the value of the injury implied by the victim's willingness to pay for prevention, given optimal insurance. The optimal fine is less if (1) markets transmit somewhat, albeit imperfectly, the value consumers place on prevention, or (2) the defendant incurs uninsurable costs of suit, such as loss of time or reputation. In principle, the fine should be paid to the state and refunded as a subsidy to consumers of the risky activity. If the fine is paid as compensation to individual victims, it provides more insurance than consumers would buy voluntarily, and therefore medical charges, which will include the cost of this insurance, would be too high. This distortion of relative prices is avoided if the fine is refunded as a subsidy (Spence, 1977).

Although the current system of compensatory plus punitive damage awards is structurally similar to this ideal two-part system, it has two defects: first, compensatory awards aim at full compensation for pecuniary plus nonpecuniary loss, regardless of consumers' willingness to pay for such insurance; and second, punitive awards are judged by the defendant's conduct rather than consumers' willingness to pay for prevention, and are paid as compensation to victims rather than being refunded to consumers. The full-compensation principle implies excessive deterrence and excessive insurance.[5]

Although the information requirements and implementation costs of this ideal two-part award system are obviously prohibitive, the basic principles do have important implications for tort reform. Most important, the fundamental tort goal of making the patient whole is almost certainly not optimal, except possibly for temporary and minor injuries that do not affect the utility of income. In this case optimal compensation is at most full coverage of monetary losses only.[6] For injuries severe enough to affect the utility of income, optimal compensation could be less or greater than full coverage of pecuniary loss, depending on whether the occurrence of the injury raises or lowers the utility of income. For injuries involving death, the optimal compensatory award may be measured by the amount of life insurance the patient would have chosen to buy on behalf of his survivors. In all cases, the incremental loss resulting from the malpractice is the relevant measure.

While theory tells us that optimal tort awards depend on willingness to pay for insurance and prevention, we must turn to empirical evidence in order to put dollar values on the theoretical constructs.

There are two sources of evidence on consumers' preferences for disability insurance. Compulsory public programs — Social Security Disability Insurance (SSDI), workers' compensation, Medicare, and Medicaid — indicate collective choices, given the costs and benefits of such programs perceived by voters and their elected representatives. Private first-party coverages indicate private preferences, given the mandatory public programs.

For wage loss, SSDI replaces 30 to 86 percent of pre-disability earnings, depending on income and family status (Meyer, 1979). All private long-term disability (LTD) and pension plans limit coverage to 60 to 70 percent of pre-disability earnings, and include offset provisions against other coverages such as SSDI to prevent total benefits from exceeding this limit. Since these replacement ratios refer to pretax earnings, coverage of after-tax earnings is virtually complete. Although a substantial fraction of wage earners have no LTD coverage, these apparent gaps appear to reflect the fact that for the majority of workers, SSDI benefits already provide the maximum permitted by private insurers.

With respect to medical expense, almost 90 percent of the population has basic health insurance, but private choices reveal an unwillingness to pay for unlimited medical care. Forty-eight percent of the population under age 65 have no private major medical expense protection, and only 36 percent of major medical plans have unlimited benefits (HIAA, 1983). Private coverage of nursing-home and other noninstitutional long-term care is virtually nonexistent (CBO, 1977). Again, the gaps in private coverage reflect a rational response to the mandatory coverage of public programs. SSDI recipients are eligible for Medicare after two years, and private insurance would cover most expenses during that interim. Long-term care is covered by Medicaid, which currently pays for more than a third of nursing home costs.

The only private disability insurance that is not a replacement of specific expenses, and thus bears some resemblance to compensation for pain and suffering, is accidental death and dismemberment (ADD) insurance, carried by 57 percent of civilian wage earners (U.S. Department of Commerce, 1981). These policies typically pay a prespecified sum in the event of a readily identifiable physical injury, such as loss of a limb. The fact that total ADD contributions by employers and employees represent less than 1 percent of total contributions to health benefits is indicative of a relatively low willingness to pay for compensation beyond income replacement and medical expense.

This evidence from private and collective choices suggests that the tort norm of full coverage of wage loss, medical expenses, and other expenses, plus pain and suffering, far exceeds the coverage that people are prepared to pay for if given the choice. However, private choices should not necessarily be taken as a guide, since they are constrained by consumer misperceptions, moral hazard, adverse selection, and loading charges. If the tort system has superior access to information, lower costs of controlling adverse selection and moral hazard, or lower loading charges, optimal compensatory tort awards would exceed these levels of private coverage. Let us examine each of these factors in turn.

It is often argued that people tend to underestimate very low probability events, and therefore buy less insurance than they would choose if better informed. This argument does not bear close scrutiny, however. To purchase appropriate first-party disability insurance, the individual does not need to know his risk from each possible source but only his overall probability of disability, which may be estimated from readily available data. This overall probability of disability is not negligibly low: in 1978, 10.9 million persons, or 8.6 percent of the noninstitutionalized civilian population aged 18 to 64, were severely disabled (unable to work altogether, or unable to work regularly), and an additional 11.0 million (8.7 percent) reported partial disability (a health condition that restricts the kind or amount of work).[7] Because most private coverage is provided through employment, information costs are drastically reduced. Even if risk perceptions underlying private choices are not perfect, individuals are better informed about their own preferences than are juries, who must make such estimates after the event.

Because tort provides compulsory insurance, it is not subject to adverse selection, but neither are large private employment-based group plans.[8] Moral hazard obviously does limit the extent of coverage that it is cost-effective for private markets to provide; this is evidenced by the limit on income replacement of 60 to 70 percent of pre-disability earnings, the integration of private LTD coverage with other public programs to prevent more than full income replacement, and the upper limits on medical coverage and exclusion of some services. But with current damage rules the compulsory insurance of the tort system is even more exposed to moral hazard than is private insurance. The tort claimant gains the full benefit of any award, net of his legal fees, whereas the cost is spread over all patients. Because there is no contract between potential plaintiff and defendant, the tort plaintiff does not choose between different levels of coverage, with prices commensurate with the degree of moral hazard expected.[9] Although legal fees constitute a sizable coinsurance percentage paid by the plaintiff, with the contingent system the fee is paid only in the event of a positive recovery. In the absence of statutory limits on awards, there is no constraint comparable to the upper limit on coverage found in most private insurance contracts. The fundamental insurance principle disallowing more than full compensation is violated by the collateral source rule, which denies evidence of coverage from other sources, and by rules that bar evidence of the tax-free status of tort awards.

Finally, with respect to administrative expense, the load on liability insurance policies, which is relevant to determining optimal tort awards, is higher than on first-party insurance. Thus there seems little justification for compensatory awards in tort to exceed levels of wage loss and medical coverage chosen in private markets.

In addition to the compensatory award, a fine or deterrent surcharge may be necessary for optimal deterrence, in the case of seriously disabling injuries. In principle, the size of the fine depends on how much patients would be willing to pay for injury prevention, given optimal compensation, and on how far this differential is internalized to physicians either through markets or through uninsured costs of being sued. The best empirical evidence on willingness to pay for injury prevention is from labor-market data on wage differentials in risky industries.[10] These data imply a value of life ranging from $500,000 to over $4 million, and a value of $27,000 to $30,000 for nonfatal injuries and illnesses (1980 dollars).[11]

These labor-market estimates obviously cannot be immediately applied to infer the willingness of patients to pay for prevention of medical injuries. First, willingness to pay depends on factors such as age, income, quality of life in the absence of injury, the degree of risk and whether it was assumed voluntarily, and the type of nonfatal injury or illness. Second, the private choices underlying wage differentials are constrained by private budgets. Most public insurance programs incorporate some income redistribution, and it is a normative issue whether the tort system should assess penalties and hence encourage differential prevention by income level. Third, labor-market choices do not internalize the cost of the public programs, which pay a large share of the costs of disability. Using a more complete theoretical model to incorporate all social costs, Arthur (1981) obtained estimates of the value of saving a life in different contexts which are all under $1.4 million (1980 dollars) for all but the youngest age groups.

Even if consumer valuations of tort injuries could be accurately measured, several factors argue against implementing them directly as fines. If the fine is insurable and premiums are not individually rated on the basis of size of loss, then the fine serves no deterrent purpose.[12] If the fine is not insurable, a payment of this size is likely to bankrupt most individual defendants. But as the prospective uninsured loss to the defendant increases, the need for a fine declines, since the optimal fine falls short of the victim's willingness to pay by the amount of any uninsured cost to the defendant.

Reform of Tort Damage Rules

DOLLAR CAPS

Fifteen states have enacted some form of dollar limit on awards. Ten states place one lower limit (typically $100,000) on the liability of an individual defendant and another higher limit (typically $500,000) on the total recovery of the plaintiff, with the difference to be paid from a patient compensation fund. Eight of these states limit the fund's contribution to all forms of compensation, while the remaining two limit recovery for noneconomic loss only. Of the five states with recovery limits but no compensation fund, most limit only the amount payable for noneconomic loss. For example, California has a limit of $250,000 for noneconomic loss. Recovery limits have been challenged in several states and in three have been declared unconstitutional, on the grounds that they deny equal protection to victims of medical malpractice and are likely to discriminate against those most severely injured and in need of compensation.

The empirical analysis (Chapter 4) of trends in severity shows that caps have been one of the most effective means of holding down awards. A cap in effect for two years was estimated to reduce average severity by 19 percent. This direct estimate is reasonably close to an indirect NAIC estimate that a ceiling of $300,000 on the total award — a more stringent cap than most actually enacted — would have eliminated 13 percent of total indemnity paid in 1975 and 20 percent of total indemnity in 1978 (NAIC, 1980, p. 31). This NAIC estimate, derived simply by measuring the percentage of actual indemnity above the selected threshold, underestimates the impact of a cap because it neglects the feedback from potential verdicts to settlements. Some cases that settle below the threshold are based on potential verdicts above the threshold. A cap would reduce the settlement on such cases, although they settled below the threshold in the absence of a cap.[13]

Measurement of the impact of caps on general damages only is frustrated by the fact that there is little public information on what fraction of verdicts or settlements is intended for general damages. In one 1975 verdict that was itemized, of the total award of $4 million to an 11-year-old boy with permanent paralysis, $1.6 million or 40 percent was for the general damages (Table 9.2). Thus the total award would have been reduced by $1.35 million, or one-third, if the $250,000 California ceiling on general damages had been in effect at that time.

The long-run effects of caps may be quite different from the estimated short-run effects based on 1975–1978 closed claims, for several reasons. Long-run effects will exceed short-run effects if the dollar thresholds are not revised upward with inflation and if the reduction in potential verdicts deters the filing of some claims. On the other hand, long-run effects may be less than short-run effects if the limit is circumvented over time by the ingenious creation of new categories of compensation. For example, while the California wrongful death statute limits the recovery of the decedent's family to pecuniary losses, the courts have defined pecuniary loss to include deprivation of society, comfort, care, protection, and companionship. Another possible evasionary device would be a more frequent use of

Table 9.2   Decomposition of a $4,025,000 award (1975 dollars)

Components of award	Award (dollars)	Annuity at 5 percent[a]	Annuity at 8 percent[a]
Lost earnings	503,570	27,596	41,162
Past medical expenses	86,240	—	—
Future medical expenses	196,902	10,790	16,095
Cost of medical supplies and equipment	41,637	2,282	3,403
Medical emergency fund	50,000	—	—
Tutoring and instruction[b]	242,643	31,423	36,161
Attendant care	1,299,637	71,220	106,236
Total economic loss	2,420,629	132,650	197,862
General damages	1,604,371	87,882	131,146
Total award	4,025,000	220,570	329,004

Note: The injury was irreparable damage to an 11-year-old boy which left him paralyzed from the neck down, but with mental and emotional capacities unaffected, and a life expectancy of 56 years.

a. Assumes life expectancy of 50 years.

b. Ten years' tuition.

punitive damages. In a 1977 case, the jury awarded $250,000 in punitive damages against a hospital even though it was found to have made only a 10 percent contribution to the injury.

Evaluation. Four possible caps must be distinguished: caps on general damages only; caps on special damages or on the total award to a single plaintiff; caps on the liability of an individual defendant in a specific incident; and scheduled awards, based on age, disability, and income. These four types will be discussed in the following paragraphs.

General damages. The case is strong for a cap on general damages. As long as the underlying principle is full compensation, there is literally no limit on the potential expansion of categories of loss or on dollar amounts, because no finite amount of money can compensate for severe physical impairment.[14] Thus in the absence of a cap, the upward trend in general damage awards is likely to continue. But as we have seen, optimal insurance would probably not attempt to compensate fully for nonpecuniary losses.

Special damages or total award. Some limit on compensation for economic loss is necessary to constrain moral hazard by claimants and juries. Even if the principle of full compensation for economic loss is maintained, it leaves a wide range of possible outcomes. There are many nonessential medical and other services available to the disabled that may improve the quality of life, but with diminishing returns. The evidence given earlier implies that ex ante, people are not willing to pay for insurance coverage of all available services, although ex post the injured plaintiff would obviously prefer them. For example, in the 1975 itemized award in Table 9.2, the $1.5 million awarded for tutoring, instruction, and attendant care would yield an annuity of $103,000, assuming a 5 percent yield. This is more generous than the private coverage most people buy. At most, optimal compensation should be sufficient to yield a marginal utility of money equal to that enjoyed prior to the injury.[15]

Because economic loss and optimal compensation vary enormously with the life expectancy of the plaintiff and severity of the injury, a common cap on economic loss applicable to all claims is inferior to a schedule of benefits based on age, injury, and possibly income. Similarly, a single cap on the total award is less desirable than scheduled benefits, because the single cap penalizes disproportionately the severely injured young claimant, who suffers the largest economic loss.

Liability of individual defendants. A cap on the liability of individual defendants to something less than the full award, with the difference paid out of a compensation fund, undermines the fundamental deterrent purpose of the tort system. It reverses the principle that the optimal fine exceeds the optimal compensation to victims and, by spreading liability costs more broadly than would self-supporting insurance mechanisms, acts as a subsidy to medical negligence. The stated purpose of shifting liability from the individual defendant to a common fund is to preserve the solvency of private insurance arrangements and ensure compensation of victims. This argument is unpersuasive. The experience of states in which no state fund exists shows that physicians do in fact buy insurance sufficient to ensure compensation of injured claimants and that private markets are able to provide such insurance. Moreover, dividing the liability for the award between the defendant (or his insurer) and the state fund undermines incentives for claim defense and is likely to lead to higher awards (subject to any ceiling that exists) than would occur if liability were not divided.

Scheduled versus individual awards. The tort system differs from the other major compulsory insurance systems — SSDI and workers' compensation — in attempting to compensate fully each individual victim, with loss measured after the occurrence of an injury. In the case of occupational injuries, foregoing the right to full compensation determined on an individual basis was viewed as a quid pro quo for replacing the negligence standard with a rule of employer liability without regard to fault. At least from the standpoint of economic efficiency, however, there is no reason why scheduled benefits should not be used for medical malpractice and other personal injury claims while retaining a negligence-based liability rule.

The economic argument against individualized awards is that they provide inefficient insurance to plaintiffs, encourage litigation expense, and add to liability insurance risk, with no offsetting gains in deterrence. From the standpoint of patients as prospective claimants, uncertainty as to the amount that will be received in the event of an injury reduces its value. To illustrate, consider a severe injury which, because of the vagaries of juries operating within imprecise rules, has an equal chance of receiving a $500,000 award and a $1,000,000 award. The risk-averse plaintiff would prefer a certain award of $750,000 — the expected value. Thus a given level of plaintiff utility can be achieved at lower cost if uncertainty is reduced. Under current damage rules, the range of uncertainty is enormous because of the discretion left to the court in determining such factors as rates of inflation of wages and medical expense, discounting, treatment of taxes, reasonable compensation for pain and suffering, and now, in some states, discretionary offset of collateral compensation and periodic payment of future damages. Moreover, the outcome is likely to be excessive compensation from the standpoint of patients as a whole. As we have seen, this is a standard problem of moral hazard. Each individual plaintiff will try to raise his award because most of the cost is borne by consumers of health care in general. Patients as a whole would probably prefer statutory limits on the compensation they could receive if injured, just as they typically buy private coverage with absolute policy limits. Further, the range of potential awards invites expenditure by both sides to influence the outcome. From the standpoint of patients as a whole, this is largely wasteful.

Finally, the uncertainty surrounding individualized awards adds to the risk borne by the defendant and his insurance carrier. The sensitivity of average claim costs to a few large awards has been documented. The greater the potential range of awards, the higher are the limits of coverage physicians will buy and the greater the insurance risk. Both factors raise the cost of liability insurance and hence the cost of health care, and the high levels of insurance coverage provide the scope for even larger awards (see Appendix to Chapter 3).

While individualized awards entail costs, because of uncertainty as to compensation, incentives to litigate, and uncertainty in pricing of insurance, they offer no offsetting benefits in terms of deterrence. Because adjudication occurs after the fact, often with many years' delay, incentives for prevention depend on the *expected* or anticipated penalty if the physician is found negligent. Even in the absence of liability insurance, the expected penalty would be the expected out-of-court settlement for that class of plaintiff or injury, which would be an average over potential verdicts. But any deterrent value of individual awards is further diluted by liability insurance. To the extent that merit rating exists, it is based on frequency rather than severity of claims precisely because large claims are such rare events that they lack actuarial credibility.

The case for scheduled versus individual awards is quite distinct from the question of whether compensation should be full or something less than full. The previous discussion suggests that medical expense should be reimbursed in full, subject to specific limits for services that are largely discretionary and exclusion of services with low marginal benefits. Compensation of wage loss up to 70 percent of pretax earnings is indicated, which on average yields full replacement of after-tax income. For individuals who have no prior history of earnings, a benefit schedule based on age and potential earnings should be established.

Whether wage replacement rates should be lower for high wage earners is a value judgment. Most mandatory insurance systems, including workers' compensation and SSDI, relate benefits to income, up to a ceiling. One argument is that because of the tax-based funding, high earners have contributed more and thus should be entitled to higher benefits. Because of the various tax and subsidy programs to health care, it is unclear whether upper-income groups contribute disproportionately to the cost of health care and therefore by that logic should be entitled to higher tort benefits. A reasonable compromise would be to award everyone the same percentage of after-tax wage loss, but to make general damage awards independent of income. Any fine or deterrent surcharge should also be unrelated to the plaintiff's income if, as an ethical matter, we do not wish to create income-related incentives for prevention.

For general damages, a schedule should be established based on the extent of disability, age, and life expectancy. The underlying principle is to maintain the marginal utility of money. Thus payments would be zero for minor or temporary injuries; they would be highest for cases of permanent disability where a reasonable quality of life could be maintained only with large additional expenditures for such items as home help or special educational aids (to the extent that these items are not explicitly included in the award for special damages).

PERIODIC PAYMENTS

Under general tort damage rules, compensation for future damages is paid in a lump sum equal to the discounted present value of the expected future payments. Since 1975, 14 states have enacted laws allowing periodic payment of awards that exceed some threshold, typically $100,000, at the discretion of the court or the request of the parties.[16] The usual plan is for a lump-sum payment to cover attorney fees and expenses incurred to date, to be followed by fixed monthly payments over a period of years. If the plaintiff dies before full payment has been made, the balance is payable to his estate or beneficiaries, minus sums intended for future medical expenses or as compensation for pain and suffering. New Hampshire has declared periodic-payment legislation unconstitutional, as a denial of equal protection, and North Dakota repealed its provision in 1980 when it declared the major part of its malpractice legislation unconstitutional. But the California Supreme Court, reversing an earlier decision, has upheld that state's provision for periodic payment of awards over $50,000.

Evaluation. Periodic payments have been advocated on several grounds. A common argument is that plaintiffs spend lump-sum awards frivolously and then become "wards of state" (Keeton and O'Connell, 1965). However, this position implies a paternalism that would deny tort victims freedom to allocate funds that are rightfully theirs, which we do not apply to individuals in general. A more cogent argument is that periodic payment reduces the cost of a large award to defendants or their insurers, and hence ultimately reduces the cost of the malpractice system to all patients. In order to provide for payment of future installments, the defendant should establish an annuity or trust fund, as is explicitly required in some states.[17] Other things being equal, the cost of an annuity for a definite term is simply the discounted present value of the future payments. In principle, this is identical to what the award would have been if calculated as a lump sum. However, there are two ways in which periodic payments can reduce costs. First, if the life expectancy of the plaintiff is uncertain, the insurer can buy an annuity from a life insurance company based on the *expected* longevity of the plaintiff. This will be less than the lump-sum tort award if it were calculated as an annuity for the *maximum* possible life expectancy. Alternatively, the insurer may recoup this difference if the law provides for unused sums to revert to the insurer upon the plaintiff's death, net of funds for support of the plaintiff's dependents. Although this transfers from plaintiff to defendant some of the savings from the plaintiff's premature death, it resembles closely the form of disability plus life insurance policy that people choose to buy when insurance is voluntary.

A second means by which periodic payments reduce costs occurs when the insurer obtains a higher rate of interest than the jury would have used in discounting future payments to present value. If this occurs, the same level of compensation can be provided to the plaintiff at lower cost. Small absolute changes in interest rate can imply large changes in present value. This is illustrated in Table 9.2, where the use of an 8 percent rather than a 5 percent rate of interest reduces the award from $4 million to $2.7 million, or by roughly one-third. Of course, the effect could go the other way, if in fact the jury uses, say, a 10 percent discount factor but available market rates are less than this.

A third rationale for periodic payments is that they may indirectly introduce a more reasonable treatment of inflation, interest, and discounting by the courts. There are two possible methods for arriving at the correct result: the first adjusts wage loss and medical expense upward by the expected rate of inflation and then discounts all future sums at the prevailing market rate of interest; the second subtracts the expected rate of inflation from the prevailing market rate of interest and applies this inflation-adjusted or real rate of discount to all future sums, unadjusted for inflation. Both methods yield the same present value if common inflation and discount rates are applied to all future streams and if the rate of inflation used by the court is that implicitly built into the market rate of interest.[18] In practice, both methods have been applied by some courts, while others adhere to the traditional rule of disallowing any consideration of future inflation. If inflation is ignored but future sums are discounted at a market (nominal) interest rate, the real purchasing power of the lump sum will be too low. On the other hand, some courts have presumed that the rate of inflation equals the discount rate, and thus disregard both. In this case the real purchasing power of a lump sum calculated by simply summing future payments at current prices, without discounting, is too high.

The great advantage of specifying the award as an annuity is that it removes the issue of discounting from the jury and transfers it to the market. Inflation can be handled by purchasing an indexed annuity. Thus the plaintiff is assured the real future purchasing power intended, and this is done at minimum cost since the insurer will presumably search out the lowest price for the annuity.

The discussion thus far applies to periodic payments of a prespecified amount. Payments are contingent on actual expenses only in the event of death, in which case payment for the decedent's medical expenses, consumption, and pain and suffering, had he lived, revert to the insurer. This is consistent with optimal insurance, since a fully informed person would not buy coverage for such items. However, some proposals—for example, the "quasi no-fault" proposal, (H.R. 5400, introduced in the 98th Congress, 2d session)—call for periodic payment of actual expenses incurred by the plaintiff. Such contingent periodic payments would indeed provide a superior form of insurance for the victim if his actual expenses were fully determined by events beyond his control. But as we have seen, many medical expenditures, home-care services, and even wage loss can be influenced by the insured. Periodic payment contingent on actual loss incurred thus creates severe moral hazard, encourages expenditure that is not worth its cost, discourages rehabilitation, and hence is unlikely to be an optimal form of insurance.

Rea (1981b) notes other disadvantages of contingent periodic payment: by eliminating all risk to the victim, it implies overcompensation to the extent that it provides more complete insurance than he would have had in the absence of the injury. Moreover, it exposes the defendant or his insurance company to an essentially open-ended liability. The fact that private first-party and liability insurance coverages almost always specify an upper limit indicates that unlimited periodic payments, contingent on actual expense, provide a level of insurance that is not worth its cost to consumers.

THE COLLATERAL SOURCE RULE

People injured in the course of medical treatment may look to other sources of compensation in addition to the tort system, such as private health and disability insurance and, in the event of serious disability, Social Security Disability Insurance (SSDI) and Medicare. The collateral source rule prohibits evidence to the jury of the plaintiff's potential compensation from these other sources. Since 1975 several states have modified the collateral source rule for medical malpractice cases to either mandate or permit, at the discretion of the court, the reduction of the award by the amount available to the plaintiff from other sources.[19] This trend toward collateral source offset is endorsed by the ABA Commission, which recommends that the judge deduct from the jury's assessment of damages all payments from government, employment-related, individually purchased, and fortuitously conferred benefits, with the possible exception of life insurance. The Commission recommends against allowing subrogation for any medical benefits, but has declined to take a position on subrogation for wage and disability payments.[20]

The main argument in favor of collateral source offset is to prevent double compensation: "The idea of a windfall runs counter to the basic end of tort law, which is to make the plaintiff whole, not to overcompensate him . . . the aim should be to assure the plaintiff fair compensation from available sources, but no more" (ABA, 1977, p. 147). Although I have argued that this principle of making the plaintiff whole should be replaced by the principle of optimal compensation, both criteria argue against double compensation.

Posner (1977) has defended the traditional no-offset rule as necessary for optimal deterrence. For example, assume that the plaintiff's only loss is $10,000 of medical expenses, all of which would be fully covered by his private health insurance. If this private coverage were simply deducted, the tort award would be reduced to zero and the defendant would incur no penalty. Further, Posner argues that any double recovery is no windfall to the plaintiff since he paid for his first-party coverage and could, presumably, have opted for a cheaper policy that excluded coverage of tort claims or assigned subrogation rights in such claims to his first-party insurer. One may add — at least in the medical or product liability context, where the victim and defendant are in a buyer/seller relationship — that the victim has also indirectly paid for the compulsory insurance provided through the tort system and thus is entitled to what he paid for.

In a world with perfect information and costless contracting, the collateral source rule is neither necessary nor sufficient for optimal deterrence or optimal insurance. Consider the case of an injury that entails a purely monetary loss, fully covered by first-party insurance, and for which the tort rule of full compensation provides optimal insurance and deterrence. If the traditional collateral source rule of no offset applies, the tort award provides optimal deterrence, and a subrogation action by the first-party insurer against the insured (the plaintiff in the tort suit) can eliminate double compensation.[21] On the other hand, if the tort rule is full reduction of the award by the amount of collateral compensation, compensation is achieved through the first-party insurance, and a subrogation action by the first-party insurer against the tortfeasor provides deterrence. Thus, in either case, two actions are necessary but together are sufficient for optimal insurance and deterrence.

In practice, under the traditional rule of no offset, subrogation mitigates but does not fully eliminate double recovery because contracting out is not costless. The law recognizes subrogation rights of medical insurers against tortfeasors or their liability insurers (Kimball and Davis, 1962), and the prevalence of subrogation clauses in medical policies indicates public preference to eliminate double coverage. But life and accident insurance has generally been denied subrogation rights on the grounds that it provides "personal" insurance rather than "indemnity" insurance, that is, life and accident policies allegedly do not compensate for explicit economic losses. As Kimball and Davis point out, however, there are significant indemnity aspects in all forms of life and disability insurance. They conclude: "Where there is an insurance against a loss measurable in economic terms, the insurer should be legally subrogated quite as readily as in fire or collision insurance once there has been full indemnification of the insured. Denial of legal subrogation should reflect the lack of adequate indemnification to the insured in the individual case, and nothing more" (p. 860). But to allow subrogation only after full indemnification could invite endless litigation, since indemnification for severe personal injury may never be complete. Unrestricted freedom to contract for subrogation in life and accident policies should be allowed, both to discourage the moral hazard created by double coverage and to permit individuals to choose their preferred level of compensation.

Subrogation rights of public programs are mixed. The Federal Medical Care Recovery Act grants the federal government a right to recover from a tortfeasor for medical expenses it incurs (Capwell and Greenwalk, 1971). Workers' compensation employers or their insurers have explicitly been accorded subrogation rights by statute in most states. However, SSDI, the primary source of disability payments, does not have subrogation rights.

Although the collateral source rule is irrelevant in a frictionless world, the optimal rule in practice depends on the costs of contracting out of double compensation and of enforcing subrogation. One obvious guiding principle is that mandatory coverage should pay in full and be denied subrogation, whereas voluntary first-party coverages should be free to include enforceable subrogation clauses, thereby enabling individuals to contract out of double coverage or supplement the mandatory coverage if they wish. This principle argues for retaining the traditional collateral source rule since tort awards are a form of compulsory insurance, but granting all first-party coverages subrogation rights. The ABA Commission argues against subrogation, on the grounds that "denying subrogation would tend to make the more efficient, high-volume accident and health insurance the primary insurance for malpractice losses and the liability insurers the secondary or excess layer insurers" (ABA, 1977, p. 148). Although it is true that liability insurers have higher overhead costs than do first-party coverages, this is not necessarily indicative of inefficiency. To the extent that litigation over liability serves the social function of deterrence as well as the private function of compensation, one cannot compare the overhead rates of liability and health insurers as a measure of their relative efficiency. The ABA argument that would design tort awards solely with a view to efficient compensation is ultimately an argument for abolishing the tort system altogether.

The principle advocated here of allowing subrogation to voluntary coverages provides no guidance for coordinating tort and other mandatory coverages, in particular, SSDI. Coordination of SSDI and tort is desirable not only to avoid excessive insurance but also to avoid reinforcing the work disincentives already built into the SSDI program. If tort awards were paid in periodic installments rather than a lump sum, a simple and efficient solution would be to reduce SSDI benefits by the amount of the tort compensation for earnings loss, should the claimant file for SSDI at a future date.[22] This system would preserve deterrence through tort, while eliminating double coverage and reducing costs to the SSDI program.

Whatever the collateral source offset rule, it should be applied as a matter of law, not at the discretion of the court. Discretionary application creates costly uncertainty for all parties involved: it becomes harder for a potential plaintiff to determine his first-party insurance needs and harder for a potential defendant to predict his liability insurance needs, while claim costs become less predictable for both first-party and liability insurers. Moreover, discretionary offset adds yet another issue that the parties will attempt to influence through litigation expenditures.

Effects of collateral source offset. As a practical matter, how much would full offset of collateral sources reduce malpractice claim costs? To answer this question one needs to know the fraction of awards that is intended to cover economic loss, and how much of this economic loss is covered by other insurance sources. Because verdicts and settlements are rarely itemized, the amount intended to cover wage loss, medical expenses, and so on can only be approximated, using data on insurers' estimates of economic loss from the closed-claim files. Unfortunately, the claim file reports of economic loss are rife with missing and erroneous data, particularly for future loss. Depending on how one adjusts for these missing data, estimates of economic loss range from 55 percent to 208 percent of awards (see Appendix at end of chapter). With a plausible set of assumptions, which allow for underreporting of economic loss and for the fact that claims settle at less than the potential verdict, I estimate that economic loss averages 61 percent of potential verdicts, of which approximately 23 percentage points is due to medical expense, 36 percentage points to wage loss, and 2.5 percentage points to other expense.[23]

Since the claim files do not report the fraction of this loss that would be covered by other public and private insurance sources, we can only make rough estimates based on population averages. Two-thirds of total health care expenditures are paid by some third-party source; the percentage is higher for hospital care (87.9 percent) than for ambulatory care, higher for routine care than for catastrophic illness and disability, and lower for the poor and for young adults aged 19–24 years. Only 37.1 percent of short-term, non-work-connected disability is covered (U.S. Statistical Abstract, 1982–83). Current data on the extent of coverage for long-term disability are less complete.[24] Only 10 percent of the population under age 65 have private LTD coverage, but over 90 percent of paid employment is covered by SSDI, which pays benefits ranging from 30 to 86 percent of pre-disability, pretax earnings. For long-term institutional care, private insurance coverage is virtually nonexistent; but a person who exhausts his private funds becomes eligible for Medicaid, which currently pays for roughly half of all long-term care (CBO, 1977).

Combining all these data, a very rough estimate would be that, if malpractice losses are representative of losses from all causes, full offset of all sources of collateral coverage might reduce malpractice claim costs by between 30 and 40 percent. This is based on two assumptions: that economic loss is 61 percent of potential verdicts, and that 60 percent of economic loss is covered by collateral sources. This estimate may be subject to downward bias if the claim files seriously underreport wage loss, as the Westat analysis indicates, and if malpractice involves a disproportionate number of severe injuries for which coverage is less complete. The estimate may be upward-biased if malpractice awards significantly discount payments for future losses (see Appendix).

This rough indirect estimate of the effect of collateral source offset is reasonably close to the direct estimate from the statistical analysis of severity trends in the period 1975–1978, that mandatory offset in effect for two years reduced average paid severity by 50 percent (see Chapter 4). Average severity may be expected to fall by more than the reduction in potential verdicts because this latter reduction would induce changes in disposition, with more cases dropped and fewer litigated to verdict. The reduction in total claim costs may therefore exceed the reduction in average severity.[25]

Conclusions

The analysis in this chapter indicates that the efficiency of the tort system would be improved by replacing the traditional norm of full compensation, for pecuniary and nonpecuniary loss, determined on an individual basis, by a schedule of more limited benefits. Patients willing to pay for more extensive benefits could do so by private contract (see Chapter 12). The basic schedule should provide for the following:

1. Compensation for medical expenses such as those found in group major medical policies, and rehabilitation costs.
2. Compensation for actual or potential wage loss up to 70 percent of pre-tax, pre-disability earnings (full replacement of after-tax earnings).

3. No offset of private insurance coverage but subrogation rights for all private insurers.
4. Reduction of SSDI benefits by the amount of tort recovery for wage loss and reduction of Medicare and Medicaid benefits by the amount of the tort recovery for medical expense.
5. A schedule of compensation for pain and suffering for serious injuries only.
6. Consistent with the principle of reducing uncertainty, statutory standards for determining inflation, interest rates, and wage growth parameters.

In addition, an uninsurable fine may be appropriate in cases of severe injury, either when consumer underestimate of risk, fraud, or breach of explicit or implicit contract is at issue, or when the defendant is fully insured. In cases where patients are adequately informed or where the defendant has incurred significant loss of time or reputation in defending the suit, deterrence incentives may be adequate without a fine. The fine should be paid to the state and used to defray the public costs of the judicial system, thereby internalizing some of these costs to activities that cause injuries.[26] To the extent that the purpose of punitive damage awards is deterrence, this analysis of the optimal fine applies directly: the optimal punitive award is simply the optimal fine. In other words, the uninsurable fine should replace, not supplement, any punitive award.

APPENDIX

Estimating Collateral Source Coverage from Claim Files

There are several problems in using claim file data to estimate how much awards might be reduced by collateral source offset.

Missing and erroneous data.[27] For 39 percent of paid claims, economic loss is either reported as zero (25 percent) or is simply missing. In some cases there may indeed have been no loss — "true" zeros — but in many cases this is not plausible. Any estimate of the adequacy of tort compensation or the effect of collateral source offset depends crucially on how these cases reporting no loss are handled. At one extreme, if all zeros are true zeros, economic loss is only 54.6 percent of total indemnity. Of this, 20.5 percent is medical expenses, 31.9 percent is wage loss, and 2.2 percent is other expenses (primarily funeral expenses). At the other extreme, if one assumes that all zeros represent missing data and that claims with missing data are no different, on average, from claims with data reported, then the estimate of economic loss is 208.4 percent of total indemnity, of which 35.5 percent is medical expense, 150.9 percent is wage loss, and 22 percent is other expense.

But consistency checks tend to reject both these extremes. The fact that claims with missing or zero reported loss receive lower awards, on average, than claims reporting economic loss suggests that at least some of the zeros are true.[28] But whereas 42 percent of cases report no medical expense, only 11.4 percent of cases involve injuries classified as "emotional only" or "temporary insignificant" and thus could conceivably entail no medical expense. Similarly, 79 percent of cases report no wage loss, whereas this can be correct for at most 45 percent, based on the age and sex of the plaintiff and the severity of the injury.[29]

An alternative approach is to assume that if no economic loss is reported there must be error, but if at least one category of loss is reported then the entire record is correct and zeros are true zeros. Under this assumption economic loss is 81.1 percent of indemnity, on average, of which medical expense accounts for 30.4 percentage points, wage loss for 47.4 percentage points, and other expense for 3.3 percentage points. This approach implicitly assumes that for cases not reporting any economic loss, the true value is lower than for cases reporting some loss but bears the same proportion to the award, on average.

Just how conservative this assumption is becomes apparent when the results are compared to those obtained in Westat (1978). For a sample of 324 claims involving either permanent total disability or death, with awards of at least $500, economic loss was computed using the following assumptions:

1. Zero medical expense was assumed false and was replaced with the mean value of medical expense on claims reporting a positive amount.
2. Wage loss was imputed using the present value of lifetime earnings, by age and sex, obtained from external sources.
3. Zero other expense was accepted as true for permanent total disability; for cases of death it was imputed from those reporting a positive value, on the grounds that funeral expenses are the primary component of other expense.

With these assumptions, the estimates imply that indemnity ranges from roughly one-quarter of economic loss for cases of death to one-half of economic loss for permanent total disability.

Discounting. The comparison with economic loss may be further biased by the fact that lump-sum awards should reflect the discounted present value of future expenses, whereas loss reported in claims files is probably not discounted. This tends to bias downward the estimate of awards relative to loss and hence bias upward the estimate of savings from collateral source offset.

Settlements. Further upward bias is created by using actual indemnity paid, primarily in out-of-court settlements, as a proxy for court verdicts. Using the estimates reported earlier, that settlements average 74 percent of the potential verdict and adjusting for the fact that 95 percent of paid claims in the NAIC sample are settled, the mean shadow award is 1.3 times the mean indemnity reported. The ratio of loss (adjusted for reporting error) to mean indemnity must therefore be adjusted down by 0.75 to obtain the ratio of loss to shadow verdict relevant to calculating the effect of collateral source offset.[30]

10

The Statute of Limitations

THE STATUTE OF LIMITATIONS defines the length of time in which a potential plaintiff may file a claim. The period allowed differs among states and among branches of law. For example, in California the basic statute of limitations for cases brought in tort is one year; for cases brought in contract, two years. But for professional and product liability, where the existence of an injury may take time to become manifest, many courts have adopted liberal discovery rules which toll (postpone) the running of the statute until the injury and its cause have been or with reasonable diligence should have been discovered. A discovery rule was applied to medical malpractice as early as 1936.[1] For persons injured at birth, the statute is often tolled until majority. For product liability actions in tort, the statute does not begin to run until the occurrence or manifestation of the injury, which may be many years after the manufacture of the product or exposure to a toxic substance. These long or deferred statutes of limitations give rise to the long tail of claims and have contributed in a major way to both the legal and the insurance problems that have occurred in medical malpractice and product liability.

Since 1975, 38 states have shortened the time allowed to file a medical malpractice claim and curtailed the previously unlimited period allowed for discovery. Such an outer limit on the time for discovery and filing is called a statute of repose. The California reform is typical; it sets a basic limit of three years from the injury or one year from discovery, whichever occurs first. But in situations involving fraud, intentional concealment, or a foreign body, the period of one year from discovery is not constrained within the overall three-year limit. For minors, the rule is three years or the eighth birthday, whichever occurs later.

Court rulings on the constitutionality of such statutes have not appreciated their effects on the overall efficiency of the tort system. As we saw in Chapter 1, shifting liability to producers or other third parties is efficient only if the gains in deterrence and risk spreading outweigh the added litigation and overhead costs. I shall show in this chapter that when standards of liability and compensable damages are changing over time, long statutes of limitations may result in excessive deterrence and an inefficient allocation of risk, in addition to even higher litigation and other overhead costs than are typical for the tort system. These costs ultimately outweigh the potential deterrence benefits of internalizing injury costs to producers, and argue for some limit on the statute of limitations.

Risk Associated with Latent Injuries and Long Statutes

The statute of limitations defines the duration of liability, that is, it determines the point at which liability for latent injuries is shifted from the physician back to the patient. In a static world such a rule would make no sense: if, on balance, placing liability on physicians is efficient because the gains in deterrence outweigh the added overhead costs, then that liability should apply regardless of when injuries are discovered. A statute of limitations would appear to defeat the purpose of full cost internalization.

In a world of imperfect information, changing technology, and changing legal rules, however, the issue is not so simple. Most obvious, delay between the injurious act and the filing of a claim leads to decay of evidence, blurs the chain of causation by adding intervening factors, and hence increases litigation overhead. The fact that claims filed late tend to involve a disproportionately large number of severe injuries confirms that the relatively high costs of proof are not worth incurring unless the potential award is large.

In addition to added litigation expense, long or deferred statutes may result in overdeterrence, an inefficient allocation of risk, and high regulatory costs. Regardless of the assignment of liability, delay between the triggering event and the manifestation of injury creates uncertainty in preventing injuries and providing for their compensation. First, delay creates technological uncertainty in establishing the connection between the triggering event and the injury. Carcinogenic chemicals and drugs with long-latent side effects are obvious examples. Second, delay introduces a financial risk in prefunding future compensation.[2] But when liability for injuries is shifted through the tort system, long statutes of limitations create a risk additional to these intrinsic risks, resulting from liability standards that not only change over time but are highly unpredictable.

To isolate the effects of perfectly anticipated change on the one hand, and uncertainty on the other, let us first assume that standards are changing but are known with certainty. For example, there may be a known upward trend in compensable damages over time or a technological advance that reduces the cost of diagnosing or treating certain conditions. The effect of such change is that the optimal level of care, defined by weighing costs and benefits, becomes ambiguous. Prevention costs occur at time 1, but damages are manifest at time 2. An action that is not negligent by the standards of time 1 may be negligent if the standards of time 2 are applied retroactively.[3]

If future liability for latent injuries is fully anticipated and internalized into the prevention and insurance decisions at time 1, this may result in too little risk taking and too much insurance, as judged by the standards prevailing at time 1. For example, with the state of knowledge at time 1, there may be only one drug available for treatment of a particular disease. Though beneficial in the majority of cases, this drug may be known to entail a risk of long-latent adverse side effects, such as increased risk of cancer. Nevertheless, because it is the only option available, at least some patients at time 1 would be willing to incur this risk in return for the chance of cure. However, drug manufacturers will take into account their expected liability costs when the adverse effects are manifest 20 years hence, which may reflect a much more advanced state of knowledge and higher standards of compensation than those prevailing when the production and utilization decisions were made at time 1. The price of the drug at time 1 must be high enough to compensate the manufacturer for the high cost of insurance against the future liability. At this price, some or all consumers may be priced out of the market, and the drug may not be produced at all. Thus with full internalization of future liability under long statutes, there may be overdeterrence and overinsurance, as judged by the standards at time 1. This distortion will fall disproportionately on providers who are at greatest risk of incurring long-latent liability and retroactive application of future standards, such as neonatologists and pharmaceutical manufacturers.

Alternatively, providers may choose not to prefund latent liability at time 1 but rather to face liability costs when they occur at time 2, with a claims-made policy. But, in a competitive industry with individually rated premiums and free entry, these costs cannot be passed on to consumers at time 2. Established firms that try to pass on current costs arising out of past liability will be undercut by new entrants. Therefore the cost of latent injuries will either fall on producers or on victims, in the event that producers go bankrupt — as evidenced by the recent bankruptcy filing of the Johns-Manville corporation, in the face of multimillion-dollar liability costs arising out of the manufacture of asbestos more than 20 years ago.

Consider now the more realistic case where liability rules — scope of liability, standard of care, rules of evidence, and size of damage awards — not only change but are unpredictable. Uncertainty as to legal rules, which I call "sociolegal risk," has two important implications for liability insurance (Danzon, 1984b). First, sociolegal risk destroys the insurer's ability to predict claim costs with any accuracy. With an occurrence policy, the insurer must predict claim frequency and severity for the duration of the discovery period plus any lag in disposition beyond that, using estimates of claim trends derived from prior experience. But experience on the most recent policy years is not fully mature, while the more mature experience on older policy years rapidly becomes obsolete in a nonstationary environment.[4] Even if statistical analysis could accurately estimate past trends, there is no guarantee that the future will replicate the past.

Second, a long statute of limitations induces positive correlation among policyholders. The expected loss per policyholder depends not only on the probability of an injury, but also on the probabilities that a claim is filed and an award made, and on the size of the award. These last three factors depend on the sociolegal climate common to all insureds. The longer the statute of limitations, the greater is the weight of sociolegal risk relative to individual risk, the greater the correlation among policyholders, and hence the greater the uncertainty in the outcome for the insurance portfolio. At the limit, with perfect correlation, the insurer's risk per policyholder, or the residual risk for the portfolio as a whole, is independent of the size of the risk pool. Long statutes of limitations in a volatile legal environment thus create nondiversifiable risk. In the case of medical malpractice, this exacerbates the risk intrinsic in the small pool of policyholders.[5]

When aggregate insurance claim costs cannot be accurately predicted, because of the small risk pool and nondiversifiable sociolegal risk, the competitive insurance premium will include a markup above expected costs. The markup depends on the uncertainty (the standard deviation) attached to the estimate of expected (mean) cost per policyholder. This standard deviation and hence the markup are larger, the longer is the statute of limitations. The necessary markup also increases with the desired safety margin. For example, if the firm will not accept a risk of premium inadequacy greater than one chance in one hundred, the markup is 2.33 times the standard deviation for large risk pools, and more for smaller groups. Evidence from medical malpractice rate hearings suggests that a standard deviation at least equal to the mean would be a conservative estimate; this would imply a "very safe" premium rate of three times the expected claim costs, plus overhead. I do not wish to imply that risk premiums of this magnitude are built into malpractice rates.[6] I do contend that, with a long duration of liability, a substantial markup for risk may be warranted even in competitive insurance markets.

If premiums include a markup for nondiversifiable risk, the expectation is that ex post there will be a net transfer from policyholders to equity owners. This raises the price of market insurance relative to self-insurance and increases incentives for risk retention by policyholders. As I have argued earlier, this is one reason for the recent dramatic growth of medical mutuals and hospital captive companies at the expense of stock insurers.

Defining the Optimal Statute

The test for an efficient statute of limitations involves weighing, at the margin, any efficiency gains and losses from extending liability, in terms of risk allocation, deterrence, and overhead costs. Obviously there is no unique optimal statute for all contexts. My purpose here is to point out how the net gain from prolonging liability of physicians through a long statute diminishes as time elapses from the triggering event.

Consider first risk spreading, which has been one of the primary justifications for extending third-party liability, particularly in the liability context.[7] The argument is that it is more efficient to assign injury costs to producers, because they can fully insure the risk and can pass on the insurance cost in product prices. In principle, this would provide an ideal distribution of risk: consumers would pay for their own insurance, with no transfer between generations of consumers and no burden on producers. This argument ignores, however, the possibility of risk spreading through first-party insurance and also ignores problems in liability insurance. The evidence from liability insurance markets suggests that such costless, distribution-neutral liability insurance is not feasible for long-latent injuries subject to sociolegal risk. If future injury costs are fully prefunded, either through an occurrence policy written at the time of the triggering event or through a claims-made policy with the physician prefunding the expected cost of a reporting endorsement, the early generation of consumers pays for the expected standards of liability and damages adopted by later generations, and for uncertainty as to those standards. If this future liability is not prefunded, these burdens on the early generation are avoided. But to the extent that current insurance costs to cover prior liability cannot be passed on, these costs fall on producers or injured victims. In the case of medical care, lack of individual rating and barriers to entry make pay-as-you-go insurance through a claims-made policy a more feasible solution. However, the allocation of risk achieved by long statutes of limitations is not necessarily preferable to that achieved with a short statute, given the availability of first-party private and public insurance.

With respect to deterrence, if the time path of liability rules entails an anticipated expansion of compensable damages or retroactive application of new knowledge, this forces early generations to pay for the standards of later generations. If liability is not only expanding but also uncertain, such that insurance premiums include a markup for nondiversifiable risk, this is equivalent to a tax on activities with potential latent injuries and results in overdeterrence, assuming that physicians buy insurance. But if physicians respond to high insurance costs by "going bare" and dispose of their assets to make themselves judgment-proof, there may be underdeterrence and incomplete compensaton of injured victims.[8] In general, if there is sufficient uncertainty about liability rules to generate significant nondiversifiable insurance risk, the value of such liability as a guide to prevention is questionable.

In addition to the direct impact on prevention and risk allocation, the uncertainty created by long statutes of limitations has generated other indirect costs. As we have seen, disagreement over the appropriate price of insurance has led to regulation of insurance premiums to levels deemed inadequate by commercial companies and to their total withdrawal from several states. Regulatory monitoring of rates is intended to ensure that they are fair, nondiscriminatory, and reasonably related to risk. The analysis here suggests that even with the full universe of potential data available, rate making will necessarily involve an element of judgment commensurate to the relative importance of sociolegal risk. Where such risk is large, uncertainty as to fair rates cannot be resolved statistically. Regulation of rates to the lower end of the feasible range is likely to destroy the voluntary market and prolong reliance on compulsory joint underwriting associations (JUAs).

In summary, indefinite liability for latent injuries tends to create inefficient risk allocation, overdeterrence, and regulatory conflict, which may outweigh any benefits from attempting full cost internalization. Efficiency considerations thus argue for a well-defined limit on the duration of liability, in the form of a statute of repose, that is, a limit on liability running from the occurrence of the injurious act rather than from the manifestation or discovery of injury. Many of the recent statutory changes, which set outer limits on the period for discovering the injury, are of this form. Defining the optimal term of the statute involves weighing the benefits of internalization against the costs of overdeterrence, nondiversifiable risk, and added litigation costs. Although the precise trade-offs will vary with the context, it is clear that the more rapid the rate of change of technology and of liability rules, the shorter is the optimal statute. Thus statutory codification of damage awards, by reducing sociolegal risk, would permit a longer efficient statute of repose. Specifically, the benefits schedule could provide that compensation for long-latent injuries should be at the rates prevailing at the time of injury, updated by the rate of return on reserves until the time the injury is manifest. This would preserve the real purchasing power of plaintiffs while curtailing sociolegal risk and retroactive application of changing standards.

The shorter the statute of repose, the greater is the incentive to conceal the occurrence of an injury. In a 1970 survey of malpractice claims, 40 percent of the files were "warning files," that is, files opened on notice by a physician to his insurer, where a claim was never actually filed (Westat, 1973). Assuming that at least some of these warning files did involve potentially valid claims, one can conclude that the tort system is functioning less efficiently than it might, in terms of both compensation and deterrence. The information that is available is underutilized because the physician, who is often best informed about the occurrence of an injury, has incentives to conceal it from the patient. Although the physician's liability insurance contract may provide for a sanction for not reporting a potential claim, for obvious reasons the insurance company will choose not to contact the patient. Currently the only sanction against concealment is that it tolls the running of the statute of limitations. However, if it is difficult to prove that the physician knew of and concealed the injury, this sanction may be weak. Thus if a relatively short statute such as the three-year California statute is adopted, a reasonable quid pro quo for this shortening of liability would be an uninsurable fine for concealing a negligent injury. This should supplement, not replace, the tolling of the statute of limitations for concealment.

Effects of a Short Statute of Repose

How many claims are likely to be barred if the statute were changed, as in California, from an unlimited period for discovery to a three-year limit from the injury or one year from discovery, whichever occurs first? The answer depends in part on how the pattern of discovery and reporting adjusts to the new limits, and partly on sociolegal trends.

To distinguish these effects, assume initially a stable sociolegal environment, that is, there are no changes in legal rules or attitudes and thus the number of claims worth filing from a given pool of potential claims is stable. Let us also make the extreme assumption that the rate of discovery of injuries is beyond the control of the potential plaintiff, but that once an injury has been discovered, filing can be accelerated if necessary to meet a shorter statute.

Under these plausible assumptions, a maximum limit on the time allowed for discovery is crucial. If the statute runs from discovery of the injury with no outer limit on time allowed for discovery, then cutting the time allowed for filing has no long-run effect on the number of claims. But if the statute runs from the time of the injury *with* an outer limit on the time allowed for discovery, then reducing this limit will cut off claims that are not discoverable earlier. Of course the impact is less, the more discovery can be accelerated.

Now add to this scenario an upward trend in awards or an expansion in liability, such as we experienced in the 1960s and early 1970s. The number of claims worth filing from a given pool of injuries is now increasing over time. Shortening the outer limit on time allowed for discovery will have greater impact when there is a pro-plaintiff trend than in a stable environment. Even without an outer limit on time for discovery, a reduction in time for filing after discovery will cut off some claims. The claims that are eliminated will be those that became worth filing only in the more pro-plaintiff environment of later years.

Previous empirical estimates of the effects of shorter statutes have been severely downward-biased because they have been based on closed-claim data. Table 10.1 shows the distribution of incidents by lag from date of incident to date of filing, for claims closed in 1974. Ninety-three percent of these closed claims were reported within three years of the incident. The ISO report therefore concludes that "reducing the statute of limitations to three years after discovery to report a claim would appear to have little effect" (ISO, 1976b, p. 32).

This inference is unwarranted for two reasons. First, since the data refer to the lag between the *incident* and the report, not the *discovery*

Table 10.1 Lag from incident to report of claim

Months from incident to report	Number of incidents (cumulative percent)	Award dollars (cumulative percent)
0	7.7	3.0
Up to 6	37.8	22.3
Up to 12	58.4	43.8
Up to 18	71.3	56.5
Up to 24	82.1	72.0
Up to 30	89.5	80.5
Up to 36	93.4	85.4
Up to 42	95.2	89.5
Up to 48	96.7	92.2
Up to 54	97.5	94.1
Up to 60	98.2	95.2
Up to 66	98.6	95.7
Up to 72	98.9	96.2

Source: Insurance Services Office, "Special Malpractice Review: 1974 Closed Claim Survey" (New York, November 1976), table 6-2a, p. 32.

and the report, any conclusion must relate to the effect of cutting the time allowed from incident to report, not from discovery. As I have argued, an outer limit running from the incident will have an impact, whereas a limit running from discovery may not. Second and most important, there is a bias in drawing this type of inference from a survey of claims closed at a particular moment in time. Assume that the total frequency of claims filed for each policy year is following an upward trend, but with a stable distribution of lags in reporting. Claims closed in any calendar year then give a misleading picture of the reporting pattern for a particular policy year. Claims reported early tend to be the more numerous minor injuries that close relatively quickly; therefore, when frequency is increasing, closed-claim data are disproportionately weighted with small claims from recent policy years. Closed-claim data yield downward-biased estimates of the number and the dollar value of claims cut off by a shorter statute, on a policy-year basis.

This conclusion is confirmed by evidence for the SOCAP program in southern California for policy years 1963–1969. Table 10.2 shows the ratio of claims reported within the first three years relative to the total reported by December 1974. If the reporting pattern were stable,

Table 10.2 Claims filed within three years, relative to total claims filed as of December 1974

Policy year	Percentage of claims filed
1963	69
1964	75
1965	70
1966	72
1967	70
1968	68
1969	63

Source: Linder (1970), and California Department of Insurance. Data are for the Southern California Physicians (SOCAP) Program.

this ratio should increase for successive policy years because the first three years represent a larger fraction of the total time from the policy year to the final observation point, for later policy years. On the contrary, with the exception of the first year, there is a steady decrease in the ratio of claims reported in the first three years to total claims reported by the end of 1974. This implies that over time the fraction of all claims that are reported more than three years after the incident increased in the late 1960s, consistent with the hypothesis that the upward trend in the net benefits of filing stimulated claims that would not have been worth filing in prior years. On the basis of these data from the pre-1975 era, when an unlimited discovery rule was in effect, one may conclude that perhaps 30 to 40 percent of the claims ultimately filed against policy year 1969 would have been eliminated if a three-year limit had been in force at that time.[9]

Conclusions

Long or deferred statutes of limitations are designed to protect victims of latent injuries. Although some late claims are surely valid under the legal rules in effect at the time of injury, others are filed late only because they become worth filing with the pro-plaintiff trend in law over time. To the extent that this latter type of case involves retroactive application of new standards, it serves no useful deterrent function but adds to the risk-bearing and overhead costs of the tort system. From the standpoint of economic efficiency, the optimal duration of liability is shorter, the more volatile are legal rules; the greater is the tendency to apply new standards retroactively; and the less frequent are injuries that are truly latent, relative to those that can be discovered earlier with more effort. Truly latent injuries are probably relatively rare in medical malpractice, except possibly for birth defects. These considerations argue for a short statute with an outer limit on time for discovery, such as the three-year limit in California, except for minors. As a quid pro quo for this protection and to offset the incentives created for concealing injuries, physicians should be required to pay an uninsurable fine for fraud or concealment of a negligent injury.

Of course many would argue that although claims filed late serve no deterrent function, they do serve an equity function and should therefore be allowed. But on the contrary, the equity and efficiency arguments seem particularly well-aligned in the case of late claims. There is little equity in holding someone responsible for damages he could not reasonably have foreseen at the time of action, or for actions that would not have been deemed negligent under the prevailing state of knowledge. Retroactive application of changed standards is surely inequitable as well as inefficient.

Thus the only argument for allowing late claims is the alleged lack of alternative sources of compensation. One solution to this perceived need is to shift liability to special funds. In some states, compensation funds already pay malpractice awards beyond a statutory threshold —typically $100,000 per defendant. Similarly, proposals for special government funds for occupational disease are proliferating. There are two general arguments in favor of such funds: first, there is said to be a need for compensation; second, where future liability was not or cannot be anticipated, government intervention to set up a special fund can force the spreading of costs to all current producers or to taxpayers, thereby protecting established firms with prior liability.

These arguments are not convincing, however. Both these purposes are served more efficiently by simply curtailing liability, through a short statute of repose, and relying on private first-party insurance and public programs to compensate injuries discovered after the running of the statute. Since these are pay-as-you-go insurance programs covering all injuries regardless of cause, the issue of nondiversifiable risk does not arise. It may be objected that private insurance coverage is inadequate, at least for those not eligible for employment-based group programs. Since this problem applies to all injuries, not just the small fraction potentially eligible for tort compensation, it argues for a general public program, which we already have in SSDI and Medicare. It is ironic and unfortunate that current rules of eligibility for SSDI require prior employment, thereby excluding precisely those people for whom private insurance markets function relatively poorly. If these employment criteria were eliminated to make SSDI a safety net for all, this would eliminate the already weak case for extending tort liability purely for purposes of compensation.

11

Costs of Litigation

COMMON CRITICISMS of the malpractice system are the high overhead costs of litigation and the delay in delivering compensation. One specific complaint is that although insurance premiums add significantly to health care costs, only a small fraction of the premium dollar actually reaches the injured party. The plaintiff's share of the malpractice insurance premium dollar has been asserted to be as low as 18 cents (Johnson and Higgins, 1975, p. 3). Even a more reasonable estimate of 40 to 50 cents (Munch, 1977a), although comparable to other liability lines such as product liability and automobile liability, is nevertheless significantly lower than the 62 cents for workers' compensation and 80 cents for first-party health insurance. These estimates are net of attorney's fees, estimated at one-third of the gross award. If the plaintiff has to pay additional court costs and other expenses, his final share may be as much as 10 percentage points lower, that is, 30 to 40 cents of the premium dollar. This chapter provides a closer look at the composition of overhead costs, analyzes the causes of expenditure on litigation, and then evaluates policies to reduce costs, specifically, regulation of contingent fees and the use of screening panels and arbitration.

Malpractice Insurance Costs in Perspective

In 1975 medical malpractice insurance premiums of physicians and hospitals cost roughly $1.4 billion. This amounted to just over 1 percent of the $132.7 billion cost of medical care, and just over 2 percent of total property/casualty insurance premiums. By 1982 malpractice insurance premiums had risen to roughly $2.4 billion, a 73 percent increase. But over the same period the cost of physician services rose 92 percent and the cost of a hospital room rose 130 percent, so that the cost of malpractice insurance declined to under 1 percent of the $322.4 billion spent on health. A 1981 survey showed that malpractice insurance costs constituted 3.6 percent of physicians' gross income, on average countrywide, ranging from 2.2 percent for general practitioners to 4.1 percent for general surgeons and 5.6 percent for orthopedic surgeons (see Table 11.1). Comparable figures in 1970 were 1.8 percent for general practitioners and 4.2 percent for general surgeons.[1] Thus although malpractice insurance costs are not trivial, the very high rates for specialists in the highest-risk areas, which attract the most public attention, create a misleading impression of the situation overall. The belief that malpractice insurance has been a major factor contributing to the high and rising cost of health care is clearly exaggerated. Nevertheless, the burden of litigation costs as a share of the total is high enough to warrant serious search for reform.

Litigation Costs

For every dollar that reaches plaintiffs as compensation, roughly 66 cents is spent by the parties on litigation. Reform measures proposed so far have tended to focus primarily on expenditure by the plaintiff (regulation of contingent fees), particularly on cases with high stakes, and on the costs of processing small claims. This focus does not appear to be justified by disproportionately high expenditures on these cases. Overall, plaintiff and defense spend roughly equal amounts, but the defense spends relatively more on small cases whereas the plaintiff spends relatively more on cases with high stakes. For claims closed in the period 1975–1978, insurer claim expense averaged over 28 percent of total indemnity paid to plaintiffs.[2] Within this overall average, insurer expense exceeded indemnity on cases awarded less than $4,000 but decreased to 5 percent of awards over $100,000. Since the defense could presumably reduce its expense by offering higher settlements, incurring expense in excess of indemnity can only be a rational strategy if adopting a tough stance on filed claims deters other potential claimants from filing. And as we have seen, potential claimants may outnumber actual claimants by as much as nine to one.

Table 11.2 shows insurer expense by stage of disposition. In the first section, which includes cases closed with and without payment to the plaintiff, expense appears to increase dramatically as a percent-

Table 11.1 Physicians' liability insurance premiums, income, and expenses, 1981 (thousands of dollars)

	General practitioners	Pedia- tricians	Obstetricians/ Gynecologists	Anesthes- iologists	General surgeons	Neuro- surgeons	Orthopedic surgeons	Total
Malpractice Premiums								
Mean	3.30	2.70	9.60	7.60	8.40	11.64	13.35	6.11
S.E.	0.24	0.26	0.78	0.72	0.54	2.73	1.75	—
N	327	99	112	76	139	11	51	815
Total Professional Expenses								
Mean	72.70	63.90	99.60	48.40	82.48	98.73	109.71	75.75
S.E.	4.30	9.20	11.90	9.20	12.18	30.19	11.22	—
N	332	101	113	74	147	11	58	836
Malpractice Premiums as Percentage of Professional Expenses								
Mean	4.5%	4.2%	9.6%	15.7%	10.2%	11.8%	12.2%	8.6%
Net Income								
Mean	72.20	65.10	110.80	118.60	123.69	132.75	127.32	94.83
S.E.	3.30	4.90	9.20	5.00	7.29	17.63	7.19	—
N	514	222	192	161	263	20	92	1464
Gross Income[a]								
Mean	144.90	129.00	210.40	167.00	206.17	231.48	237.03	170.58
Malpractice Premiums as Percentage of Gross Income								
Mean	2.2%	2.1%	4.6%	4.6%	4.1%	5.0%	5.6%	3.6%

Source: 1982 Core Survey, Socioeconomic Monitoring System, American Medical Association.
a. Gross Income = Total Professional Expenses + Net Income.

Table 11.2 Awards and adjustment expense, by stage of disposition, 1974

Disposition	Average award	Average expense	Expense as percentage of award
Claims Closed with and without Payment			
Prior to suit	$1,892	$95	5.0
In suit[a]	$10,156	$2,604	25.6
Verdict	$9,715	$6,231	64.1
All incidents	$6,841	$1,841	26.9
Claims Closed with Payment Only[b]			
Prior to suit	$5,742	$95	1.7
In suit[a]	$17,044	$2,604	15.3
Verdict	$44,466	$6,231	14.0
All incidents	$14,696	$1,841	12.5

Source: Insurance Services Office, Special Malpractice Review: 1974 Closed Claim Survey, November 1976, pp. 59–60.
a. Claims closed after filing suit, prior to verdict.
b. Allocated expense is for all cases. Expense for claims closed with payment only is not reported.

age of award for more advanced stages of disposition: it increases from 5 percent of the award for claims closed prior to suit to 26 percent for claims settled or abandoned after suit but before verdict, and 64 percent for cases litigated to verdict. However, the lower section reveals that the apparent pattern of increase in litigation expense relative to award, for cases going to verdict, results from the much larger fraction of verdicts closed without payment to the plaintiff, which pulls down the average award. Separating out cases closed with payment to the plaintiff shows that although trial to verdict entails larger total expense, this total is nevertheless smaller relative to the stakes than for cases settled out of court, presumably because optimal expenditure is a decreasing proportion of higher-valued cases which are more likely to go to trial. Thus just as we found that a simple comparison of jury verdicts and settlement amounts is inappropriate because cases that go to verdict are atypical, similarly the comparison of the costs of trial relative to settlement is biased by the "self-selection" of high-valued, difficult cases to trial.[3]

Much less comprehensive information is available on litigation expense for the plaintiff. Plaintiff attorneys typically handle medical malpractice — and all other personal injury litigation — on a contin-

gent-fee basis.[4] A 1971 survey of attorneys handling medical malpractice cases shows that of respondents using a fixed-percentage
contingent fee, the most common amount is 33⅓ percent of the award,
the mean and median are 36 percent, and the range is 25 to 50 percent.
For attorneys using a sliding scale, the most common amount is 33⅓
percent of the award if the case is settled before trial and 40 percent if
it goes to trial or appeal, but the range runs from 20 percent before
trial to 50 percent through appeal (Dietz, Baird, and Berul, 1973).

This survey did not report whether fees typically vary by size of
case, but other evidence suggests that the percentage decreases in
cases with larger awards. In a 1957 survey of contingent fees for 3,000
personal injury cases in New York City (Franklin, Chanin, and Mark,
1961), the average fee ranged from 41 percent on cases under $1,000 to
29 percent on cases over $25,000, with an overall mean of 36 percent
— comparable to the mean for the 1971 malpractice survey. This less
dramatic decline in expense relative to award, by size of case, for
plaintiff than for defense confirms the inference drawn from the
claim disposition analysis, and the inference of "deterrent" expenditure by the defense to discourage potential claimants. The tendency
for expense to decrease relative to award, the higher the award, is in
fact greater than it appears because large awards are more likely to
include a discounted present value of compensation for future damages, and thus total compensation includes investment income on the
initial lump-sum award.

Litigation expenditure as a choice. In evaluating the likely effect
of measures to reduce litigation expense, it is crucial to note that the
amount actually spent reflects the voluntary choices of the litigants,
given the opportunities and constraints they face. Any measure to
reduce litigation expense must operate through these incentives and
constraints. Under the simple assumption of rational behavior, each
side would be willing to spend to the point where the marginal dollar
spent on legal fees, expert witnesses, and so on has an expected payoff
of at least one dollar—an increase in expected recovery for the
plaintiff, a decrease in expected payout for the defense. It follows that
each side will expend more effort, the greater the potential effect on
the outcome, and the lower the cost per unit of litigation input. Thus,
one of the expected savings from adopting scheduled benefits rather
than attempting to compensate each plaintiff for his individual loss is
that schedules limit the range of potential outcomes and hence reduce incentives to spend to influence the outcome. By contrast, measures that reduce the cost per unit of litigation input may have muted
if not perverse effects on total expenditures, depending on the price

elasticity of response. If quantity purchased were very sensitive to price, total expenditure could actually increase in response to a reduction in cost per unit. In fact, rough estimates indicate that a 10 percent reduction in cost per unit of legal services would lead to a 3.3 percent increase in the quantity purchased, so that total expenditure per case would fall by 6.7 percent.[5]

The possibility of settling out of court creates a distinction between the maximum the parties would be willing to spend — determined by expected payoff, relative to cost — and the amount they actually spend. If settlement occurs, actual expenditure is less than the potential maximum. Because the incentive to settle is greater, the higher the potential maximum costs of proceeding with litigation, measures designed to reduce these costs of litigating to verdict will tend to reduce actual expenditure by *less* than might have been anticipated. This was demonstrated in Chapter 3, using the model of claim disposition (Danzon and Lillard, 1983) to simulate the effects of hypothetical changes in the cost of going to verdict, such as might result from a change in rules of procedure or the introduction of pretrial screening panels or arbitration. We first assumed that the litigation costs of settlement are zero but that the costs of going to verdict are 30 percent of the potential verdict for each party. We then simulated the effects of a procedural reform that cuts the cost of going to verdict by one-third. Although, by assumption, cost per case is reduced by 33 percent, total expenditure on litigation falls by only 18 percent. In response to the reduced cost per case, there is an increase in the number of cases going to verdict, which partially offsets the reduction in cost per case. If the costs of settling are not zero but, say, 10 percent of the potential verdict for each party, before and after the change, then total saving on litigation is only 3 percent, because fewer cases are dropped and more incur settlement costs. And these estimates still omit the additional costs that will be incurred as more cases are filed.

Private versus social optimum. If predicting the full ramifications of measures intended to reduce costs is problematic, evaluating their overall efficiency is even more uncertain. Actual expenditure on litigation is determined by private utility-maximizing decisions. The private optimum may differ from the social optimum because of divergence of private and social benefits and costs. On the benefit side, adjudication through the courts serves both a private and a social purpose: the private benefit is resolution of private disputes and determination of rights to compensation; the social benefit is formulation and enforcement of rules of law. In the case of professional liability, this latter function consists of clarifying the standards of due care and imposing sanctions on those found in violation. As we have seen, for liability rules to provide effective and accurate incentives, injured patients must sue and courts must make accurate findings of liability and damages.

On the cost side, private and social costs may diverge for several reasons. Each party, by incurring costs himself, imposes costs on the public and on the opposing party. First, to the extent that courts are financed out of the public fisc rather than by user fees, litigants impose cost on taxpayers. Second, because scarce court resources are rationed by queues rather than fees, each pair of litigants who enter the queue impose a cost on other users. Third, each side in a case imposes costs on the other, to the extent that expenditure by one merely nullifies the other's influence rather than adding new information. In fact, each side has an incentive to impose costs on the other to enhance his bargaining position in settlement. As the model of the settlement process showed, the plaintiff can increase the maximum a rational defendant would offer by increasing the latter's expected costs, and conversely the defendant can decrease the minimum the plaintiff would settle for and increase the likelihood of his dropping the case by increasing his costs of proceeding. The incentives for strategic behavior are obviously reduced if the other side can retaliate in kind, since then the expected net payoff may be zero or even negative. But such strategic tactics, with negative social payoff, surely exist and pose a difficult policy dilemma. In practice there is no clear distinction between legal actions that generate information and promote more accurate deterrence, and those that serve purely strategic purposes. Taking depositions and filing interrogatories obviously impose costs on the other side but also generate information. Thus, although there may be savings in litigation from such measures as limits on the discovery process, the net savings, including effects on accuracy of outcome, may be much smaller.

Previous analyses of incentives to bring suit have concluded that plaintiff litigation costs result in suboptimal private incentives to sue (Ordover, 1978; Shavell, 1982c). This conclusion is based on the assumption that the plaintiff's expected payoff is the expected award, net of his litigation costs. Positive costs of suit for the plaintiff are viewed as a tax that leads to underinvestment. But this view neglects the litigation costs of the defense: since the maximum offer in settlement is the expected award *plus* defense costs of going to court, defense costs act as a subsidy to the plaintiff, raising the potential payoff in settlement above the expected award, other things being equal. Thus the effects of plaintiff and defense litigation costs tend to be offsetting. If plaintiff and defense costs were equal and if settlements typically split the difference between the ask and the offer, these two effects would offset each other precisely: settlement would be for the expected verdict (probability of winning times the potential verdict). This would provide the socially correct incentive to sue, ignoring the external benefits of law enforcement and assuming that settlement for the amount were certain.

In fact, although the distortion due to costs may be lower than indicated by previous analyses, the necessary conditions for zero distortion do not hold in practice. If defendants can be forced to settle closer to the maximum offer, as the estimates in Chapter 3 indicate, this would encourage too many suits, other things being equal. Moreover, litigation costs are not precisely equal. Defense costs tend to exceed plaintiff costs on low-valued cases and vice versa on high-valued cases, with the result that settlements are closer to the potential verdict on low-valued cases—the familiar "overcompensation" of small cases. But since the probability of winning a positive settlement is lower on small cases, one cannot say a priori whether the net effect of litigation costs is to encourage too few or too many suits, or how the distortion varies by size of case. Certainly the evidence in Chapter 2 shows that far fewer than the potential number of suits are filed, and that costs are an important deterrent to filing. In view of this shortfall and the positive deterrent benefit from law enforcement, there is some justification for a public subsidy to private litigation, such as public provision of the courts. Whether the current subsidy is too high or too low is an important but difficult policy question that remains unresolved.

Delay: Causes and Cures

For claims closed in the period 1975–1978, the average number of months from report to disposition of the claim was 25 months for paid claims and 18 months for unpaid claims, with an overall average of 21 months. With an average lag from incident to report of 16 months for paid claims and 14 months for unpaid claims, this adds up to an average lag from incident to disposition of 41 and 32 months, for paid and unpaid claims respectively, or an overall average of 36 months (NAIC, 1980). These are averages over a skewed distribution: 42 percent of claims closed within a year of filing and 66 percent within two years, but 5 percent took over five years. Adding the lag in claim reporting, 21 percent closed within a year of the incident, 40 percent closed within two years, and 15 percent took more than five years.

Delay is longer on cases with higher stakes, and it is more than twice as long for permanent total disabilities as for minor temporary injuries.

Delay is often cited as a self-evident defect of the tort system. But in fact, like other litigation expense, delay has both positive and negative effects, and determining the socially optimal amount is exceedingly difficult. In fact finding, as in most activities, speed can be costly. Gathering information may be more costly if the parties are rushed — for example, if the physician or attorney must cancel other commitments to respond as soon as a claim is filed. Moreover, time may be valuable in determining the true extent of the patient's injuries. On the other hand, to the extent that an award is based on medical expense and wage loss incurred at the time of trial, delay creates moral hazard by reducing the patient's incentives for rehabilitation and return to normal life.

Delay in receiving compensation is also costly to patients if the law disallows prejudgment interest, that is, interest on the judgment over the period from injury to disposition. Given the uncertainty about the timing and size of an award, if any, borrowing against the expected award to cover current costs may be difficult. Moreover, there is some evidence that more time does not necessarily improve the quality of the proceedings. One study of the effects of judicial case management to expedite disposition found that the same amount of attorney preparation was compressed into a shorter time span, and the quality of the outcome improved because evidence was fresher (Flanders, in Adler et al., 1982, p. 20).

Although it is impossible to define the optimal time for disposition, it is possible to identify factors that create incentives for nonoptimal behavior. Most obviously, the rule against prejudgment interest creates incentives for the defense to delay. This should be replaced with a simple rule requiring payment of interest at current market rates, from the date of filing. Payment of interest from the incident to filing might be awarded at the discretion of the court in cases where reporting was delayed through no fault of the plaintiff. In general, however, withholding interest prior to filing may be justified as a means of encouraging the plaintiff to file promptly. Delay in filing is costly to insurers because it lengthens the tail of claims and makes the pricing of insurance more uncertain; moreover, plaintiffs may delay filing in anticipation of favorable changes in law, and this may result in inefficient retroactive application of new standards.

Another factor is that plaintiff attorneys have an incentive to prefer long delays because this permits them to have a large portfolio of cases; such diversification provides a form of insurance to the attorney paid on a contingent basis. Clearly, large caseloads may be the cause as well as the result of long delays. If the private incentives of attorneys to expedite disposition tend to be socially suboptimal, this can be corrected by active judicial management, setting short times to prepare for trial, and denying unreasonable requests for continuances.

Contingent Fees

As we have seen, contingent fees are the dominant form of payment for plaintiff attorneys in personal injury litigation. With a contingent fee the attorney receives some fraction of the award, usually agreed upon by prior negotiation with his client, only if there is a positive recovery. By contrast, defense attorneys are typically paid on an hourly basis for time actually spent, regardless of the outcome of the case. Thus with a contingent fee the attorney finances the litigation and bears the risk of zero return on the investment.

There is a long tradition of hostility toward contingent fees. They are prohibited in England and Canada and have been singled out for regulation in the United States. The Federal Tort Claims Act limits contingent fees on claims against the government to a flat 25 percent, and contingent fees on worker's compensation cases are also regulated. Since 1975, 18 states have enacted limits on contingent fees for medical malpractice cases, whereas no such restrictions have been placed on hourly fees paid by the defense. The rationale for this traditional hostility is summarized in MacKinnon (1964): (1) giving the attorney the right to finance litigation allegedly promotes "nuisance" suits with little legal merit; (2) contingent fees are said to be excessive; and (3) the attorney's stake in the claim allegedly creates a conflict of interest with the client that impedes settlement—the attorney is believed to be more prone to gamble.

The traditional view, that contingent fees stimulate "excessive" litigation, differs sharply from the conclusion reached by previous economic analysis. Using as a benchmark what a fully informed, risk-neutral plaintiff would choose if paying an attorney by the hour (which may not be the social optimum, for the reasons discussed earlier), Schwartz and Mitchell (1970) conclude that the contingent fee results in less attorney effort per case and consequently in lower gross recoveries and lower fees. Essentially the argument is that whereas the client would be willing to buy attorney time to the point where the expected payoff is equal to the attorney's hourly wage, with a contingent fee the attorney decides how much time to spend. His optimal decision rule is to devote time only to the point where his share of the payoff is equal to his hourly wage rate (the opportunity cost of his time). This decision rule would imply less effort per case and hence a lower plaintiff win rate and award than would result if an informed, risk-neutral plaintiff purchased attorney time by the hour, as does the defense.

I have argued elsewhere that both these extreme views are incorrect (Danzon, 1983a). Competition in the market for legal services can lead attorneys paid on a contingent basis to act exactly as would be preferred by fully informed clients paying an hourly wage.[6] If competition is imperfect, however, there may be some tendency toward less attorney effort than the client would prefer, as a result of the effect noted by Schwartz and Mitchell.

The number of suits filed is certainly likely to be higher if contingent fees are available, not because the contingent fee creates incentives for attorneys to bring frivolous suits—this incentive is surely higher with an hourly fee that is paid regardless of the outcome—or because contingent fees are excessive, but because the contingent fee protects the plaintiff from risk. Many risk-averse plaintiffs with meritorious claims would be unwilling to incur the sure costs of litigation with an hourly fee when the payoff is uncertain. The following example illustrates this point. In 1976 the average malpractice award was $29,456. With plausible assumptions about risk aversion, I estimated that a plaintiff with assets of less than $20,000 would be unwilling to hire an attorney on an hourly basis to bring a malpractice suit of average value, if the odds of winning were less than two chances in three. In fact, plaintiffs won only 41 percent of cases in 1976. This suggests that abolition of contingent fees could deter a large number of cases. The plaintiffs most affected would be those with low income and high costs of borrowing, those most averse to risk, and those with low estimates of their chances of winning. Even with a contingent fee, risk aversion will eliminate some meritorious suits if time costs and filing fees are significant factors for the plaintiff.

Do contingent fees lead risk-preferring attorneys to stir up suits? The limited truth in this allegation is that a risk-preferring attorney would accept a case that would be rejected by a risk-neutral attorney and would charge an expected fee less than the opportunity cost of his time. Because attorney risk tolerance tends to benefit clients, competition tends to eliminate risk-averse attorneys from contingent fee litigation. Note, however, that the contingent nature of the fee, such that the attorney recoups his costs only if he wins, generally acts as a deterrent to stirring up suits, relative to an hourly wage that is paid regardless of the outcome.

If there is some minimum time required to handle a case, regardless of the stakes, small cases may be effectively barred—and the evidence from claim filings and disposition tends to confirm this. But this is a result of the rules of procedure and possibly the strategy of the defense, not the contingent fee per se. This situation may be exacerbated by constraints on contingent fees, both explicit regulation and the unwritten rule that contingent fees may not exceed 50 percent (MacKinnon, 1964). But in cases where the contingent fee necessary to cover the opportunity cost of the attorney's time would exceed 50 percent of the expected recovery, the client could presumably pay on an hourly basis. The fact that such contracts are so uncommon must be attributed to plaintiff risk aversion, inability to monitor attorney effort, and higher cost of borrowing, all of which make the contingent fee the preferred contract from the client's perspective.

Are contingent fees excessive? It is widely—and correctly—believed that one-third of a multimillion-dollar award typically exceeds the opportunity cost of the attorney's time spent on the case. However, it does not follow that, on average, attorneys paid on a contingent basis earn above competitive returns. In setting the fee percentage ex ante, a risk-neutral attorney will charge the same expected fee on a contingent or an hourly basis. But ex post the actual fee for cases won will exceed the cost of his time by a multiple that is the inverse of the probability of winning, ex ante.[7] Roughly 60 percent of medical malpractice cases with attorney representation obtain some positive award. If this outcome is correctly anticipated, contingent fees on average will appear to overcompensate attorneys by 66 percent for their time spent on cases won. Plaintiffs who win therefore realize a lower net recovery than they would, other things being equal, if they paid an hourly fee. Nevertheless, plaintiffs are better off with a contingent fee for the same reason that any insurance makes people better off: you pay a premium if your income is high (you win the case) in order to avoid a loss if your income is low (you lose the case).

In response to the malpractice insurance crisis, 18 states enacted limits on contingent fees. Five states prescribed a sliding scale, with the maximum percentage decreasing with the size of the award.[8] The remaining 12 states granted the court discretion to determine a reasonable fee, either on its own motion or at the request of the plaintiff or plaintiff's attorney.

Sliding-scale limits are likely to fall unevenly on different types of cases. For example, the California sliding scale is 40 percent of the first $50,000; 33 percent on the next $60,000; 25 percent of the next $100,000; and 10 percent on any amount over $200,000. This yields an average percentage of less than one-third on cases over $140,000. The maximum allowed on an award of $1 million would be 14 percent, or roughly one-third of the typical free-market fee for a case taken to trial. In general, sharply decreasing sliding scales are most likely to be binding on cases with large potential awards, which tend to be cases of severe injury to young claimants. Regulations that do not follow the market pattern of a higher fee for cases taken to trial will discourage litigation to verdict and appeals. Flat ceilings are most likely to be binding on small cases and cases with weak evidence for the plaintiff; the magnitude of the effect depends on the shortfall between the regulated and the unregulated fee. Theoretical analysis suggests that if the fee is cut by half, the plaintiff's expected recovery would fall by roughly 25 percent. The empirical analysis of fee ceilings introduced in the mid-1970s (Danzon and Lillard, 1983) is broadly consistent with this estimate: we found that fee ceilings reduced average settlement size by 9 percent, increased the proportion of cases dropped without payment from 43 to 48 percent, and reduced the proportion of cases litigated to verdict from 6.1 to 4.6 percent.[9]

This evidence suggests that unconstrained contingent fees do not convey rents at the margin and hence that controls not only reduce the attorney's fee but also reduce compensation to plaintiffs. It confirms survey evidence that hourly earnings of plaintiff and defense attorneys are similar (Dietz, Baird, and Berul, 1973), despite their different forms of payment. Indeed, any other result would be surprising in view of the mobility of attorneys between contingent-fee and hourly business. Thus, in the absence of any evidence or presumption that the number of suits is excessive, from a social standpoint, there is no case for regulating contingent fees — particularly if expenditure by the defense is unconstrained.

Screening Panels

Since 1975, 30 states have introduced pretrial screening of medical malpractice claims by special review panels, and federal legislation to promote screening has recently been proposed.[10] These panels are intended to make use of legal and medical expertise to eliminate frivolous actions, promote prompt settlement of valid claims, and assist in trial preparation. Typically, panels are composed of three to seven members, including an attorney, a physician (usually of the same specialty as the defendant) and a judge or attorney chairman appointed by the court. Hearings are informal, without strict rules of evidence and procedure. Approximately two-thirds of the panels are authorized to make a finding only with respect to liability, while the remainder also award damages. Unlike arbitration, the findings of a review panel are not binding on the parties: either party may accept the panel decision, negotiate a settlement, or proceed to a jury trial. But to discourage further litigation, some statutes make the findings of a panel admissible at a later trial, while others assess monetary costs against a party who rejects the panel finding and fails to prevail at trial.[11]

Proponents of panels hoped that an early review of cases by an informal panel of experts would facilitate fair and speedy disposition. But theory and evidence suggest that the panel model, which interjects another, nonbinding step in the dispute resolution process, may be fatally flawed. Panels designed as voluntary, pre-complaint hearings with little formal power do not appear to be used very often. On the other hand, mandatory panels with formal hearings and real power to discourage appeal to jury trial run the risk of incurring the cost and delay of a real trial, as well as the risk of constitutional challenge. Common to four of these successful challenges was the claim that the statutes denied reasonable access to the courts, either on their face or in practice because of severe backlogs in the processing of claims. However, two-thirds of the states with functioning mandatory panels have withstood constitutional challenges.[12]

The impact of panels can be analyzed in the context of the model of dispute resolution developed in Chapter 3, which implies that rational litigants will continue to trial if the costs of proceeding are less than the difference between their expectations of the outcome. Consider how the operation of a panel might affect this calculation. A panel will narrow divergence of expectations about the outcome at verdict only if it is a reasonable replication of a jury trial. But this means using formal rules of evidence and allowing full discovery, which entail the costs and delay that panels are intended to prevent. Moreover, once the costs of a panel hearing have been incurred, the incremental costs of proceeding to trial are reduced, which tends to encourage litigation. This is particularly true in cases where the panelists or nonmember expert witnesses can be called at trial, effectively providing expert testimony free of charge. This reduction in the incremental costs of litigating to verdict may be offset by penalties imposed on a losing appellant; but the model implies that if the incremental costs of litigation fall by more than the reduction in divergence in expected outcomes, screening could increase the number of claims litigated to verdict. Consistent with this, evidence from Arizona suggests that screening tends to increase delay in disposition and raise total litigation costs because fewer claims are closed with zero litigation expense (National Center for State Courts, 1980).

Another dilemma of the panel approach is that in order to economize on the cost of expert testimony, at least one panelist must be a physician. But assuming that the other panelists are neutral, this may bias outcomes against plaintiffs, particularly in cases where the panel is composed solely of physicians and where the medical panelist must come from the same locality as the defendant.

Data are not available for a detailed empirical evaluation of panels. Most studies to date are descriptive rather than controlled statistical analyses, and there is a tendency to compare screened cases with unscreened cases tried to verdict, whereas the appropriate base of comparison is *all* unscreened cases, of which verdicts are a tiny, atypical subset.[13] In some states (Massachusetts and New Jersey), panels are reportedly processing cases efficiently and disposing of them at the hearing stage; others report serious backlogs and administrative problems. Limited evidence on the impact of screening is available from the NAIC data on claims closed in the period 1975–1978 (Table 11.3). Of the 71,782 claims, panels are reported to have been utilized in only 606, or less than 1 percent. Panels found for the plaintiff in 36 percent (216) of screened cases, whereas 38 percent of all claims closed with some payment to the plaintiff. Twenty-two percent (134) of screened claims were appealed and subsequently resolved by court disposition (121) or binding arbitration (13), compared to 13 percent of all cases. The great majority (84 percent) of the appeals against the panel decision were brought by the plaintiff, but the court reversed the panel's findings in only 13 percent of cases. Whereas plaintiffs won 14 percent of the 9,325 claims taken to verdict or binding arbitration, plaintiffs won only 9 percent (12) of such cases that had been subject to prior screening.

Although the number of cases is too small for firm conclusions, taken at face value the evidence is consistent with the prediction that panels may tend to increase the number of cases litigated to verdict, to be weakly biased against the plaintiff, and to reduce the plaintiff's chances in subsequent appeals. This last effect may be stronger than these data would suggest because, to the extent that it can be anticipated, only cases with an above-average chance for the plaintiff will proceed to appeal after an adverse panel finding.

The only other attempt so far to measure systematically the effect

Table 11.3 Costs and outcomes, by forum, 1975–1978

Variable	Settlement/ Abandoned	Court disposition	Binding arbitration	Review panel
Claims Closed with and without Payment				
Number of claims	62,210	9,086	239	606
Percentage for plaintiff	41.3	13.5	38.9	35.6
Claims Closed with Payment				
Average indemnity	$19,696	$54,438	$20,865	$29,501
S.E.	(356)	(3,864)	(4,610)	N/A
N	25,662	1,229	93	182
Average expense	$3,949	$8,322	$4,794	$4,272
S.E.	(144)	(311)	(784)	N/A
N	18,362	1,134	81	155
Average delay (months)	18	26	19	21
Claims Closed without Payment				
Average expense	$1,860	$5,229	$2,708	$2,398
S.E.	(134)	(381)	(282)	N/A
N	16,016	6,938	120	323
Average delay (months)	12	21	16	13

Source: NAIC (1980), p. 75.

of panels is the analysis of trends in claim frequency and severity reported in Chapter 4. That study found no significant effect of voluntary or mandatory screening on average claim frequency and severity.

A full evaluation of panels in the context of the overall purpose of the tort system must consider their impact on incentives to file, on the accuracy of findings with respect to liability and damages, and hence on deterrence. Even if the effect of expert evaluation is to reduce the divergence of the parties' expectations of the outcome and encourage settlement, there is a net efficiency gain only if any saving in litigation expense exceeds the possible loss of accuracy resulting from systematic bias or less thorough investigation, and the consequent impairment of deterrence.

It is also not clear whether specially instituted panels are more effective than other court efforts to expedite dispute resolution. For example, Cook County in Illinois has established a special malpractice court with emphasis on the pretrial stage, a time limitation for discovery, and tight scheduling of early trial. This program has apparently greatly accelerated the disposition of malpractice litigation (ABA, 1977; Ebener et al., 1981).

Arbitration

Thirteen states have enacted legislation providing for voluntary binding arbitration of medical malpractice claims. Of these states, four will enforce only those arbitration agreements made after the plaintiff claims injury,[14] while the remainder enforce both post-claim and pre-claim agreements. Puerto Rico, which has no state constitutional guarantee of jury trial in civil suits, provides for mandatory arbitration of malpractice claims. In states that have no specific legislation authorizing arbitration of medical malpractice claims, it may be permissible under general arbitration statutes that have been adopted in thirty-six states.

Some courts have refused to enforce arbitration agreements because of potentially unequal bargaining power between the parties, particularly in cases where the agreement was signed by the patient before treatment was given. To protect patient interests and avoid judicial findings of adhesion or unconscionability, statutory provisions typically require that arbitration agreements must comply with a special format, including large print and explicit language, designed to ensure that there has been a knowing waiver by the plaintiff of the right to jury trial. Inpatient hospital agreements typically apply to a single admission, while ambulatory care agreements (covering outpatient and physician office visits) are primarily based on an ongoing relationship or may remain in force for a specific time period. Several states have ruled that signing an arbitration agreement cannot be made a precondition to a patient's receiving medical care. Others provide that in cases where an arbitration agreement has been signed before injury is claimed to have occurred, the plaintiff may rescind within a period of 30 to 60 days after the execution of the agreement or the completion of treatment, whichever comes later.

Although arbitration resembles screening in using less formal rules of procedure and evidence, they differ in certain key respects. Whereas screening is mandatory, arbitration is voluntarily chosen by the parties, either prior to treatment (in which case either party may have an opportunity to rescind the agreement to arbitrate within a specified time) or after the occurrence of a potential dispute.[15] Arbitration decisions are binding, whereas findings of screening panels can be appealed to the courts, albeit with a penalty in some cases.

Arbitration findings include both liability and damages. The statutes vary as to the size, composition, and source of arbitration panels and the freedom of detail left to the choice of the parties; some require the inclusion of physician, attorney, judge, or public members. But all leave some choice to the litigants, since a key objective of arbitration is the selection of a tribunal acceptable to the parties and suited to determine the issues.

In the NAIC data on claims closed in the period 1975–1978, only 239 (or one-third of 1 percent) were closed by binding arbitration. Of these, 39 percent were decided for the plaintiff, compared to 38 percent of all claims closed with payment to the plaintiff and 13.5 percent of court dispositions. The average arbitration award was $20,865, similar to the average for all claims of $21,257 and much lower than the average court award of $54,438. The higher plaintiff win rate and lower award in arbitration than in court suggests that, consistent with the model of rational settlement behavior, the lower costs of arbitration induce more parties to seek a decision by a third party rather than settling between themselves. The average litigation expense of the defense on cases closed by binding arbitration ($3,549) is significantly less than on cases taken to court verdict ($5,663) but exceeds the average expense of settlement ($2,976). Unfortunately, these data do not permit a full comparison of the litigation costs of arbitration relative to the judicial process because they do not report information separately for those cases settled in anticipation of arbitration. Moreover, the conclusions are tentative because of the small sample of cases and the possibility of nonrandom selection.[16]

On the grounds of economic efficiency and freedom of choice, a strong case can be made for permitting patients and physicians to enter into voluntary but binding arbitration agreements. Arbitration offers a less formal, potentially cheaper private forum than the courts. When arbitration services are privately provided in competition with the publicly subsidized court system, there is some presumption that the rules and procedures of arbitration will be designed to maximize the value of the service to potential litigants (Landes and Posner, 1979).[17] Arbitration will be voluntarily adopted only where the (private) saving in expected litigation costs exceeds any costs associated with forgoing the right to a jury trial.

The presumption that arbitration procedures will be optimally designed and adopted only where they increase efficiency requires that the parties to the agreement be well-informed and operate in competitive markets. If a medical provider has sufficient monopoly power to force arbitration on patients as a precondition of providing services, or if patients are uninformed, suppliers of arbitration services would have incentives to design procedures to favor physicians. These are the concerns underlying court refusals to enforce arbitration agreements, on grounds of adhesion (unequal bargaining power) or unconscionability, particularly where signing is made a condition of treatment.

However, statutory specification of the terms and format of arbitration agreements seems adequate to handle the problem of patient ignorance, and competition among providers is surely adequate to protect a source of medical services offering patients the court option, if that is indeed preferred by a substantial group. Denying providers the right to make arbitration a condition of treatment means that they have to offer both judicial and arbitration options. This in turn raises contracting and billing costs, reduces the potential saving in malpractice insurance costs (by making claim costs less predictable), and forces all patients to pay for legal protections they might be willing to forgo in return for lower medical costs.

The slow adoption of arbitration so far is due at least in part to the lack of incentive for the individual patient to opt for the cheaper form of dispute resolution, under the current fee-for-service health care system. It is yet another instance of moral hazard: any individual who gives up his tort rights realizes only a fraction of the saving. This situation should change with the growth of health insurance contracts that limit beneficiaries to prespecified groups of providers (health maintenance organizations, exclusive or preferred provider agreements), which internalize to consumers the saving from opting for arbitration. Courts have been—and should be—more willing to uphold binding arbitration agreements included in such health insurance contracts than those signed just prior to treatment. The feasibility of contracting out of various tort rights is discussed more fully in the next chapter.

Deterring Frivolous Claims: Countersuits

By filing suit, a plaintiff imposes on the defendant the alternative of incurring costs of defense or buying out by a settlement offer. Whether this becomes a serious form of extortion in the legal system depends on whether the rules of procedure require that the plaintiff incur significant costs before the defense. If so, the defense can call the plaintiff's bluff simply by waiting. The most extreme allegations of frivolous suits are belied by the fact that 38 percent of all claims are closed with zero litigation expense to the defendant and, of claims closed out of court, 62 percent were abandoned without payment to the plaintiff (NAIC, 1980). Given this uncertainty of recovery, the contingent-fee basis of payment must give plaintiff attorneys an incentive to screen out claims with a very low probability of success.

One remedy becoming increasingly available to physicians who are groundlessly sued is a countersuit, most commonly for malicious prosecution. An action based on malicious prosecution must show all of the following: the institution or continuation of judicial proceeding without probable cause; malice; termination of the suit in the defendant's favor; and damage to the defendant arising out of the suit. A minority of states require, in addition, that the countersuing defendant show some special damages, such as arrest or interference with property, other than those normally incident to defending a court action.[18]

Clearly there is a fine line to be drawn between groundless harassment and filing a potentially valid claim with great uncertainty as to the outcome, particularly in a field of uncertain standards of appropriate care such as malpractice. The stringent requirements for success in an action for malicious prosecution reflect this concern to preserve open access to the courts: "Honest litigants are to be encouraged to seek justice and not to be deterred by fear of an action in return . . . the good citizen must endure any resulting expense or damage as an inevitable burden to be borne under his government" (Prosser, 1964).

A countersuit may be brought against the malpractice plaintiff or his attorney. Because of his role as an officer of the court, the attorney is held to a higher standard of care than his nonattorney client.[19] A California court has clarified the attorney's obligations as follows: "An attorney has probable cause to represent a client in litigation when, after a reasonable investigation and industrious search of legal authority, he has an honest belief that his client's claim is tenable."[20] In the case of medical malpractice the plaintiff's attorney must show that he investigated the facts, by examining the records and consulting with expert physicians, and that "reasonable" legal colleagues would have agreed, after an adequate investigation, that there was a reasonable basis for the claim (Singer, 1977). Thus lawyers, like physicians, have an obligation to follow the prevailing standards of their profession.

However, courts have stopped short of holding that an attorney owes a duty of care and could be liable in negligence to the defendant physician, since this would create a conflict of interest with his duty to represent his client.[21] In *Weaver v. Superior Court of Orange*

County, the court held that although malice could be inferred from the lack of probable cause — itself a significant relaxation of the burden on the countersuing defendant — "the quantum of culpable conduct which must be proved to prevail as a plaintiff in a malicious prosecution case is significantly greater than that required to prevail in a case alleging only negligence." Just what constitutes a "quantum of culpable conduct" was left undefined. Nevertheless, the consensus of commentators is that the obstacles to countersuit are being reduced. This trend is also reflected in an expansion of the grounds for countersuit for abuse of process to include filing with the ulterior purpose of coercing a nuisance settlement.[22]

Both compensatory and punitive damages have been awarded in successful countersuits. In *Bull v. McCuskey*, the court upheld an award of $35,000 in compensatory damages for damage to the physician's reputation, embarrassment, humiliation, mental suffering and inconvenience, as well as $50,000 in punitive damages, arguing that there were sufficient grounds for the jury to infer that the attorney acted out of malice (Taub, 1981).

Although a case can be made for limiting countersuits by imposing a higher burden of proof than in an action for negligence, the minority position of requiring proof of special injury does not provide a useful deterrent to harassment through countersuit, since the occurrence of a special injury does not distinguish meritorious from frivolous cases or even those where the greatest damage was inflicted. As noted in a dissenting opinion in *Friedman v. Dozorc*, which upheld the special-injury requirement, this requirement is comprehensible only because of an unstated though correct premise: most litigation does not involve special injury.[23]

While concern with frivolous claims may be legitimate, it is more rarely noted that the ability to impose costs is two-sided. The fact that the defense spends much more on small claims than does the plaintiff suggests that we should be equally concerned about the possibility of the defense deterring legitimate claims by its defense strategy, as we are about nuisance claims.

A more even-handed reform than encouraging countersuits would be to adopt the English rule that imposes the legal costs of both sides on the losing party. Such a rule tends to discourage a plaintiff from bringing suit where his likelihood of winning is low (Shavell, 1982b) and thus should deter suits brought purely with the hope of extracting a settlement offer, assuming that the collection of costs from a losing plaintiff can be enforced. In fact, this deterrence to filing may go too far: if plaintiffs are risk-averse, the English rule also discourages potentially valid claims, defined as claims where the plaintiff has at least an even chance of winning. This danger of discouraging potentially valid claims could be reduced by allowing contingent-fee contracts to include a provision that the attorney would assume liability for the defendant's costs, in the event that the suit was unsuccessful. Permitting freedom of contract on this point would probably result in attorneys assuming this risk in return for a higher fee if successful, and such sharing of the risk is potentially efficient. If the English rule were adopted, it would provide an additional reason for permitting unregulated determination of the contingent-fee percentage.[24]

Conclusions

Litigation expense is one of the most troublesome areas of the tort system, and neither theory nor evidence gives us much guide for reform. Some litigation expense is pure waste, but some contributes to the accuracy and efficiency of deterrence. Because of divergence between private and social costs and benefits, there is no clear benchmark of the optimal expenditure on litigation. Moreover, because the actual amount spent depends on the expected net payoff, reforms designed to reduce costs may lead to unanticipated cost increases.

If the intent is simply to reduce expenditure on litigation, since plaintiff and defense spend comparable amounts overall there is little basis for directing regulation primarily at contingent fees for plaintiff attorneys, especially on large awards, and leaving defense expense unconstrained. Granted that large awards probably do provide excessive compensation, it is more efficient to limit the award directly than to limit the attorney's incentive to go after it.

Excessive delay can be deterred by the award of prejudgment interest from the time of filing the claim, and by active judicial case management. Mandatory pretrial screening is almost certainly inferior to facilitating private contracting for alternative forums of dispute resolution, such as arbitration. The English rule (the loser pays all legal costs) is a potentially useful reform for deterring nuisance suits; but to avoid imposing undue hardship on risk-averse plaintiffs, it should be combined with freedom to contract for sharing the risk with the attorney, in return for a higher fee percentage if the claim is successful. This is an added reason for removing constraints on contingent fees.

12

Alternatives: Private Contract and No-Fault

THERE IS widespread dissatisfaction with the existing negligence-based system of liability for iatrogenic injury. Some of the criticisms replicate those that were applied to the automobile liability system in the 1960s and motivated the switch to a no-fault standard in some states. The negligence system is said to provide incomplete and unequal protection to victims of iatrogenic injury, allegedly overcompensating a tiny minority and undercompensating the great majority, with unacceptable delay and excessive administrative cost. The claimed benefit of deterrence is said to be illusory because courts in practice cannot make efficient findings of liability, and because court sanctions, even if correct, are undermined by insurance. On the contrary, to the extent that the liability system does influence the standard of care, it is said to encourage excessive defensive practices, designed more to protect the physician against suit than the patient against injury.

Those who believe that the existing system is inherently incapable of performing efficiently its twin goals of compensation and quality control, and that the problems are too fundamental to be resolved by piecemeal statutory reforms, have proposed changes in the basic rule of liability. These radical alternatives fall along a spectrum, ranging from a contractual rule with individual freedom for patients and providers to contract for any assignment of liability, to a statutory no-fault rule — with mandatory provider liability for all iatrogenic injury, regardless of fault. This chapter evaluates some variants of these proposals.

The Contractual Approach

The case for a private-contract approach to assigning liability for iatrogenic injury has been stated most cogently by Richard Epstein. His fundamental premise is that

> We have been mistaken all along in looking at the problem of personal injury in malpractice cases as though it were a problem of tort law. Instead, we should both permit and encourage private agreements between physicians, hospitals, and patients to set the terms on which medical services are rendered . . . Although most courts have not expressly stated the extent to which specific provisions in the physician-patient contract are void and unenforceable for reasons of public policy, some uneasy combination of the doctrines of unequal bargaining power, contracts of adhesion, economic duress, and unconscionability today block any private effort to contract out of the judicially mandated liability rules for medical malpractice (1978, p. 255).[1]

Epstein argues that in expanding the scope of physicians' liability, by liberal use of such doctrines as informed consent, res ipsa loquitur, and a broader locality rule, and in expanding the standard of compensable damages, the courts have established rules of liability and compensation that patients would probably not be willing to pay for if given the choice. Private agreements to contract out of the judicially mandated medical malpractice rules should therefore be honored by the courts, as explicit evidence of the preferences of the parties involved. The costs of contracting over liability rules for iatrogenic injury are relatively low because, unlike automobile or many product-related injuries, physician and patient are already in a direct contractual relationship. Failure to honor private contracts represents an unwarranted intrusion upon the principle of freedom of contract.

Epstein surmises that two types of contracts would probably emerge. First, patients might opt for no rights to compensation, taking medical services on an "as-is" basis, no matter how adverse the outcome. Under such agreements physicians would be constrained only by market forces: patients would be more selective in their choice of physician, knowing that they had no legal recourse in the event of an injury. Of course, other quality-control mechanisms — licensure, hospital accreditation, and oversight — would remain in place and might even be strengthened in response to an increased market demand for quality control.

Alternatively, patients might opt for some contractual protection such as liability for willful harm or gross negligence. A gross-negligence standard would allow actions for egregious errors such as amputation of the wrong leg or failure to take some universally recognized precaution, but would repudiate all of the recent judicial extensions of malpractice liability, including actions for failure to disclose risks under an informed-consent theory, the extensive use of *res ipsa*, and attacks on the standard of custom of the medical profession.

But regardless of the specific types of contract that might emerge, Epstein supports this approach as a matter of principle: "The strength of contracts is that they allow individuals to determine solutions for themselves that are better than any we, as legislators, economists, or lawyers might wish to impose." Private parties might make mistakes, but so does regulation—whether judicial or administrative. Whatever the problems confronting private individuals in evaluating and pricing services, they are problems that any scheme of regulation must face as well.

Part of the logic of Epstein's argument for private contracts is unassailable: individuals are indeed better judges of their preferences for risk and for different health outcomes than are regulators or courts. Individuals also know better their willingness to pay for compensation in the event of injury. Nevertheless, the case for private contracting, like the case for the custom standard, requires that patients be well-informed. If patients systematically underestimate risks—and the financial incentives of physicians in the absence of liability discourage full disclosure—then private contracting will result in a lower quality of care and lower levels of compensation than patients would choose if fully informed; this is one reason for placing liability, by law, on physicians. Another reason is that patients cannot monitor the quality of performance, so tort liability is a way of requiring physicians to guarantee that their product conforms to the custom of the profession. In principle, of course, public regulation—judicial or otherwise—is superior only if the public monitor has and uses superior information in setting standards of care and compensation than would emerge from private contracts. If in fact the courts simply enforce the custom standard, because they lack the expertise to do otherwise, then the case for contract remains strong despite the potential problem of consumer misperceptions.

Even if patients were granted the freedom to contract for different levels of liability coverage, the current fee-for-service system of medical care would seriously undermine their incentives to contract for less than maximum coverage. Since medical malpractice premiums represent less than 5 percent of the physician's gross income, they account for a correspondingly small fraction of the total fee; thus the fee reduction the patient could expect by opting for less extensive liability coverage would be trivial. This already small incentive to opt for lower liability coverage is further undermined by health insurance. If the patient typically pays 20 percent of ambulatory costs out of pocket, and if malpractice premiums constitute 5 percent of the average fee, then forgoing all malpractice coverage would only reduce out-of-pocket costs of a medical service costing $100 from $20 to $19.

However, the feasibility of a contract approach to malpractice liability is becoming much stronger as the traditional fee-for-service system with unrestricted choice of providers breaks up under pressures for cost containment. An incentive-based approach to health care reform — a direction in which there is already considerable progress — would result in consumers being faced with a choice among health insurance packages offering different levels of coverage at different prices, with some plans restricting coverage to designated groups of physicians. These range from self-contained, prepaid group practices (health maintenance organizations or HMOs) to loosely organized networks of primary care physicians (PCNs) with designated specialists for referrals. A conceivable component of any of these "alternative delivery" health insurance plans might be explicit stipulations of the terms of liability coverage and means of dispute resolution.

Stipulating liability coverage as part of health insurance coverage offers three advantages. First, since more than 85 percent of private health insurance is employment-based, it would economize on the transaction costs and the information problems inherent in contracting for liability coverage on a service-by-service, patient-by-patient basis, as required under the traditional fee-for-service system with unrestricted choice of providers. Second, courts are more willing to uphold contractual modifications of tort rights entered into by employers on behalf of employees than to uphold contracts entered into by individual patients immediately prior to treatment.[2] Third, by linking liability coverage to health insurance coverage, the patient would receive the full saving from lower liability coverage in the form of a lower health insurance premium, not just the copayment fraction of those benefits.

Moreover, the cost of coordination to prevent double coverage of health expenses would be greatly reduced if the health insurer also provided the remedial health services. Provision could, of course, be made to allow the patient to switch from the defendant provider to another provider within the same insurance network. To make an informed choice between medical insurance plans offering different liability coverages, the patient would need to know the probability of injury under each plan and the expected amount of compensation in the event of an injury. Competitive pressures might lead insurers to supply such information, which would enormously strengthen the advantages of a contractual approach and encourage physicians to compete on quality as well as price.

Freedom to contract over malpractice liability may not only be facilitated by the growth of alternative delivery health insurance plans but may, in fact, be essential if such plans are to realize their full potential for improved efficiency and cost containment in health care delivery. One way in which alternative delivery plans reduce costs is by restricting patients to physicians who eliminate "unnecessary" services. For example, it is well known that HMOs reduce costs by reducing hospitalizations.[3] But any departure from the fee-for-service, "all extras" norm runs the risk of liability for negligence if alternative delivery groups are judged by the customary practice of the unrestricted, fee-for-service market — despite the fact that this customary standard has evolved in response to inefficient incentives. Thus denying patients the right to contract out of traditional tort liability limits their ability to contract for more cost-effective forms of health care delivery and financing.

Of course there is a fine line to be drawn between recognizing legitimate differences in quality of medical care and allowing each provider group to define its own standards, such that the possibility of finding malpractice is ruled out. either by definition or by the impossibility of obtaining expert testimony as to the relevant standard from outside the group of potential defendants. This dilemma may be resolved, at least partially, by recognizing different standards for different forms of health care delivery and financing — with lower standards for less costly coverages — and by honoring contractual modifications of tort standards, for example, excluding claims based on specific legal doctrines or claims arising out of specified procedures or outcomes. Because contracting costs make it prohibitively expensive to cover all possible contingencies by prior agreement, a grievance procedure with arbitration as the ultimate step may be the optimal way of giving operational meaning to necessarily vague contractual terms. Thus a system of private medical jurisprudence might arise, just as the system of private industrial jurisprudence has arisen out of the arbitration of collective labor contracts (Bovbjerg, 1975).

Greater contractual freedom over the assignment of liability for iatrogenic injury should not be viewed as an alternative to the reforms in tort law — scheduled awards, shorter statute of limitations, and so on — proposed earlier in the book. Rather, tort reform and greater contractual freedom should be seen as complementary. The reason is that, as the Coase theorem shows, the rule of liability does not matter only when contracting around it is costless. When contracting is costly, the basic liability rule provides the norm, and private contractual modification will occur only if the expected benefits exceed the added contracting costs. Legislation explicitly authorizing private contractual agreements can usefully reduce the uncertainty and hence the implicit costs surrounding private contracting. Nevertheless, to reduce to a minimum the need for private contracting, there remains an overwhelming case for modifying the basic law to resemble as closely as possible the conditions that most people would voluntarily choose with full information about benefits and costs.

Thus if most people do not voluntarily insure against all pecuniary and nonpecuniary losses, as I argued earlier, the tort norm should be a limited schedule that more closely resembles revealed willingness to pay for insurance. But private contracting for the more extensive benefits of current tort law should be permitted. Physicians and hospitals who perceive a demand for such coverage can make it a basic condition of the service package they offer, through the insurers who contract to pay for their services. In that case people who want more extensive tort coverage would pay the full cost through higher insurance premiums, except to the extent that cost shifting occurs through the tax subsidy to health insurance. If we do not wish to subsidize tort compensation through the tax system, any contractual modification for benefits more generous than the basic norm should be sold as a rider to the health insurance package and not be eligible for the tax subsidy. Other providers might in principle choose to offer the more expensive tort coverage as an optional rider to be purchased at the beginning of treatment, separately from the basic health insurance and compensation package — much as extended warranties for automobile maintenance are available as an optional extra. This outcome seems less likely, however, because of the risk of adverse selection and the added contracting costs.

No-Fault Plans

A second alternative to the negligence-based malpractice liability system is a system of provider liability for iatrogenic injury without regard to fault. Patients would be compensated for any injury arising out of medical care, regardless of whether it was caused by negligence of the physician or whether it was an "unavoidable" risk of normal care. Thus medical causation rather than negligence would be the criterion for compensation.

It is important to note that the so-called no-fault plans for iatrogenic injury differ in crucial respects from no-fault automobile plans, although the analogy is often drawn. In no-fault automobile plans, the injured party is compensated without regard to his fault through his own first-party insurance. Thus, in effect, third-party liability through tort is replaced by mandatory first-party insurance. In the medical context, by contrast, the proposal is to make medical providers liable without regard to their fault. This might more correctly be called strict provider liability, akin to strict liability of employers for work-related injuries under workers' compensation.

Despite these differences, proponents claim many of the same advantages for medical no-fault as have been claimed in the automobile context. It is hoped that eliminating the issue of negligence would reduce expenditure on litigation and permit more timely compensation. The deterrent value of such litigation costs are viewed as pure waste because of erroneous findings and liability insurance. The saving in litigation expense could be used to compensate the victims of normal risk, who are denied compensation under the fault principle. Incentives to practice defensive medicine would allegedly be eliminated, assuming the no-fault insurance premiums were not experience-rated. Finally, from a legal standpoint, providing compensation on a no-fault basis might be a necessary quid pro quo for some limitation on damage awards, although from an efficiency standpoint there is no necessary connection between the rule of damages and the rule of liability.

Despite its apparent simplicity, however, it seems unlikely that no-fault liability for medical injuries would realize a significant saving in litigation costs per case. The occurrence of a compensable event is easy to identify in the case of automobile accidents and work-related accidents.[4] But the occurrence of iatrogenic injury is much harder to identify, because of the difficulty of distinguishing an adverse outcome due to medical care from the prior condition for which medical care was sought. The original medical no-fault proposals used a definition of the compensable event adapted from the definition of a work-related injury as an injury "arising out of or in the course of employment." For medical injuries, the following definition has been proposed:

"Compensable injury" is defined as any physical harm, bodily impairment, disfigurement or delay in recovery which (i) is more probably associated in whole or in part with medical intervention rather than with the condition for which such intervention occurred, and (ii) is not consistent with or reasonably to be expected as a consequence of such intervention, or (iii) is a result of medical intervention to which the patient has not given his informed consent . . .

"Medical intervention" shall include the rendering as well as the omission, of any care, treatment or services provided within the course of treatment administered by, or under the control of, a health care provider or within a health care institution (Roth and Rothstein, 1973, p. 460).

As Epstein and others have pointed out, making causation rather than negligence the test for compensation might increase rather than reduce the administrative burden. Any less than perfect recovery might become potentially compensable if there were in principle any alternative judgment, any possible omission, or any better treatment, at any cost, that might have improved the patient's condition. Similarly, all adverse side effects might become compensable if the notion of patient assumption of risk for possible adverse effects of adequate medical treatment were abolished, or might be open to litigation if the standard attempted to preserve assumption of normal risk. In practice, if a line is to be drawn between a medical injury insurance system and a universal health insurance system, the negligence issue would probably not be eliminated. Proving negligent performance would be one way of showing that the injury in question was due to the medical intervention rather than the patient's natural condition. This phenomenon is common in product liability litigation: although manufacturers are strictly liable for injuries caused by defective products, proving that the product was defective often entails proving negligence.

Thus as long as a line is to be drawn between compensable and noncompensable cases, litigation over borderline cases will remain. And note that it is the clarity of the dividing line that determines the extent of litigation: cases that fall clearly within whatever boundary is set will be settled with relatively little litigation. Basing compensation on medical causation rather than negligent performance will reduce average litigation expense per case only if the demarcation between medically-caused and non-medically-caused adverse outcomes is clearer than the demarcation between negligent and non-negligent care.

But an evaluation of the efficiency of a no-fault system relative to a negligence system does not turn solely on litigation cost per case, but rather on a comparison of the total costs of injuries, injury prevention (including defensive medicine), overhead costs, and uninsured risk. With respect to prevention, the elimination of fault would reduce useful incentives to avoid negligence, while defensive practices might well increase. Even if liability insurance premiums were not experience-rated, physicians would incur time costs in litigating claims and hence would have incentives to avoid patients or procedures with a high risk of adverse outcome.

With respect to compensation, timely compensation can be achieved more efficiently through the existing framework of first-party public and private programs. As we have seen, the great majority of Americans have private first-party coverage of medical expense and short-term wage loss, and are eligible for public programs — SSDI and Medicare — in the event of permanent total disability. These programs cover injuries regardless of cause. It is true that there are holes in this safety net, especially for those who lack the employment history necessary to qualify for SSDI, and it should be an item of high priority on the social insurance agenda to close these holes. But with such a system of no-fault first-party coverages in place, it would entail costly duplication of coverage to add compulsory insurance for iatrogenic injuries through no-fault provider liability. Retaining a separate system of compensation for iatrogenic injuries could be justified only on grounds of market deterrence, that is, the costs of iatrogenic injuries would be built into the cost of health care, through the no-fault insurance premiums, and health care utilization would reflect this full social cost. But in view of the highly inelastic demand for health care, changes in utilization would probably be small. In that case the welfare gains from internalizing the costs of iatrogenic injuries are unlikely to outweigh the added overhead expense of operating the separate system.

The program costs of a comprehensive no-fault system of compensation for iatrogenic injury could indeed be staggering. Using the CMA count of iatrogenic injuries, the number of potentially compensable events would be between 75 and 150 times the number of injuries currently compensated through tort.[5] And this is almost certainly a conservative estimate, being based on a review of hospital records by medical-legal experts. Because of the difficulty of distinguishing an iatrogenic injury from any less than perfect health outcome, the number of claimants could be much larger. The underestimation is particularly severe for the over-65 population, who have a lower rate of claims relative to injuries under the current system, and probably a higher rate of imperfect cure relative to true iatrogenic injury. Thus, the incremental cost of a no-fault compensation program for the Medicare population could be even higher.

The proponents of no-fault plans hope to offset these additional costs by savings from three sources: reduced litigation per case, scheduled awards in place of unlimited, individualized tort awards, and offset of collateral benefits. As I argued earlier, litigation saving per case may be negligible, and the benefits of scheduled awards can be realized without abandoning the negligence-based liability rule. Although collateral source offset would produce significant saving, there is a real question of why the offset should not be total — in other words, why should we mandate compulsory insurance for iatrogenic injuries over and above that which we choose to buy, through private or public programs, for injuries from other sources? And why should we mandate that this additional coverage be provided through the relatively inefficient means of strict producer liability?

Limited No-Fault: Designated Compensable Events

In recognition of the problems of an open-ended no-fault system, Havighurst and Tancredi (1974) have proposed a limited no-fault plan, medical adversity insurance (MAI), which would compensate patients without regard to fault for a list of "designated compensable events" (DCEs). Those outcomes would be designated as compensable which are more often than not associated with negligent treatment. Compensation for DCEs would be determined by a schedule of benefits, and other iatrogenic injuries not on the list would continue to be handled under the existing tort system. Providers would carry both DCE and liability insurance. To preserve incentives for injury prevention, DCE premiums would be experience-rated, with mandatory deductibles if necessary.

There are several reasons why the saving in litigation expense from such a system might be small or nonexistent. First, by confining automatic compensation to those events in which there is a strong presumption of negligence, this approach would remove only those cases where the issues are clear-cut, which are precisely the cases that do not entail large litigation costs under the current system. The empirical analysis of claim disposition in Chapter 3 confirmed the conventional wisdom that cases involving obvious error tend to be settled out of court, with relatively low litigation costs. Under MAI, cases where the issue of negligence is in doubt, which are those that entail large litigation expense because the parties cannot agree to settle and thus litigate to verdict, would remain in the tort system. Thus the DCE system might merely make automatically compensable those events that are already de facto compensated automatically under the negligence system. If so, the added costs of operating two systems would be pure waste.

Second, the closed-claim surveys show that medical malpractice cases involve many different injuries. The number of well-defined events which experts could agree were more probably than not due to negligence would not account for a significant fraction of current claims.[6] Third, it seems unlikely that events could be defined sufficiently clearly to prevent extensive litigation over whether a particular case should fall within the no-fault or the tort system. The more severe the injury, the greater would be the plaintiff's incentive to allege that it is not a DCE, if the DCE schedule pays less than full tort compensation. And the less certain the issue of negligence, the greater would be the plaintiff's incentive to try to prove that the injury is a DCE, thereby claiming a right to compensation regardless of negligence. Of course the incentives for the defense are precisely the opposite: to attempt to accord DCE status to severe injuries, but deny it to minor ones or those of doubtful merit.

Finally, although there may be distortions in medical care resulting from defensive medicine and inadequate deterrence under the negligence system, these distortions might well be greater under a partial no-fault system. If physicians' no-fault insurance premiums were not experience-rated, incentives for injury avoidance would be reduced. But if they were experience-rated, as proposed under the DCE plan, or if the time costs of defending claims were high, then physicians would have incentives to avoid high-risk patients or high-risk procedures unless they could charge commensurately higher fees to cover the higher liability risk. But as argued earlier, differentiating medical fees for patients posing a high risk of adverse outcome may not be feasible because of lack of objective evidence of risk propensity and the consequent risk of moral hazard that such a fee system would pose to health insurers. But without the ability to pass through higher insurance costs, physicians might be unwilling to treat precisely those patients most in need of care.[7]

Perhaps the most appealing approach to no-fault liability is to recognize no-fault coverage as an elective option (O'Connell, 1975). The freedom to contract for liability coverage, as part of the contract for medical services, could permit election of no-fault compensation for all or any subset of injuries.

Conclusions

Freedom to contract out of standard tort rights should be permitted, particularly where the modification is part of the basic health insurance contract. In fact, allowing such contractual limits on tort liability may be a necessary condition of achieving significant cost containment through alternative delivery health insurance plans. If tort damage awards and statutes of limitations are reduced, as I have proposed, those individuals willing to pay for more extensive benefits could do so by private contract.

Mandatory no-fault plans are unlikely to generate a significant saving in litigation cost per case, to offset the possible hundredfold likely increase in number of claims compensated and the increased costs of defensive medical practices. No-fault compensation for iatrogenic injury would simply add a costly compensation system that would largely duplicate the private and public insurance mechanisms already in place.

Summary and Conclusions

FROM THE STANDPOINT of economic efficiency, the medical mal-practice system makes no sense if its sole function is compensation. Compensation can be effected more cheaply and arguably more equitably through first-party health and disability insurance, which operate on lower overhead, pay in a more timely fashion, and pay all victims without regard to cause of the injury. Our negligence-based system of liability for iatrogenic injury can be justified, if at all, only on grounds of deterrence — that is, assigning liability to those best placed to prevent injuries results in savings in injury costs that out-weigh the added overhead costs of litigating over cause and fault.

The need for such a liability system arises only if consumers are relatively uninformed about risks and cannot monitor quality of care. In that case there is a potential market failure: consumers may incur more risk and receive a lower quality of care than they would be willing to pay for if fully informed. We do not know just how serious misperceptions of risk and quality are in practice, nor is the status quo immutable. If insurance against adverse outcomes were less com-plete, patients might well take the trouble to become better informed, with the result that other market mechanisms to guarantee quality might develop in medical care just as they do for other professional services and goods where quality is not readily observable.

Nevertheless, since assuring quality either directly or through one of these surrogate mechanisms does not come free, the tort system deserves serious consideration. Although most physicians may well act in their patient's best interests most of the time, even without the threat of liability, nevertheless the incidence of medical negligence is too common to be ignored. The evidence from 1974 suggests that almost 1 percent of hospital admissions resulted in a mishap due to negligence, and that only 1 in 25 of these injured patients was compensated through the tort system. Even if the ratio of claims to injuries has doubled—and we have no current data—these estimates suggest that the cost of negligent injuries is several times larger than the cost of malpractice insurance premiums. Concern for quality control is not redundant.

Alternative control systems do exist: medical licensure and hospital accreditation, state boards of quality assurance, and hospital oversight committees. But these systems provide only gross filters, designed to eliminate the seriously incompetent physician; they lack the information to monitor care to each patient on a day-to-day basis, and to the extent that they rely on peer review, they lack strong incentives to take disciplinary action. All professions are notoriously reluctant to police their members, and medicine is no exception.

In theory, tort liability is uniquely designed to provide an ongoing system of quality control, without direct regulation, because each patient is the enforcer in his own case. He has the right to initiate an investigation and to seek redress, through a legal suit, in the event of breach of due care. The damage award provides an incentive for the plaintiff to incur the costs involved. In principle, the tort system can define a standard of due care and a measure of damages that provide physicians with optimal incentives for care and patients with optimal insurance and compensation.

In practice, as we have seen, the malpractice system departs significantly from this theoretical ideal, but the most extreme criticisms are unfounded. Far from being excessive, the number of claims falls short of the number of incidents of malpractice. The disposition process follows the precepts of the law to a significant degree. Court awards are strongly influenced by the economic loss of the plaintiff and by the law of compensable damages. Outcomes in out-of-court settlement reflect the expected outcome at verdict, with cases settling on average for 74 percent of their potential award. Disposition is distorted to some extent by the heavy burden of costs, but the allegation that insurers can be forced to pay on any claim, no matter how specious, in order to buy out of higher litigation costs is belied by the fact that more than 50 percent of claims are dropped without payment. The costs of filing clearly bar many small but potentially meritorious claims.

In view of the strong evidence that legal standards affect both the propensity to file claims and their disposition, the design of these standards is of key importance. For the standard of care, there is no practical alternative to deferring to professional custom. However, because custom may not be optimal in an imperfectly informed market, courts should retain the discretion to define negligence by weighing social costs and benefits. To facilitate the development of less costly modes of health care delivery, the heterogeneous standards of different delivery systems should be recognized, together with patients' and providers' freedom to contract out of tort rights, in part or completely.

With respect to awards, the tort norm of full compensation for pecuniary and nonpecuniary loss almost certainly implies more compensation than people would be willing to pay for, if given the choice — and the bill. The efficiency of tort as a compulsory insurance system would be increased by replacing individualized awards with scheduled benefits in order to reduce uncertainty. The schedule should provide benefits comparable to those people buy voluntarily: compensation of medical expenses, up to limits such as those found in typical major medical health insurance policies, and up to 70 percent of pretax wage loss, which on average implies full replacement of after-tax income. Compensation for pain and suffering should be paid only in cases of severe injury and should be a scheduled amount based on age, disability, and characteristics of the injury that affect the marginal utility of income. Benefits should be determined at the time of trial but paid periodically. Compensation from other private sources of insurance should not be offset, but private first-party insurers should be allowed subrogation rights; however, benefits payable from SSDI and Medicare should be reduced by the amount of the tort payments for wage loss and medical expense. These measures are designed to eliminate double coverage while preserving deterrence. In addition to the compensatory award, in cases of severe disability the defendant should be liable for an uninsurable fine, to be paid to the state. This fine would replace, not supplement, punitive damage awards; it is intended to correct for the fact that in cases of severe disability, the optimal fine for deterrence purposes exceeds the optimal compensatory award.

To prevent retroactive application of new standards and to limit insurance risk, the statute of limitations should be short — say, three years for adults, longer for minors — and should run from the date of the injurious act, not from the discovery of the injury. But the running of the statute should be tolled in cases of fraud or concealment, and an uninsurable fine should be imposed. To ensure some source of compensation for those who might be cut off by a shortened statute,

SSDI should be made generally available without regard to prior employment status. This step is recommended quite apart from its intersection with malpractice reforms, in order to provide a safety net for those currently covered by neither SSDI nor employment-based private insurance programs. It would reduce the pressure to expand compensation through tort and through special government programs for victims of occupational hazards and exposure to toxic substances.

With respect to costs, the contribution of malpractice insurance premiums and defensive medicine to the total cost of health care has often been exaggerated. The high overhead cost of malpractice insurance, relative to first-party or no-fault coverage, is not necessarily indicative of inefficiency when the liability system is viewed as providing deterrence as well as compensation. Nevertheless, any measure that would reduce uncertainty as to court outcomes would improve cost effectiveness, by reducing incentives for litigation expenditures and reducing insurance risk and hence the cost of malpractice insurance. Scheduled awards and short statutes of limitations offer gains on this front.

Procedural reforms that simply reduce the cost to the litigants of trying to influence the outcome may actually increase total expenditure on litigation. This can be explained by the "freeway effect": if the cost per ride falls, more people choose to travel. Regulation of contingent fees does not simply increase the plaintiff's share of the gross recovery. On the contrary, fee ceilings tend to reduce attorney effort and hence reduce the plaintiff's likelihood of winning, the gross recovery, and the net to the plaintiff. The limited evidence available on the operation of screening panels suggests that strict judicial management of the pretrial process may be more effective in controlling costs and expediting disposition. Requiring defendants to pay interest on the award from the date of filing to judgment would reduce delay. Contracting out of the tort system should be allowed, and it is expected to increase with the growth of HMOs and other preferred-provider health plans . These contracts might include such measures as modification of the rule of liability or the standard of due care, modification of the measure of damages, and arbitration of disputes. Replacing the negligence system with a no-fault rule of liability, on the other hand, could result in more than a hundredfold increase in the number of paid claims, a negligible saving in litigation expense per case, increased defensive practices, and diminished incentives for cost-effective precautions.

There is strong evidence that the medical malpractice insurance market is competitive and able to handle the risks involved without government intervention. The huge premium increases of 1975 were largely a catching-up process following a lag in rates behind rapidly rising claim costs over the preceding four or five years. The surge in claims was due in part to the expansion of health care utilization in the late 1960s, in part to the pro-plaintiff shift in legal doctrines. The crisis in availability of insurance was caused by state regulatory intervention to deny the rate increases deemed necessary by private carriers.

Of the tort reforms adopted in response to that crisis, caps on awards and mandatory offset of collateral compensation appear to have slowed the growth in awards in states enacting such changes. But countrywide, awards have continued to outpace the rate of inflation. Moreover, although claim frequency tapered off in 1976–77, this can apparently not be attributed to the tort reforms, and since 1978 the upward trend has resumed, although at a slower pace than in the early seventies. The evidence that many potential claims are not filed implies that there may be further increases in claims, even assuming no change in the underlying rate of injury. However, the shorter statutes of limitations and limits on discovery periods that have now been adopted in most states provide some safeguard against a surge in claims from prior practice, should another pro-plaintiff shift in law occur (assuming, of course, that the courts uphold these changes in the statute of limitations).

The formation of mutuals and introduction of the claims-made policy represent a potentially efficient reallocation of risk and protection against problems of insurance availability. Although joint underwriting associations may have been warranted as a stopgap measure to ensure availability at the time of the crisis, as a permanent institution they are unnecessary provided adequate rates are allowed for a voluntary market to function. To the extent that JUAs have assessment or loss write-off provisions which effect a subsidy, either among groups of physicians or from policyholders in other lines of insurance to medical malpractice, they defeat the cost-internalization purpose of the tort system and ultimately subsidize medical negligence.

In conclusion, the fault-based system is worth retaining if the benefits, in terms of injuries deterred, exceed the costs of litigating over fault and other associated costs, such as defensive medicine. Unfortunately, a full cost-benefit evaluation is impossible because we cannot measure the number of injuries that are prevented as a result of the additional care exercised by medical providers in response to the threat of liability. But we can make a very rough calculation of the benefits, in terms of injury reduction, that would be required to offset the additional costs of operating the tort system, rather than simply compensating victims through first-party insurance and forgoing all aim at deterrence. To make this calculation, let us assume initially that both tort and first-party programs fully compensate victims, and that 80 cents of every health insurance premium dollar reaches the patient as compensation, compared to only 40 cents of every malpractice insurance premium dollar. Thus the 40 cents spent litigating to assign fault through the malpractice system is an additional cost worth incurring only if it results in at least equivalent deterrence benefits. In other words, if the tort system deters at least one injury of comparable severity for every injury currently compensated, the deterrence benefits outweigh the additional costs of the liability system.

We do not know how many injuries are actually deterred, but we can estimate the percentage reduction in the rate of negligent injury that is required. Using the 1974 estimate that 1 in 10 incidents of negligence leads to a claim and 1 in 25 receives compensation, only a 4 percent reduction in the rate of negligent injury is required to justify the costs of the tort system. If the rate of compensation per negligent injury is currently, say, twice as high as it was in 1974, then an 8 percent reduction in the rate of negligent injury would be required. Similarly, if the tort system entails significant costs other than the litigation costs considered so far — such as defensive medicine, public costs of operating the courts, time and psychic costs of litigation to patients and providers — then the deterrence benefits would have to be higher. On the other hand, to the extent that the compensation received by victims through tort understates their willingness to pay for injury prevention, the deterrence necessary to justify the system is less.

This rough calculation suggests that if the number of negligent injuries is, generously, 20 percent lower than it otherwise would be because of the incentives for care created by the malpractice system, the system is worth retaining, despite its costs. But this is not grounds for inaction. The malpractice system could be made more cost-effective for purposes of both deterrence and compensation, through reforms such as the restructuring of awards, freedom of private contract, redefinition of the standard of care, and short statutes of repose. These reforms would represent a radical change in traditional tort law and raise the obvious question of why medical malpractice should be singled out for special treatment. My answer would be that it should not; that—where relevant—these reforms should also apply to other areas of tort law, in particular to product liability. Unless such changes are enacted, the growing frustration over the more visible costs of the tort system may lead us to abandon entirely what is potentially a valuable system of quality control.

Abbreviations

AAI	Alliance of American Insurers
ABA	American Bar Association
AIA	American Insurance Association
AIRAC	All-Industry Research Advisory Committee
AMA	American Medical Association
CBO	Congressional Budget Office
CMA	California Medical Association
CPCU	Chartered Property & Casualty Underwriters
HIAA	Health Insurance Association of America
ISO	Insurance Services Office
NAIC	National Association of Insurance Commissioners

References

Acton, J. 1973. Evaluating Public Programs to Save Lives: The Case of Heart Attacks. Santa Monica, Calif.: The RAND Corporation.

Adler, J. W., W. F. Felstiner, D. R. Hensler, and M. A. Peterson. 1982. The Pace of Litigation. Santa Monica, Calif.: The RAND Corporation. R-2922-ICJ.

Alliance of American Insurers (AAI). 1984. Medical Malpractice: Status of Malpractice JUAS (unpublished report). Chicago.

All-Industry Research Advisory Committee (AIRAC). 1979. Automobile Injuries and Their Compensation in the United States. Chicago: Alliance of American Insurers.

A. M. Best Company. 1982. Management Reports. Oldwick, New Jersey.

———Aggregates and Averages: Property Liability (various years). Oldwick, New Jersey.

Amemiya, T., and F. Nold. 1975. A Modified Logit Model. Review of Economics and Statistics 57:255.

American Bar Association (ABA). 1977. Report of the Commission on Medical Professional Liability. Chicago.

———1979. Designated Compensable Event System: A Feasibility Study. New York.

American Insurance Association (AIA). 1976. Special Malpractice Review: 1974 Closed Claim Survey. New York: Insurance Services Office.

American Medical Association (AMA). 1963. Professional-Liability Survey. Reprinted in Medical Malpractice: The Patient vs. the Physician. U.S. Senate, Committee on Government Operations, 91st Cong., November 1969.

———1983. Report of the Board of Trustees: Study of Professional Liability Costs. Chicago.

Andrews, G. M. 1968. A Note on the Use of Statistics in Rate Determination. Journal of Risk and Insurance 35:320.

Arrow, K. J. 1963. Uncertainty and the Economics of Medical Care. *American Economic Review* 53:941.

——— 1970. Insurance, Risk, and Resource Allocation. In *Essays in the Theory of Risk Bearing*. Amsterdam: North-Holland.

Arthur, W. B. 1981. The Economics of Risk to Life. *American Economic Review* 71:54.

Bernzweig, E. P. 1973. Defensive Medicine. *Appendix to the Report of the Secretary's Commission on Medical Malpractice*. Washington, D.C.: DHEW Publication no. OS:73–89.

Bolsen, B. 1982. Medical News: Influence of Laboratory Testing. *Journal of the American Medical Association* 247:1235.

Bovbjerg, R. 1975. The Medical Malpractice Standard of Care: HMOs and Customary Practice. *Duke Law Journal* 1975:1375.

Brown, J. P. 1973. Toward an Economic Theory of Liability. *Journal of Legal Studies* 2:323.

Calabresi, G. 1970. *The Cost of Accidents*. New Haven, Conn.: Yale University Press.

California Citizens' Commission on Tort Reform. 1977. *Righting the Liability Balance*. Los Angeles.

California Medical Association (CMA). 1977. *Medical Insurance Feasibility Study*. San Francisco: Sutter Publications.

Capwell, R., and T. E. Greenwalk. 1971. Legal and Practical Problems Arising from Subrogation Clauses in Health and Accident Policies. *Marquette Law Review* 54:281.

Carlin, P. E. 1980. Medical Malpractice Pre-Trial Screening Panels: A Review of the Evidence. Intergovernmental Health Policy Project. Washington, D.C.: George Washington University.

Coase, R. 1963. The Problem of Social Cost. *Journal of Law and Economics* 3:1.

Congressional Budget Office (CBO). 1977. *Long Term Care for the Elderly and Disabled*. Washington, D.C.: Government Printing Office.

Conley, B. C., and G. M. Flick. 1978. Toward an Objective Valuation of Pain and Suffering. Unpublished manuscript, Graduate School of Business Administration, University of Southern California.

Cook, P. J., and D. A. Graham. 1977. The Demand for Insurance and Protection: The Case of Irreplaceable Commodities. *Quarterly Journal of Economics* 91:143.

Cooter, R. D. 1982. Economic Analysis of Punitive Damages. *Southern California Law Review* 56:79.

Cummins, J. D. 1974. Insurer's Risk: A Restatement. *Journal of Risk and Insurance* 41:147.

Danzon, P. M. [*See also* Munch, P.]. 1980a. Why Are Malpractice Premiums So High—or So Low? Santa Monica, Calif.: The RAND Corporation. R-2623-HCFA.

——— 1980b. The Disposition of Medical Malpractice Claims. Santa Monica, Calif.: The RAND Corporation. R-2622-HCFA.

——— 1982. The Medical Malpractice Insurance Crisis Revisited: Causes and Solutions. Stanford, Calif.: The Hoover Institution. E-83-11.

———— 1983a. Contingent Fees for Personal Injury Litigation. *Bell Journal of Economics* 14:213.

———— 1983b. Liability Insurance and the Tort System: The Case of Medical Malpractice. Stanford, Calif.: The Hoover Institution. E-83-14.

———— 1984a. The Frequency and Severity of Medical Malpractice Claims. *Journal of Law and Economics* 27:115.

———— 1984b. Tort Reform and the Role of Government in Private Insurance Markets. *Journal of Legal Studies* 13 (3):517.

Danzon, P. M., and L. Lillard. 1982. The Resolution of Medical Malpractice Claims: Modeling and Analysis. Santa Monica, Calif.: The RAND Corporation. R-2792-ICJ.

———— 1983. Settlement Out of Court: The Disposition of Medical Malpractice Claims. *Journal of Legal Studies* 12:2.

Diamond, P. 1974. Accident Law and Resource Allocation. *Bell Journal of Economics* 5:366.

Dietz, S., B. Baird, and L. Berul. 1973. The Medical Malpractice Legal System. *Appendix to the Report of the Secretary's Commission on Medical Malpractice.* Washington, D.C.: DHEW Publication no. OS:73-89.

Ebener, P., et al. 1981. Court Efforts to Reduce Pretrial Delay. Santa Monica, Calif.: Institute for Civil Justice. The RAND Corporation. R-2732-ICJ.

Ehrlich, I., and G. S. Becker. 1972. Market Insurance, Self-Insurance and Self-Protection. *Journal of Political Economy* 80:623.

Elligett, T. 1979. The Periodic Payment of Judgments. *Insurance Counsel Journal* 46:130.

Epstein, R. A. 1973. A Theory of Strict Liability. *Journal of Legal Studies* 2:151.

———— 1976. Medical Malpractice: The Case for Contract. *American Bar Foundation Research Journal* 76:87.

———— 1978. Medical Malpractice: Its Cause and Cure. In *The Economics of Medical Malpractice,* ed. Simon Rottenberg, American Enterprise Institute.

———— 1982. Manville: The Bankruptcy of Product Liability Law. *Regulation,* September/October 1982.

Fairley, W. B. 1979. Investment Income and Profit Margins in Property Liability Insurance: Theory and Empirical Results. *Bell Journal of Economics* 10:192.

Feldman, R. 1979. The Determinants of Medical Malpractice Incidents: Theory of Contingency Fees and Empirical Evidence. *Atlantic Economic Journal* 7:2.

Flanders, S. 1982. The Pace of Litigation: Conference Proceedings, ed. J. W. Adler et al. Santa Monica, Calif.: The RAND Corporation. R-2922-ICJ.

Franklin, M. A., R. H. Chanin, and I. Mark. 1961. Accidents, Money and the Law: A Study of the Economics of Personal Injury Litigation. *Columbia Law Review* 61:1.

Gould, J. P. 1973. The Economics of Legal Conflicts. *Journal of Legal Studies* 2:279.

Greenspan, N. T. 1979. A Descriptive Analysis of Medical Malpractice Insurance Premiums, 1974–77. *Health Care Financing Review* 1(2):65.

Hammond, J. D., A. F. Shapiro, and N. Shilling. 1979. Analysis of an Underwriting Decline: 1972–1975. *The Society of Chartered Property & Casualty Underwriters (CPCU) Journal* 32(2):66.

Harris, M., and A. Raviv. 1978. Some Results on Incentive Contracts. *American Economic Review* 68:1.

Havighurst, C. 1975. Medical Adversity Insurance: Has Its Time Come? *Duke Law Journal* 75:1233.

Havighurst, C., and L. Tancredi. 1974. Medical Adversity Insurance: A No-Fault Approach to Medical Malpractice and Quality Assurance. *Insurance Law Journal* 613:69.

Health Insurance Association of America (HIAA). 1983. *New Group Health Insurance Policies.* Washington, D.C.

Henderson, J. A. 1981. Coping with the Time Dimension in Products Liability. *California Law Review* 69:919.

Hershey, N. 1972. The Defensive Practice of Medicine: Myth or Reality. *Milbank Memorial Quarterly* 1:1.

Hill, R. D. 1979. Profit Regulation in Property-Liability Insurance. *Bell Journal of Economics* 10:172.

Holder, A. R. 1975. *Medical Malpractice Law.* New York: Wiley.

Institute for Judicial Administration. 1970, 1972, 1974. *Calendar Status Study.* New York.

Insurance Services Office (ISO). 1975. *Compilation of General Liability Experience: Professional Liability.* New York.

——— 1976a. *Product Liability: 1976 Closed Claim Survey.* New York.

——— 1976b. *Special Malpractice Review: 1974 Closed Claim Survey.* New York.

Johnson and Higgins of California. 1975. *Patient's Compensation: An Alternative to the Medical Malpractice Liability System.* Los Angeles.

Keeton, R. E. 1973. Compensation for Medical Accidents. *University of Pennsylvania Law Review* 121:590.

Keeton, R. E., and J. O'Connell. 1965. *Basic Protection for the Traffic Victim.* Boston: Little, Brown.

Kendall, M., and J. Haldi. 1973. The Medical Malpractice Insurance Market. *Appendix to the Report of the Secretary's Commission on Medical Malpractice.* Washington, D.C.: DHEW Publication no. OS:73-89.

Kimball, S. L., and D. A. Davis. 1962. Extension of Insurance Subrogation. *Michigan Law Review* 60:7.

Komesar, N. 1974. Toward a General Theory of Personal Injury Loss. *Journal of Legal Studies* 3:457.

Landes, W. M. 1971. An Economics Analysis of the Courts. *Journal of Law and Economics* 14:61.

Landes, W. M., and R. A. Posner. 1979. Adjudication as a Private Good. *Journal of Legal Studies* 8:235.

Larson, L. W., and J. F. Burton, Jr. Special Funds in Workers' Compensation (unpublished manuscript). School of Industrial and Labor Relations, Cornell University.

Linder, J. 1970. *A Study of Professional Liability Coverage in Southern California*. New York: A. S. Hansen.

Linnerooth, J. 1979. The Value of Human Life: A Review of the Models. *Economic Inquiry* 17:52.

Longshore, W. L. 1981. Medical Malpractice: Constitutionality of Statutory Mediation Panels. *American Journal of Trial Advocacy* 4:816.

MacKinnon, F. B. 1964. *Contingent Fees for Legal Services*. Chicago: Aldine.

McGovern, F. E. 1981. The Variety, Policy and Constitutionality of Product Liability Statutes of Repose. *The American University Law Review* 30:579.

Meltzer, N. 1975. *Helling v. Carey:* A Landmark or Exception in Medical Malpractice? *N.E. Law Review* 11:301.

Meyer, C. W. 1979. *Social Security Disability Insurance*. Washington, D.C.: American Enterprise Institute.

Mossin, J. 1968. Aspects of Rational Insurance Purchasing. *Journal of Political Economy* 76:4.

Mueller, M. 1976. The Economics of Medical Malpractice: Claims, Awards and Defensive Medicine. Paper presented at the American Economic Association Meetings.

Munch, P. 1976. [*See also* Danzon, P. M.]. An Economic Analysis of Eminent Domain. *Journal of Political Economy* 84:473.

———1977a. The Costs and Benefits of the Tort System if Viewed as a Compensation System. Santa Monica, Calif.: The RAND Corporation. P-5921.

———1977b. Issues in Professional Liability: Multiple Defendants (unpublished research). Santa Monica, Calif.: The RAND Corporation.

———1978. Causes of the Medical Malpractice Insurance Crisis: Risk and Regulation. In *The Economics of Medical Malpractice*, ed. S. Rottenberg. Washington, D.C.: American Enterprise Institute.

———1980. Solvency Regulation in the Property-Liability Insurance Industry: Empirical Evidence. *Bell Journal of Economics* 11:261.

Munch, P., and D. E. Smallwood. 1979. Professional Liability. Staff Background Paper, California Citizens' Commission on Tort Reform.

———1981. Theory of Solvency Regulation in the Property and Casualty Insurance Industry. In *Studies in Public Regulation*, ed. G. Fromm. Cambridge, Mass.: MIT Press.

National Association of Insurance Commissioners (NAIC). 1980. *Malpractice Claims*, 2(2). Brookfield, Wis.

National Center for State Courts. 1980. *Medical Liability Review Panels in Arizona: An Evaluation*. San Francisco.

O'Connell, J. 1975. An Elective No-Fault Liability Statute. *Insurance Law Journal* 628:261.

Oi, W. Y. 1973. The Economics of Product Safety. *Bell Journal of Economics* 4:3.

Ordover, J. A. 1978. Costly Litigation in the Model of Single Activity Accidents. *Journal of Legal Studies* 7:243.

Pashigian, P. 1977. The Market for Lawyers: The Determinants of the Demand for and Supply of Lawyers. *Journal of Law and Economics* 20:1.

Pauly, M. V. 1980. *Doctors and Their Workshops: Economic Models of Physician Behavior.* Chicago: University of Chicago Press.

Peltzman, S. 1976. Toward a More General Theory of Regulation. *Journal of Law and Economics* 19:211.

Peterson, M. A. 1984. Compensation of Injuries: Civil Jury Verdicts in Cook County. Santa Monica, Calif.: The RAND Corporation. R-3011-ICJ.

Peterson, M. A., and G. L. Priest. 1982. The Civil Jury: Trends in Trials and Verdicts, Cook County, Illinois. Santa Monica, Calif.: The RAND Corporation. R-2881-ICJ.

Posner, R. A. 1972. A Theory of Negligence. *Journal of Legal Studies* 1:1.

——— 1973. An Economic Approach to Legal Procedure and Judicial Administration. *Journal of Legal Studies* 2:399.

——— 1977. *Economic Analysis of Law.* Boston: Little, Brown.

Priest, G. L. 1977. The Common Law Process and the Selection of Efficient Rules. *Journal of Legal Studies* 6:65.

Professional Liability Newsletter. 1975. Vol. 7(3), ed. D. S. Rubsamen. Berkeley, Calif.: Professional Liability Newsletter, Inc.

Prosser, W. 1964. *Handbook of the Law of Torts.* St. Paul: West Publishing Company.

Rea, S. A., Jr. 1981a. Private Disability Insurance and Public Welfare Programs. *Journal of Public Finance* 36:84.

——— 1981b. Lump Sum versus Periodic Damage Awards. *Journal of Legal Studies* 10:131.

——— 1982. Nonpecuniary Loss and Breach of Contract. *Journal of Legal Studies* 11:35.

Rhem, S. D., and N. L. Trusch. 1977. Malicious Prosecution Suits as a Counterbalance to Medical Malpractice Actions. *Journal of Legal Medicine* 77:43.

Rolph, J. E. 1981. Some Statistical Evidence on Merit Rating in Medical Malpractice Insurance. *Journal of Risk and Insurance* 48:247.

Rolph, J. E., with J. K. Hammitt, R. L. Houchens, and S. S. Polin. 1984. Automobile Accident Compensation: I. Who Pays How Much How Soon? Santa Monica, Calif.: The RAND Corporation. R-3050-ICJ.

Roof, L. S. 1982. *Fringe Benefits: Social Insurance in the Steel Industry.* Beverly Hills, Calif.: Sage Publications.

Rosenberg, C. L. 1984. Doctor-Owned Malpractice Carriers: Who's Winning, Who's Losing. *Medical Economics* (Oct.) 1:62.

Roth, E., and P. Rothstein. 1973. Non-Fault-Based Medical Injury Compensation Systems. In *Appendix to the Report of the Secretary's Commission on Medical Malpractice.* Washington, D.C.: DHEW Publication no. OS:73-89.

Rothschild, M., and J. Stiglitz. 1976. Equilibrium in Competitive Insurance Markets: An Essay on the Economics of Imperfect Information. *Quarterly Journal of Economics* 90:629.

Rubin, P. H. 1977. Why Is the Common Law Efficient? *Journal of Legal Studies* 6:51.

—— 1982. Common Law and Statute Law. *Journal of Legal Studies* 11:2.

Sandor, A. A. 1957. The History of Professional Liability Suits in the U.S. *Journal of the American Medical Association* 163:459.

Schwartz, A., and L. L. Wilde. 1979. Intervening in Markets on the Basis of Imperfect Information: A Legal and Economic Analysis. *Pennsylvania Law Review* 127:630.

Schwartz, G. 1983. Retroactivity in Tort Law. *New York University Law Review* 58:796.

Schwartz, M. L., and D. J. B. Mitchell. 1970. An Economic Analysis of the Contingent Fee in Personal Injury Litigation. *Stanford Law Review* 22:1125.

Schwartz, W. B., and N. K. Komesar. 1978. Doctors, Damages and Deterrence: An Economic View of Medical Malpractice. *New England Journal of Medicine* 298:1282.

Shanley, M. G., and M. A. Peterson. 1983. Comparative Justice: Civil Jury Verdicts in San Francisco and Cook County, 1959–1980. Santa Monica, Calif.: The RAND Corporation. R-3006-ICJ.

Shavell, S. 1979. On Moral Hazard and Insurance. *Quarterly Journal of Economics* 93:541.

—— 1980. Strict Liability vs. Negligence. *Journal of Legal Studies* 9:9.

—— 1982a. On Liability and Insurance. *Bell Journal of Economics* 13:120.

—— 1982b. Suit, Settlement and Trial: A Theoretical Analysis under Alternative Methods for the Allocation of Legal Costs. *Journal of Legal Studies* 11:55.

—— 1982c. The Social versus the Private Incentive to Bring Suit in a Costly Legal System. *Journal of Legal Studies* 11:311.

Singer, R. A. 1977. Countersuits: They're Starting to Make Lawyers Sweat. *Medical Economics* (May) 2:76.

Spence, M. 1977. Consumer Misperceptions, Product Failure, and Product Liability. *Review of Economic Studies* 64:561.

Spence, M., and R. Zeckhauser. 1971. Insurance, Information and Individual Action. *American Economic Review* 61:380.

Steves, M. F., Jr. 1983. Medical Professional Liability. In *Professional Liability: Impact in the Eighties.* Malvern, Pa.: The Society of Chartered Property & Casualty Underwriters.

Steves, M. F., Jr., and A. McWhorter, Jr. 1975. Notes on the Malpractice Insurance Market. *CPCU Annals* 28:4.

Sweetland, P. 1984. Cited in Florida Doctors Seek Malpractice Referendum, *Professional Agent* 80:81.

Taub, S. 1981. Malpractice Countersuits: Succeeding at Last? *Law, Medicine and Healthcare* 9(6):17.

U.S. Department of Commerce. 1978. *Interagency Task Force on Product Liability, Final Report.* Washington, D.C.: Government Printing Office.

U.S. Department of Commerce, Bureau of the Census. 1981. *Statistical Abstract of the United States.* Washington, D.C.: Government Printing Office.

U.S. Department of Labor. 1980. *An Interim Report to Congress on Occupational Disease.* Washington, D.C.: Government Printing Office.

U.S. Department of Transportation. 1970. *Automobile Insurance and Compensation.* Washington, D.C.: Government Printing Office.

U.S. House of Representatives. 1979a. Committee on Interstate and Foreign Commerce, Subcommittee on Consumer Protection and Finance. *Problems Associated with Product Liability.* June 26, Sept. 27, and Oct. 16.

U.S. House of Representatives. 1979b. Committee on Interstate and Foreign Commerce, Subcommittee on Consumer Protection and Finance. *The Nature and Causes of the Product Liability Problem.* 96th Cong.

U.S. Senate. 1969. Committee on Government Operations, Subcommittee on Executive Reorganization. *Medical Malpractice: The Patient versus the Physician.* 91st Cong., 1st sess. Washington, D.C.: Government Printing Office, 35-461-0.

U.S. Senate. 1975. Committee on Labor and Public Welfare, Subcommittee on Health. *Continuing Medical Malpractice Insurance Crisis, 1975.* 94th Cong., 1st sess. December 3.

Venezian, E. C. 1983. Insurer Capital Needs under Parameter Uncertainty. *Journal of Risk and Insurance* 50:19.

Victor, R. B. 1982. Workers' Compensation and Workplace Safety: The Nature of Employer Financial Incentives. Santa Monica, Calif.: The RAND Corporation. R-2979-ICJ.

Viscusi, W. K. 1983. *Risk by Choice: Regulating Health and Safety in the Workplace.* Cambridge, Mass.: Harvard University Press.

Waltz, J. R., and F. E. Inbau. 1971. *Medical Jurisprudence.* New York: Macmillan.

Westat, Inc. 1973. *Study of Medical Malpractice Claims Closed in 1970.* Rockville, Md.

———— 1978. *Medical Malpractice Closed Claim Study, 1976.* Rockville, Md.

Wiley, J. 1981. The Impact of Judicial Decisions on Professional Conduct: An Empirical Study. *Southern California Law Review* 55:345.

Wittman, D. 1983. The Price of Negligence: An Econometric Study of Civil Jury Trials (unpublished paper). Merrill College, University of California, Santa Cruz.

Zeckhauser, R. 1970. Medical Insurance: A Case Study of the Tradeoff between Risk Spreading and Appropriate Incentives. *Journal of Economic Theory* 2:10.

Notes

1. TORT LIABILITY AS A SYSTEM OF QUALITY CONTROL

1. Variants of these three basic liability rules include strict liability with the defense of contributory negligence (the injurer is liable unless the victim failed to meet a due care standard); negligence with the defense of contributory negligence (the injurer is liable if he failed to meet a due care standard and the victim was nonnegligent); and comparative negligence (liability apportioned in proportion to fault).

2. This analysis assumes that the patient personally pays all the costs of treatment. Complications due to the fact that most patients carry extensive health insurance and thus do not personally bear the cost of care, at least at the point of purchase, will be introduced later.

3. Arrow (1963) discusses institutional responses to information asymmetry in the market for medical care. It may not be necessary for all consumers to be informed, provided producers cannot distinguish informed from uninformed. The existence of a subgroup of informed consumers is less likely to protect the uninformed in the case of a service than in the case of a standardized product. Schwartz and Wilde (1979) argue that if consumers are heterogeneous in their tastes, providing information may be better than setting uniform standards.

4. Consumer misperceptions are used to justify the rule of strict liability in, for example, Calabresi (1970) and Spence (1977).

5. 159 Federal Reporter 2d 169 (1947).

6. See Shavell (1980). Although strict liability and negligence can in principle correct for consumer misperception of costs inclusive of risk, they cannot correct for consumer misperception of benefits. Further, if the cheapest way of preventing injuries requires precautions of more than one party, efficiency under either strict liability or negligence requires a contributory negligence defense, that is, the defendant is not liable if the plaintiff failed to meet his standard of due care. See Brown (1973).

7. Part of the saving in overhead costs under workers' compensation may result from the use of scheduled awards rather than elimination of the negligence issue.

2. MALPRACTICE: A PROBLEM OF INJURIES OR CLAIMS?

1. The study defines a disability caused by health care management as follows. (a) A disability is a temporary or permanent impairment of physical or mental function (including disfigurement) or economic loss in the absence of such impairment. (b) Causation is established when the disability is more probably than not attributable to health care management. (c) Health care management includes both affirmative actions (commission) and inactions (omission) of any health care provider or attendant whether or not such actions constitute legal fault.

The study identified injuries that were "discoverable" in 1974. For brevity I refer to injuries "occurring" in 1974.

2. The investigators were highly or reasonably confident of their decision in 72 percent of the cases in which they assigned liability.

3. The claim and injury data are not perfectly comparable in several respects. First, the definitions of age brackets and severity categories are similar but not identical in the two studies. Second, the NAIC reports claims *closed* by calendar year, which include claims *filed* in several prior calendar years. The average lag from filing to disposition is roughly two years, but more serious injuries take longer to settle. To estimate the number of claims filed as a result of injuries discoverable in 1974, I assumed a two-year lag from discovery of an injury to closing of a claim for temporary minor injuries (severity categories 1 and 2), that is, closure in 1976; a three-year lag for temporary major and fatal injuries (categories 3, 4, and 8), that is, closure in 1977; and a four-year lag for permanent injuries (categories 5–7), that is, closure in 1978. The total number of claims closed nationwide fluctuated substantially over these years: 23,240 (estimated) in 1975, 17,683 in 1976, 15,556 in 1977, and 17,238 in 1978. The estimates of claims relative to injuries are therefore quite sensitive to which year of closure is used. Although not all insurers participated for the full duration of the study, nonparticipation is not a serious problem in California.

4. One-third of the injuries occurred outside the hospitals in the sample. The investigators also examined a sample of 928 outpatient records, which revealed only two injuries, both of minor severity.

5. The first two categories would not constitute a cause of action under negligence law, unless they resulted in some damage to the patient.

6. Of the patients who died, 25 percent had unrelated underlying conditions that were considered likely to be terminal within one year.

7. These conclusions are particularly tentative because of the extremely small sample for severe injuries.

8. On the other hand, the estimated ratio of claims to injuries is down-

ward-biased to the extent that the claim universe excludes incidents occurring outside hospitals, but the injury universe includes injuries occurring outside hospitals if they resulted in hospitalization in the sample hospitals. Thirty-one percent of all injuries occurred outside the sample hospitals. With the extreme assumption that all these occurred in office-based practice, the ratio of claims to injuries would be only 1 in 7.

9. The National Association of Insurance Commissioners (1980, p. 420) reports a risk index of *claims* per procedure, by comparing the number of paid claims to countrywide hospital discharge figures.

10. The investigators note that because of the need for confidentiality, which precluded tracing patients or questioning physicians, the number of diagnostic incidents may be understated.

3. THE DISPOSITION OF MALPRACTICE CLAIMS

1. Estimates that malpractice plaintiffs receive only 17 cents of the premium dollar are exaggerated. For a summary of evidence on the allocation of the premium dollar for various lines of insurance, see Munch (1977a).

2. See, for example, American Insurance Association (1976), U.S. Department of Transportation (1970).

3. For statistical reasons we did not attempt in this analysis to measure the effect of other reforms. These are discussed in Chapter 4.

4. For medical malpractice, see Westat (1973, 1978), AIA (1976), NAIC (1980). For automobile liability, see U.S. Department of Transportation (1970), AIRAC (1979).

5. A full technical description of the methodology and results is given in Danzon and Lillard (1982). A sequential probit analysis is used to compute correction factors analogous to an inverse Mills ratio. These correct for successive stages of self-selection: (1) the decision to drop or pursue the claim; (2) the decision to settle or litigate, conditional on not having dropped; and (3) a positive award, conditional on not having dropped or settled.

6. In states that have adopted the principle of comparative negligence, the courts must also apportion liability between multiple defendants and, possibly, the plaintiff, if he was contributorily negligent. Since the data do not report the apportionment of liability, this issue cannot be addressed in the empirical analysis.

7. For expositional simplicity these examples presuppose that the parties are risk-neutral, but this is not a necessary assumption of the model.

8. Specific allegation of *res ipsa* is known for the 1974 data set only, whereas type of error is known only for the 1976 data set. Cases of obvious treatment error in the 1976 data were classified with the 1974 *res ipsa* cases.

9. These estimates are from Danzon (1980). The differential is measured relative to the average over all other cases, for which the specific allegations are not known.

10. NAIC (1980) ran regressions using actual dollar values of awards and

economic loss, whereas we used a logarithmic transformation. Using actual dollar values effectively assigns a dominant weight to the few very large cases, whereas the logarithmic transformation weights all cases more equally, regardless of dollar value, and is more appropriate if binary variables (such as laws) and all unmeasured factors included in the residual have proportional effects on awards.

11. For a substantial percentage of claims, the data on economic loss are either missing or obviously erroneous or incomplete (AIA, 1976; NAIC, 1980). Underreporting is most severe for future wage loss. Even where a plausible figure for future loss is reported, it is presumably undiscounted, whereas awards should represent the discounted present value of future sums. If awards are discounted but loss is not, this would bias toward a spurious finding of undercompensation on cases with large loss. In an attempt to control for reporting errors, we excluded cases of obvious error and included an indicator variable for cases with suspiciously low loss (under $100). To control for discounting error, we estimated separate coefficients for cases of permanent disability. The implied elasticities remained significantly below unity (Danzon, 1980).

12. Court congestion is measured as the average number of months between service of answer and jury trial in the urban areas of the host state.

13. These are indirect estimates, derived from the relation between the shadow verdict and settlement. They assume risk neutrality, unbiased expectations, and a range of possible values of litigation costs and bargaining strength. See Danzon and Lillard (1982).

14. Contingent fees are discussed more fully in Chapter 11 and in Danzon (1981).

15. Evidence from a 1970 closed-claim survey indicates that disagreement as to liability is more important than disagreement as to size of damages in the decision to go to verdict. In that survey, the insurer acknowledged liability in 80 percent of cases settled, as opposed to 20 percent of cases litigated to verdict. The insurer believed the damages were as severe as claimed in 60 percent of cases settled, as opposed to 50 percent of cases litigated (Danzon, 1980).

16. This procedure controls for the fact that states with relatively high awards in 1974 were more likely to enact changes. Assuming no such changes, these states could be expected to have high awards in 1976. If we simply compared the level of awards in 1976 in states that did and did not enact changes, we would underestimate the effects of the changes. For example, awards in California remained higher than awards in Maine, although tort reforms reduced awards in California relative to what they would have been with no reforms.

17. Using a different data set (see Chapter 4) I find similar effects for dollar caps, no effect for periodic payments, and significant effect for mandatory collateral source offset.

18. Rolph, Hammitt, Houchens, and Polin (1984) report that 90 percent of

automobile tort claimants receive full payment for economic loss. Of those receiving payment less than economic loss, 4 percent were constrained by policy limits.

19. In California the ratio declines from roughly 4 to 1, for claims with loss under $200, to 2 to 1, for claims with loss over $3,000.

4. THE FREQUENCY AND SEVERITY OF MALPRACTICE CLAIMS

1. Changes in doctrine affecting medical malpractice are described in Dietz, Baird, and Berul (1973). Changes affecting all lines of tort liability are described in California Commission (1977).

2. This estimate is based on the AMA report of 1.3 claims per physician for those reporting claims and their assumption that the average physician had been in practice for 16 years (AMA, 1963). Sandor (1957) provides an interesting history of medical malpractice, including a survey of all appeal cases from 1794 through 1955.

3. Westat (1973) estimates a total of 9,057 claims closed in 1970. Of these 28 percent were "warning" files, established by insurance companies on the basis of notification by physicians, which were subsequently closed without payment. For the remaining 6,521 claims, the median opening year was 1968. The corresponding physician population was 238,481.

4. Personal communication from Tom Swain, vice president of the St. Paul Insurance Company, to Terry J. Miller, senior consultant to the Senate Committee on Insurance and Financial Institutions, California legislature.

5. As the main rating bureau for the property-liability insurance industry, the ISO collects data on loss experience from member companies, adjusts for trends, and publishes advisory premium rates. Although ISO data are not comprehensive, they are probably representative of experience for the entire industry.

6. For a detailed account of how the ISO calculates incurred claim frequency and severity, see U.S. Senate (1975) and Appendix A in Chapter 6. The claim experience available as of the date of the estimate is "developed" to create a projection of ultimate experience, using development factors derived from past experience.

7. The automobile data are on a calendar-year basis but are comparable with policy-year data for other lines because lags in filing automobile claims are negligible.

8. The average lag from filing to disposition increased from 18 months for claims closed in 1975 to 25 months for claims closed in 1978. This may reflect a reduction in the filing of minor claims, which close relatively quickly, or longer lags in disposition, possibly due to the uncertainty created by the changes in law.

9. Claims closed in a given calendar year include claims filed in several prior calendar years. The data underlying these estimates are described later

in Chapter 4. The growth rate between 1970 and 1975 reported in Table 1.1 is probably upward-biased because the 1970 sample is incomplete, by as much as 30 percent. For the period 1975–1978, claim counts in some years for some states may be incomplete. Since data were only collected for July–December 1975, the estimate used here for 1975 frequency is two times this six-month count.

10. Washington, D.C., was an extreme outlier in 1975, with claim frequency twice that of the second-ranked state, California. Correlation coefficients between year-to-year growth rates and level in the initial year range from -0.2 to -0.4 for frequency, and -0.3 to -0.5 for severity.

11. For example, *Helling v. Carey*, 519 Pacific Reporter 2d 981 (1974).

12. If local physicians are unwilling to testify against each other—the alleged "conspiracy of silence"—abolition of the locality rule reduces the cost to the plaintiff of obtaining expert testimony.

13. The net effect of these alternative forums is highly uncertain a priori, since they may change expected recoveries as well as costs. They are described in Ebener (1981) and discussed in Chapter 11 of this volume.

14. The recent surge of asbestos claims stems from a similar retroactive application of new standards in product liability law.

15. The 1970 survey is described in Westat (1973); the 1975–78 survey is described in NAIC (1980). The 128 participating insurers include some of the new medical mutual companies, joint underwriting associations, and hospital captive companies, but not all insurers participated throughout the survey. An indicator variable identifying states with known underreporting was not significant in the regressions. In both surveys, claims against physicians are probably more fully represented than claims against hospitals because of hospital self-insurance. Claims against multiple defendants arising from the same incident have been consolidated.

16. The data consist of four annual cross sections (five for claim frequency). To allow for an unconstrained autoregressive process with endogenous explanatory variables, I used generalized least squares (GLS) or three-stage least squares (3SLS) applied to the pooled cross sections, with weighting to correct for heteroscedasticity. Danzon (1984a) reports details of the methodology and the laws adopted in each state.

17. Constraining coefficients to be equal across years effectively quadruples sample size and thus would increase estimation efficiency if the assumption of a constant effect is correct. In the reduced-form equations of Table 4.3, this assumption is not strictly appropriate for variables that affect claims both directly and indirectly through their effect on tort reform. Using an F-test, the hypothesis of equal coefficients could not be rejected.

18. The higher incidence of claims against surgeons that is observed in aggregate data may in part reflect a concentration of surgeons in states where claims are high for other reasons.

19. Since roughly 80 percent of reported malpractice claims arise in hospitals, the number of hospital admissions per capita was included as an explan-

atory variable. Its coefficient was often negative but was very sensitive to the specification. Hospital admissions may be an inaccurate measure of exposure because of variation in the type of treatment for which hospitalization occurs, depending on the availability of insurance and outpatient facilities.

20. Court delay was measured by average time from service of answer to trial in personal injury litigation in federal courts in the major urban areas of the state (Institute for Judicial Administration, 1970, 1972, 1974).

21. If lawyers per capita and membership of the ABA are included as the sole regressors, the elasticity of frequency with respect to lawyer density is .275 and significant at $p = .05$.

22. This evidence is consistent with Pashigian's conclusion from time-series analysis of the market for legal services (1977), that increases in the number of lawyers reflect demand rather than exogenous supply shifts. Between 1959 and 1969 the number of lawyers per capita increased, but mean and median annual earnings of lawyers rose relative to those of other salaried male workers.

23. For example, see U.S. Senate Committee on Labor and Public Welfare, Subcommittee on Health (1975, p. 142).

24. The effects of these laws on severity are positive but not statistically significant, which on theoretical grounds is not surprising. By expanding the scope of liability, three of these doctrines — informed consent, abolition of charitable immunity, and expansion of respondeat superior — will induce the filing of claims that would not otherwise have been filed. The mean true damages of claims filed may rise or fall. The possibility of naming hospitals as codefendants on claims against physicians will tend to raise potential awards by raising defense costs. Abolition of the locality rule expands liability and reduces the cost of establishing liability, which may raise the plaintiff's optimum legal effort and thus raise potential awards on all claims but induce more marginal claims, with an ambiguous net effect on observed severity.

25. Statutes of limitations are measured in years for filing for adults. If there is a discovery rule with no outer limit, the statute of limitations is assigned a value of 10. This is inaccurate to the extent that courts in fact recognize a discovery rule even in states where no such rule is enacted in statute. A discovery rule tolls the running of the statute until the injury is or "with reasonable diligence" should have been discovered. Many states have exceptions to the basic statute for cases involving minors or fraud and concealment by the physician.

26. 1975 LAWS $= \sum_{j=1}^{12} M_j$, where $M_j =$ number of months prior to December 1978 the jth law was in effect. The twelve laws are as follows: caps on awards, collateral source offset, limits on ad damnum, periodic payments, patient compensation fund, reinstatement of locality rule, limits on res ipsa or informed consent, limits on contingent fees, change in statute of limitations, arbitration, and pretrial screening panels. States enacting each of these laws are listed in Danzon (1984a).

5. THE MALPRACTICE INSURANCE MARKET

1. The range in premiums overstates the range in expected claim costs to the extent that physicians choose different limits of coverage as a result of differences in risk preference, or if premium differentials overstate actuarial differences.

2. These states are California, Florida, Illinois, Michigan, Pennsylvania, New York, and Texas (NAIC, 1980, p. 119).

3. Sociolegal risk and the statute of limitations are discussed more fully in Chapter 10.

4. Some occurrence policies provided for rebates if claim costs were less than anticipated, thereby retaining some sharing of pricing uncertainty between insurer and insureds. Such rebates were confined to the group programs and were prorated across all members of the group, regardless of their individual claim experience.

5. One exception to this is that a carrier might gain experience through writing a society program for some years and then continue writing individual coverage after leaving the program. For example, Pacific Indemnity continued to write individual coverage in southern California after writing the society program for several years and losing it to The Hartford Insurance Co. in 1969.

6. Although the insurer in theory retains the right to refuse coverage, in practice the underwriting function is turned over to the medical society (personal communication from an underwriter at a major company). See also the testimony of Robert S. Hansen, vice president of the Aetna Life and Casualty Co., in explaining the Aetna's preference for writing through medical associations: "By writing the association, you get a much better penetration of the available market, which gives you a better spread of risk, which automatically enhances your opportunity for profit" (*Owens v. Aetna Life and Cas. Co.*, 654 F.2d 218, 1981).

7. See the testimony in *Owens v. Aetna*: "[It is] extremely important to have the support [of the medical association] when you attempt to secure . . . adequate rate levels from an insurance department."

8. The ISO advisory rates can be used by new entrants and thus provide some check on the monopoly power of incumbent carriers. But since they are not tailored to a specific group of policyholders, they are likely to be less accurate.

6. THE 1975 INSURANCE CRISIS

1. A 1983 survey by the American Medical Association showed an average rate increase of 47 percent over the preceding three years by 20 of the mutuals (*Medical Liability Monitor*, vol. 8, August 29, 1983).

2. I use 1969 as a base year because it corresponds to an approximate peak in the rate cycle. Changes in basic limits rates for the decade 1965-1974 were as follows: 5.3 percent, 14.4 percent, 14.3 percent, 33.1 percent, 33.4

percent, 6.8 percent, 14.1 percent, 11.8 percent, 8.3 percent, 52.5 percent. The severity trend of 10.2 percent was the exponential curve of best fit applied to 1969–1973 paid claims. The frequency trend was an exponential trend of best fit for 1966–1973 policy year incurred claims.

3. Target loss ratios in the range 0.66 to 0.7 were used in different contexts. The projected loss ratio is on a total limits basis, whereas the target loss ratio, severity trend, and rate increases are for basic limits coverage ($25,000 per claim, $75,000 for the policy year).

4. These are rough estimates because the data available to me do not permit a consistent weighting procedure. The 1969 actual loss ratio and the frequency and severity trends are based on countrywide losses and premiums and thus effectively weight each state's experience in proportion to loss or premium volume, whereas the average recommended rate increase is an unweighted average of the individual state recommended increases. It is unclear whether the average realized rate increase reported by the ISO is weighted or unweighted.

5. The reason is that the average payment for claims *closed* in a given calendar year is a weighted average of claims *filed* in several prior calendar years. Since minor claims are settled more quickly, they constitute a larger fraction of claims closed in successive calendar years when claim frequency is rising, assuming a constant severity distribution of claims and lag in closure.

6. The estimates of frequency for policy years 1968 and 1969 that were made in calendar years 1972 and 1973 were revised *downward* in 1975 and 1976 on the basis of experience during calendar years 1972–76, although these were the years of peak frequency increase. But estimates of frequency for policy years 1970 and 1971 made in 1972 and 1973 were revised upward by roughly 50 percent by 1975. Since this pattern of upward revision of initial estimates (through the 51-month evaluation) followed by downward revisions thereafter is followed consistently throughout the decade and is not confined to this period of frequency increase, it does not resolve the question of whether trends in frequency were underestimated in the early 1970s.

7. The annual trend factor was used to project incurred losses for policy years ending December 1972 and December 1973 to one year beyond the anticipated effective date of July 1, 1975. Using a 23.5 percent trend, the factors are $(1.235)^{4.5} = 2.58$ for 1972 and $(1.235)^{3.5} = 2.09$ for 1973. The resulting loss ratios at current rates were weighted by 0.3 and 0.7, respectively, and then compared to the target loss ratio to obtain the indicated increase in current rates.

8. Phase I (Aug. 15 to Nov. 14, 1971) was a 90-day total freeze on wages, prices, and rents. Phase II (Nov. 14, 1971 to Jan. 11, 1973) permitted the customary treatment of "factors that reflect experience incurred in all actual costs, including commissions on other than a percentage of premium basis," factors that reflect changed conditions of risk, or loss adjustment expenses, taxes, fees, and percentage commissions "to the extent consistent with rul-

ings of the Pay Board and Price Commission." Controls focused on the trend factor and on the margin for general expenses and profit. Specifically, trend factors were limited to zero for the Phase I period and to ⅚ of the rate of inflation that would otherwise be used for any period after Nov. 13, 1971. Phase III (Jan. 11 to June 12, 1973), applied voluntary standards on a self-administered basis; for insurance, Phase II guidelines remained in place. A second 90-day freeze was in effect June 13 to Aug. 11, 1973. Under Phase IV (Aug. 12, 1973, to April 1974) the restrictions on trend factors were as follows: zero for Phase I, ⅚ of the rate calculated by customary practice for Phase II, ⅚ of this rate for the period Jan. 11 to Aug. 12, 1973, and ⅞ of this rate from Aug. 12, 1973, through the end of the projection period. Under Phase II the prospective dollar amounts for general expenses, other acquisition expenses, underwriting profit, and contingency could not increase by more than 2.5 percent over their previous level. Under Phase IV the 2.5 percent continued to apply to profit, but a 5 percent increase for administrative expense was permitted. Federal Register, vol. 37, no. 6; Code of Federal Regulations, Title 6 (various dates), Government Printing Office.

9. Since the ISO does not file rates in all states, the maximum number of potential filings is 48, including Alaska, Hawaii, and Puerto Rico.

10. For example, in Rhode Island the 1974 indicated rate increase was not filed because the 1973 increase became effective in July 1974, and the ISO staff considered it futile to file another increase immediately.

11. Similarly, in the 1968–69 period of relatively large rate increases, large filings by independent carriers preceded large filings by the ISO (Steves and McWhorter, 1975).

12. Munch (1978). In the light of hindsight, the 1970 rates were inadequate but the 1976 rates were excessive, because the latter were based on a projected continuation of the 40 percent annual rate of growth of claim costs of the early 1970s, whereas in fact frequency actually fell after 1976.

13. Average annual yields on high-grade municipal bonds rose from 5.18 in 1973 to 6.89 in 1975; the yield on 10-year U.S. Treasuries increased from 6.84 in 1973 to 7.99 in 1975. To indicate rough orders of magnitude, an increase in interest rates from 6 percent to 7 percent implies a 16.7 percent decrease in the value of a perpetuity. Thus if insurers' bond holdings were primarily long-term, there was an additional decrease in market value of total assets of roughly 8 percent.

14. The premium/capital ratio is a meaningful measure of financial strength only when applied to a single group of companies over a timespan sufficiently short to preclude distortions due to changes in rate levels or in the composition of liabilities or assets. Hammond, Shapiro, and Shilling (1979) estimated that given the distribution of combined ratios in 1975 for medical malpractice insurers, the probability of ruin at a 4:1 premium/surplus ratio was 0.32. This exceeds the comparable probability for all other property liability lines except air and reinsurance. Venezian (1983) showed how uncertainty about the parameters of the loss distribution raises insolvency risk for a given premium/surplus ratio.

15. U.S. Senate (1975). The St. Paul, which was the leading carrier nationwide in 1974, began writing only claims-made coverage as of March 1975. It withdrew from states where approval of this policy was denied but has reentered where approval has since been granted, as in New Jersey.

16. Most of the mutuals are reinsured either through commercial reinsurers or through the reinsurance facility established by the American Medical Association, AMACO, but their retained risk is larger than insurers of comparable size writing other lines of general liability (Steves, 1983).

17. "Potential remedial legislation has been enacted in California in the past 36 months in an effort to bring about stability in professional liability insurance rates; however the insurance industry has not yet reflected this in its rate-making process due to uncertainties of the ultimate effects of such legislation. Should the legislation result in a significant reduction in loss, premiums (net of any claim payments) which have already been paid to non-physician-owned insurance companies may simply pass through to the stockholders of the respective insurance companies . . . The mutual concept insures that excess premiums belong to the member physicians." Ivan C. Neubauer, president, Norcal Mutual, in "What Every Physician Should Know about Claims-Made Liability Insurance," March 1978.

18. This hypothesis would predict higher excess limits factors (more nonlinear pricing) for claims-made coverage. Consistent with this, one carrier prohibits the upgrading of policy limits for claims arising out of prior practice. Some companies reduce the risk to the physician by providing the reporting endorsement free of charge in the event that the physician dies or is totally disabled prior to age 65 or retires after age 65, if he was insured in the previous five years. These are clearly circumstances where adverse selection risk is minimal.

19. To compare the full cost of claims-made and occurrence coverage, one cannot simply compare the premiums for mature claims made and occurrence policies in a single year because they do not provide equivalent coverage. Assuming that claims are filed over a period of five years, so that the claims-made policy is mature after five years, the correct calculation compares the present value of five years of occurrence coverage with five years of claims-made coverage plus the reporting endorsement.

20. Calculated from data reported in *Best's Aggregates and Averages*, various years. These loss ratios are not strictly comparable because some companies are writing claims-made policies, which have a lower expected loss ratio, and some mutuals may report discounted losses.

7. INSURANCE VERSUS PREVENTION

1. For example, "The extent to which the defendant must respond in damages is better measured by the plaintiff's harm than by the degree of the defendant's fault . . . the notion of a wrongdoing defendant is increasingly anachronistic in this age of widespread malpractice insurance" (ABA, 1977, p. 147).

2. A secondary function of insurance is to enable individuals, including those who are not risk-averse, to meet costs that may be many times their income in the event of a catastrophic loss. For example, take a physician who is risk-neutral and is faced with a 1 in 100 chance of a $5 million judgment: he may be willing to pay more than $50,000 (1 percent of $5 million) for insurance against such a loss because he could not pay that amount from his own resources. This example is adapted from Zeckhauser (1970).

3. Self-insurance is a third alternative, not explicitly considered here.

4. Without the lock, the expected loss is $10 (0.01 × $1,000); with the lock the expected loss is $1 (0.001 × $1,000). Thus the expected benefit from installing the lock is $9.

5. Experience-rated premiums also have other advantages. First, in situations where the insurance carrier can better estimate the value of risk reduction measures, because of a wide pool of experience, experience rating serves to convey that information to the insured. The fact that he is offered a lower premium if he adopts certain procedures or installs specific equipment implicitly informs him of their value in terms of loss reduction. Second, experience-rated premiums have appeal on grounds of equity: without experience rating, good risks effectively subsidize bad risks.

6. This conclusion presupposes that the utility of income is independent of whether or not a loss occurs. In order to achieve efficient prevention, it is necessary that the formula for loading insurance costs onto the pure premium, to arrive at the total premium, accurately reflects the costs actually incurred. The most common formula appears to be a proportionate loading —the complement of the target loss ratio. If costs in fact are less than proportionate because, for example, claim adjustment costs are a smaller fraction of large claims, then an experience-rated premium with a proportional load would induce excessive investment in prevention.

7. This assumes that efficient resource allocation is the only objective of public policy. Regulation of insurance markets is sometimes adopted in the name of equity or income redistribution. For example, rating of automobile insurance on the basis of age and sex has been prohibited in some states.

8. The term "error" is used for brevity. In fact, because the appropriate treatment in any circumstance is often uncertain, the courts must adopt a probabilistic standard, finding liability where it is more probable than not that the injury was due to negligence. Even if the standard were correct on average, the risk-averse physician would have an incentive to insure even if his practice were nonnegligent, that is, if he adopted all cost-effective preventive measures.

9. This is analogous to the result in the first-party context, that optimal coverage approaches complete coverage if the cost of care is very high (Shavell, 1980).

10. In the first-party context, there are two analogs of insurer moral hazard. First, the insurer has an incentive to try to deny valid claims, but this incentive is mitigated rather than exacerbated by the insured's retention of

risk. Thus copayment provisions do not create a trade-off between policy-holder and insurer moral hazard in the first-party context. Second, a monop-olistic insurer may have suboptimal incentives to encourage loss prevention, if the demand for insurance falls by more than the cost when losses are reduced. In the liability insurance context, this analysis applies to both legal defense and injury prevention.

11. The enforcement value of private litigation is discussed in Ordover (1978) and Shavell (1982b).

12. Personal communications from underwriters. A policyholder might be penalized for noncooperation in settlement; but he would not be penal-ized for a claim where, in the opinion of the reviewers, an award or settle-ment was made simply to compensate a severely injured plaintiff without evidence of medical negligence, that is, an invalid claim. Even in companies with merit-rating programs, typically fewer than 5 percent of physicians are subject to surcharge at any one time.

13. On average, physicians spend 2.7 days per claim for depositions, court appearances, and so on (AMA, 1983). Some policies cover the policyholder's out-of-pocket expenses and a per diem expense for trial appearance.

14. Additional amounts for punitive damages, ranging from $6,000 to $50,000, have also been awarded. To the extent that uninsured costs vary with the severity of the injury, because severe injuries take longer to settle and are more likely to go to court, there is a hidden coinsurance rate. In addition, if pricing for high levels of coverage were nonlinear, it would act as a crude form of individual rating (Rothschild and Stiglitz, 1976).

15. Relating reimbursement rates to patient characteristics would create a moral hazard risk to health insurers.

16. The maximum fee increase each year is based on a cost index, of which average malpractice premiums are one component.

17. This argument presupposes collusion by physicians in choosing their malpractice insurance coverage. Such collusion is not implausible in view of the role of the medical societies in running malpractice insurance programs.

18. Personal communication from underwriter.

8. THE STANDARD OF CARE

1. A more precise definition of the Learned Hand test—and one also more descriptive of how courts actually apply the test—would be phrased in terms of the marginal costs and benefits of reducing the probability of injury. See Brown (1973) and Posner (1977).

2. *The T. J. Hooper*, 60 F.2d 737, 740 (2d Cir. 1932).

3. 83 Wash. 2d 514, 519 P.2d 981, 983 (1974).

4. 1975 Wash. Laws, 1st Ex. Sess., Ch. 35-1, which revised the state's Code of Civil Procedure, Wash. Rev. Code 4.24.290 (Supp. 1975). Wiley (1981) provides interesting empirical evidence on the effects of the Helling decision; he shows that there was no uniformly accepted standard, so the court in the

Helling case may be viewed as adopting a substantial minority standard rather than rejecting all customary standards.

5. With imperfect information, relative prices will be only a rough guide to relative qualities. Oi (1973) shows that liability could drive out either high-quality or low-quality products.

6. In October 1983 a prospective payment system was introduced for payment to hospitals under Medicare. Payment is a fixed rate, per admission, for each of 467 diagnosis-related groups (DRGs). Initially, hospital-specific and regional differences received some weight, but these will be phased out by 1985.

7. *Caldwell v. Knight*, 92 Ga. App. 747, 89 SE2d 900, 1955.

8. *McCurdy v. Hatfield*, 30 Cal. 2d 492, 183 P2d 269, 1947.

9. In *Canterbury v. Spence* (464 F2d 772, CA DC, 1972), the courts applied an objective reasonable-man standard. In *Cobbs v. Grant* (8 Cal. 3d 229, 502 P.2d 1, 104 Cal. Rptr. 505, 1972) the standard referred to the particular patient.

10. If a defendant "succeeds in establishing that the plaintiff's pre-existing condition was bound to worsen . . . an appropriate discount should be made for the damages that would have been suffered even in the absence of the defendant's negligence." *Evans v. S. J. Groves and Sons Co.*, 315 F.2d 335, 348 (2d Cir. 1963).

11. The introduction of panels of tests has led to some ambiguity in measuring trends in testing. *Laboratory Management*, the leading source of data on test volume, counts multiple tests in a panel as separate tests. From an economic standpoint, this is not necessarily the relevant measure. Typically, the tests in the panel are joint products — that is, once the cost of performing one test has been incurred, the marginal cost of performing the additional tests in the panel is negligible. Joint production increases the efficient frequency of ordering at least one test. The efficient decision is to order the panel if the sum of the values of the individual tests exceeds the cost of the panel, even if the value of any individual test is less than the cost of the panel.

12. In 1969 a consent decree between the Department of Justice and the College of American Pathologists barred pathologists from preventing independent pricing by laboratories and from suggesting uniform fee schedules.

9. SIZE AND STRUCTURE OF AWARDS

1. NAIC (1980), pp. 31, 58. This adjustment is based on the GNP deflator, which rose 19.6 percent, while the medical-care component of the Consumer Price Index rose 26.9 percent and unit labor costs rose 20.3 percent.

2. NAIC (1980), p. 104. This average increase overstates somewhat the increase for a given type of claim because there were relatively fewer minor claims in the later years.

3. For example, the Illinois Supreme Court held, in *Wright v. the Du Page Hospital Association*, 347 N.E. 2d 736 (1976), that the statutory ceiling on

recovery ($500,000) is void, as being contrary to the Illinois constitutional provision against special privileges.

4. This conclusion ignores social benefits from private enforcement of laws.

5. Compensation for pain and suffering, if correctly calculated as willingness to pay for prevention, would provide optimal deterrence but excessive compensation. Willingness to pay as a measure of compensation for pain and suffering is discussed in Conley and Flick (1978). They do not distinguish between the optimum award for purposes of compensation and that for purposes of deterrence.

6. In theory, optimal coverage is less than full coverage on account of the positive loading charge.

7. U.S. Statistical Abstract (1982–83), p. 336. An additional 1.8 million persons under age 65 (0.9 percent of the under 65 population) were in nursing homes.

8. This feature of tort might be undermined if contracting out of tort rights were permitted. See Epstein (1976) and Chapter 12.

9. The contributory negligence defense (total bar to recovery) and the comparative negligence reduction in the award in proportion to the plaintiff's fault provide some incentive for care by the potential tort plaintiff, comparable to lower limits of coverage in private contracts for events within the control of the policyholder.

10. Workers' compensation benefits reflect a collective insurance choice in which employers and unions have a significant input, and may be supplemented by industry-specific collective bargaining agreements, which also set wage levels and may determine safety measures. Thus with the exception of SSDI and other public sources of compensation, labor markets reveal choices of injury prevention and insurance when costs are fully internalized, insurance premiums are widely experience-rated, and potential victims, through unions, are reasonably well informed about injury risks.

11. Viscusi (1983). The $4 million is estimated at a risk of 6×10^{-4} (6/100,000) per year, and the mean annual risk of nonfatal injury was 1/30. To see how wage premiums for risk are translated into implicit values for injury, consider the following example. If a worker receives $500 annually in return for a 1/30 chance of injury, dividing $500 by 1/30 yields an implicit value of $15,000 for an injury. This does not mean, however, that the worker would accept certain injury for $15,000.

12. Such merit rating as exists is based on frequency rather than size of loss, because large losses are too infrequent for statistical credibility.

13. Similarly, the ABA Commission underestimates the impact of caps: "As a practical matter it is very doubtful if the actual ceilings which have been enacted are low enough to be of any benefit from an actuarial point of view" (ABA, 1977, p. 57). The reason given is that, with the exception of Idaho, the limits imposed are at least $500,000 for a single injury. "Statistics compiled by the NAIC indicate that in the states in which ceilings have been

enacted, very few claims involved payments in excess of these ceilings." Again, this ignores the fact that caps affect potential verdicts and hence reduce settlements below the threshhold. It also underestimates the potential impact of caps on total claim costs because the cases affected, although few in number, account for a large fraction of total dollar outlay.

14. However, some courts have rejected the idea that pain and suffering should be measured in terms of the sum of money an average person would voluntarily accept in exchange for a particular painful experience (*Zibbel v. Southern Pacific Railway*, California Supreme Court, 1911).

15. Common reports that tort plaintiffs fritter away their awards on "trivia," if true, are consistent with the argument that current standards of damages lead to excessive compensation.

16. Wisconsin and South Carolina provide for mandatory periodic payments when an award is to be paid from patient compensation funds that have been depleted below a specified level.

17. California, Florida, Maryland, and Washington (Elligett, 1979).

18. Since medical costs have historically risen more rapidly than wages or other goods and services, and since the prevailing market rate of interest is a precise indicator of the potential return on sums invested, the former method gives a more accurate calculation of the amount required to yield the desired level of real future benefits.

19. Alaska, Florida, Idaho, and New York mandate the deduction of all collateral compensation, at least for expenses already incurred. Ohio, Pennsylvania, and Tennessee mandate deduction only of compensation from public sources such as SSDI. Nebraska and New York deduct private medical insurance proceeds but credit the plaintiff with premiums paid for such insurance. In the remaining states the presentation of evidence is discretionary, except in South Dakota where it is mandatory.

20. ABA (1977), p. 146. Subrogation refers to the right of one insurer to recover expenses it incurs from another insurer, the tortfeasor, or the plaintiff.

21. The subrogated insurer may simply receive part of the proceeds from any judgment or settlement. Optimal compensation might be achieved without the supplementary subrogation action if the first-party insurance simply excluded coverage of any injury with recovery against a third party. But such contracts tend to provide inferior insurance because of the uncertainty of tort recoveries and are less common than contracts providing subrogation rights.

22. SSDI has similar offset provisions against some workers' compensation programs.

23. This is reasonably close to the rule of thumb that calls for a one-third markup for general damages. It is an overestimate of net compensation for economic loss after deduction of the plaintiff's litigation expense. Assuming attorney's fees absorb one-third of awards on average and that the plaintiff incurred other additional out-of-pocket costs, these crude calculations suggest that malpractice awards slightly undercompensate for economic loss on average. However, reasonable estimates for the adequacy of compensation

for permanent total disability and death (Westat, 1978) indicate that awards range from roughly one-quarter of economic loss for cases of death to one-half for permanent total disability.

24. A 1972 survey of severely disabled adults aged 20–64 years shows that families with a severely disabled adult had an average annual income almost 50 percent lower than the national average. Public and private programs account for one-third of total family income for families with a disabled adult. Of these families, only 1 percent had private insurance, compared to 48 percent receiving SSDI and 22 percent receiving public welfare (U.S. Department of Labor, 1980, pp. 55–61). Note that this evidence shows less complete coverage than might be expected from the facts cited earlier on SSDI and LTD benefit levels at 60 to 70 percent of pre-disability earnings. The discrepancy arises in part because the 1972 survey data predate the 1977 increases in SSDI benefit levels, in part because some people are ineligible for SSDI because of the prior employment requirements.

25. Note that these estimates based on closed-claim data cannot be applied directly to obtain the reduction in insurance premiums that might be warranted by the introduction of mandatory offset. That calculation must take into account lags in claim disposition and hence effects on investment income.

26. Although this would reduce the plaintiff's incentive to litigate, the effect may be negligible since a fine only applies in cases of severe injury where the compensatory award is large.

27. "Economic loss amounts were often not known by insurance companies and consequently were included on the report for only 61% of paid incidents. In addition, some reports include only past medical expense and wage loss, without allowance for future costs" (NAIC, 1980, p. 48).

28. The mean award is $37,416 for claims reporting some loss, $29,802 for claims where data are simply missing, and $28,297 for claims reporting zero loss (NAIC, 1980, table 2.6, p. 51). Claims closed without payment are excluded.

29. This assumes zero wage loss for all persons over age 65, all injuries classified as emotional or temporary insignificant, and all major but temporary injuries to persons under 18. For persons aged 18–64 with injuries at least as severe as temporary minor, no wage loss is assumed for the proportion not in the labor force in 1977 (42 percent for women, 12 percent for men).

30. Reported Indemnity = 0.05 Verdict + 0.95 Settlement, = 0.05 Verdict + 0.95 (0.74) Verdict, therefore Verdict = 1.328 Reported Indemnity.

10. THE STATUTE OF LIMITATIONS

1. *Huysman v. Kirsh*, 6 Cal. 2d 302, 57 P2d. 908.

2. The financial risk arises because of uncertain timing rather than delay per se. A certain time schedule of future payments could be matched with the maturity schedule of financial assets, thereby eliminating financial risk.

3. In *Beshada v. Johns-Manville Products Corp.*, 90 N.J. Sup. Crt., 191, 447

A2nd 539 (1982), the New Jersey supreme court ruled that a manufacturer can be held liable for its failure to warn even if the hazard in question was unknowable at the time of the product's sale. Retroactivity in tort is discussed in Henderson (1981) and Schwartz (1983).

4. If the statute of limitations is 10 years, it requires 10 years to determine whether an increase in the number of claims filed in the first report period represents accelerated reporting of a given number of claims — in which case estimates of unreported claims should be decreased — or an increase in underlying frequency — in which case estimates of unreported claims should be increased. Moreover, the longer the statute of limitations, the greater is the backlog of claims that will be filed in response to any pro-plaintiff legal change, and the greater the amplitude of year-to-year fluctuations in claim filings.

5. Residual risk for a given line of insurance, resulting from either a small risk pool, parameter uncertainty, or positive correlation among policyholders, can in principle be diversified through a multiline firm writing different lines of insurance with negatively correlated experience, or through stock markets. The capital asset pricing model (CAPM) implies that residual insurer risk is nondiversifiable *only* if it is systematic, that is, if underwriting turns bad when the stock market as a whole turns bad.

6. The formula used by the Insurance Services Office to calculate advisory rates incorporates only a 5 percent markup over losses plus expenses, for profit and other contingencies. But other components of the formula — in particular, projected losses — are sufficiently judgmental to accommodate an implicit allowance for risk.

7. For example, see Justice Traynor's concurring decision in *Esola v. Coca Cola Bottling Co.*, 150 P., 2d 436 (1944), "The cost of an injury . . . may be an overwhelming misfortune to the person injured, and a needless one, for the risk of injury can be insured by the manufacturer and distributed among the public as a cost of doing business." See also *Greenman v. Yuba Power Products, Inc.*, 27 Cal. Rptr. 697, 377 P2d 897 (1962).

8. AMA (1983) reports that only 2.6 percent of all physicians go bare, primarily in the low-risk specialties (general and family practice).

9. This assumes that no substantial number of claims that are filed after three years are on behalf of minors or involve fraud or intentional concealment, and thus would be exempt from the three-year limit.

11. COSTS OF LITIGATION

1. The small sample sizes in Table 11.1 for some specialties make conclusions tentative. The 1970 figures are from Kendall and Haldi (1973). Since 1981, some states have experienced malpractice rate increases in excess of the rate of inflation of other health care costs (Rosenberg, 1984), so currently premiums may be a slightly higher percentage of physicians' gross income or total health care costs.

2. NAIC (1980). Insurer claim expense is defined as "expenses paid to all defense counsel plus all other claim adjustment expenses specifically allocated to a particular claim against a particular defendant . . . Since some overhead costs are not allocated to particular claims, the cost of handling and defending malpractice claims is understated." (p. 42).

3. It is interesting to note in Table 11.3 that on cases tried to verdict, the defense spends less on those it ultimately wins than on those it loses. If the average potential verdict in each group were equal, this would imply that the defense has some idea which cases it will win and therefore puts less effort into these.

4. With a contingent fee the attorney receives a prespecified percentage of the award if his client wins, zero otherwise.

5. The elasticity of quantity with respect to a change in price can be estimated from the ratio of legal expense to award, assuming maximization of net value (Danzon, 1983b).

6. The argument is that an attorney will compete for cases by bidding an expected award and fee percentage that maximize the expected net recovery of the client, consistent with covering the opportunity cost of his time. The implied level of effort is precisely that which would be chosen by an informed, risk-neutral client paying an hourly fee. Competitive monitoring of the actual recovery relative to the amount bid is necessary to enforce delivery of the implicitly promised level of effort. The conclusion that the outcome is invariant under an hourly wage and contingent-fee contract presupposes risk neutrality. When the plaintiff is risk-averse, his expected utility is unambiguously higher with a contingent fee, but attorney effort, the win rate, and gross recovery may be higher or lower, depending on parameters of the utility and production functions (Danzon, 1983a).

7. Ex ante, the fee percentage (k) times the expected award (pA) is equal to the cost of time (wL): $kpA = wL$. Ex post, on cases won, $kA = wL/p$.

8. California, Delaware, New York, Oregon, and Pennsylvania. Fee limits were declared unconstitutional in New Hampshire, as interfering with freedom of contract and discriminating against malpractice claimants. Indiana allows a fee of no more than 15 percent of any part of an award over $100,000 that is paid from the state's compensation fund.

9. For technical reasons we were unable to estimate the effect of fee ceilings on verdicts and the plaintiff's probability of winning and thus could not perform a direct test of the theoretical proposition.

10. S. 189, 98th Cong., 1st sess., January 26, 1983. Voluntary panels existed in New Jersey and New Mexico prior to 1975. Illinois, Missouri, Florida, Pennsylvania, and New Hampshire have subsequently declared their statutes unconstitutional; Arkansas has abolished its panels under state sunset laws, and Connecticut and Hawaii use them rarely. Of the remaining 22 states with functioning panels, screening is mandatory in all but Delaware, Kansas, Maine, and Virginia. See Ebener et al. (1981).

11. The former is true in Alaska, Arizona, Delaware, Florida, Indiana,

Louisiana, Maryland, and Massachusetts. In Alaska, Illinois, Rhode Island, and Wisconsin, the court may assess panel or court costs, or both, against a party found to have made a frivolous claim or frivolously denied liability. For details of panel characteristics by state, see Carlin (1980).

12. The constitutionality of panels has been challenged on three primary grounds: as a violation of the equal protection and due process clauses of the Fourteenth Amendment, as a denial of the Seventh Amendment right to trial by jury, and as an improper delegation of judicial authority. But most courts have held such legislation a valid exercise of the police power granted to the state by the Tenth Amendment. See Longshore (1981), and cases cited therein.

13. See, for example, Carlin (1980), National Center for State Courts (1980).

14. Alabama, Georgia, North Dakota, and Vermont.

15. Alaska, Louisiana, and Ohio have mandatory screening of malpractice claims, as well as provision for arbitration, while Virginia and Maine have voluntary screening and arbitration. Wisconsin, which has mandatory screening, allows parties to stipulate that panel findings shall constitute binding arbitration. Arbitration is mandatory by inclusion in subscriber contracts in the California Ross-Loos and Kaiser Health Maintenance Organizations.

16. Because arbitration, in contrast to screening, is voluntarily chosen, sometimes after the occurrence of an incident, cases going to arbitration may be a nonrandom sample of all incidents. If arbitration reduces costs relative to the expected award by more for minor injuries, these cases will be disproportionately represented in the sample of cases closed by arbitration.

17. A comparison of the social costs and benefits of arbitration relative to the courts is complicated by the fact that courts provide social benefits in defining liability rules, which are used in arbitration and out-of-court settlements, but are also subsidized out of the public fisc.

18. For example, *Friedman v. Dozorc*, Michigan Sup. Ct., *Michigan Reports* 412:1–80.

19. A.L.R. 639, 643 (1926), cited in Rhem and Trusch (1977).

20. *Tool Research and Engineering Corp. v. Henigson*, 120 Cal. Rptr. 291 (Cal. App. 1975).

21. If legal negligence were defined as filing if the expected award were less than the sum of litigation costs to both parties, such a standard might induce too few suits for optimal deterrence. In fact it is unlikely that holding attorneys liable for negligence would deter many filings. By the Hand standard, based on private benefits and costs, negligence would be defined as bringing a suit if the expected payoff exceeds the costs of filing, that is, the expected net recovery of the plaintiff is positive. But an attorney paid a contingent fee would require that his share of the expected payoff exceed the costs, a more stringent condition.

22. *Bull v. McCuskey*, 615 P. 2d 957, Nev. 1980.

23. *U.S. Law Week,* 12/8/81, 50 LW 2331.

24. The English rule has recently been adopted in Florida, but it is too soon to judge its effect. Allegedly, the inability to collect defense costs from unsuccessful malpractice claimants undermines the power of the rule as a deterrent to frivolous claims.

12. ALTERNATIVES

1. See, for example, *Tunkl v. Regents of University of California,* 60 Cal. 2D92, 32 Cal. Rptr. 33, 383, P.2d 441 (1963).

2. *Doyle v. Guiliucci,* 62 Cal. 2d 606, 401 P.2d 1 (1965); *Madden v. Kaiser Foundation Hospitals,* 17 Cal. 3d 699, 552 P.2d 1178 (1976).

3. In HMOs, the physician's incentive to control cost stems from the prepaid, capitation form of reimbursement. But a similar principle applies, if to a lesser degree, under fee-for-service, preferred-provider contracts.

4. Litigation costs in workers' compensation are much higher for occupational-disease claims, where occupational hazards are hard to distinguish from environmental or genetic factors, than for traumatic injuries.

5. The 150-fold estimate is based on the assumptions that 1 in 25 negligent injuries were compensated in the mid-1970s, and that these negligent injuries constituted 17 percent of all iatrogenic injuries. The 75-fold estimate assumes that the ratio of claims to injuries has doubled since 1978 (see Chapter 2).

6. The ABA Commission's feasibility study of MAI (1979) noted the lack of medical literature with good statistical or epidemiological information on the association between medical interventions and adverse outcomes. Evaluations were based largely on the personal experience of medical panelists. Of course, this lack of data also undermines an accurate negligence standard.

7. The ABA Commission (1979) discusses subsidizing providers who treat high-risk patients. But the difficulty of objectively identifying high-risk patients applies equally to a government subsidy program as it does to private insurers.

Index